"Josh Hammer's book *Israel and Civilization* is an extraordinary accomplishment from beginning to end. Hammer makes an overwhelming case that Judaism, based on God's word known through the Torah, scholarly treatises of old, and ancient history, is essential to the acknowledgement and embrace of eternal truths, right reason, and morality, and, as a result, gave birth to Western civilization and the civil society. He explains that man's 'creation in God's image' is about living a good, righteous, and faithful life in support of community and individual fulfillment. And he discusses the inextricable link between Judaism and Christianity and Judeo-Christian values. But this is not what one might consider a religious book per se. Hammer takes on much more.

"Hammer emotionally describes how Jews have suffered so horribly through the ages, noting his own visits to the gas chambers of Europe and the killing fields of October 7. He writes about the present-day explosion of anti-Semitism and violence against Jews throughout the Western world, including the United States. And here is where this excellent book is at its most profound: Through several chapters, Hammer comprehensively explains that as Judaism and the Jewish people go, so goes the rest of the West. What we are witnessing and experiencing, writes Hammer, is the degradation of and, if we do not act, ultimately the dissolution of the West as we know it. This is why Israel, and the Jewish people, are facing such an outbreak of terror. They are the point of the spear. And their fight is, as Hammer states, the battle of and for Western civilization and the values and beliefs that undergird it. The State of Israel's survival is essential not only to the Jewish people but the rest of the free world. Rather than turning on Israel, Western governments should be providing their full support—for their own sake—and putting down the rise of anti-Jewish hate and violence in their own countries. Hammer emphasizes that the US–Israel and Jewish–Christian alliances are imperative to saving the West.

"I have barely touched the surface of *Israel and Civilization*. It is a superb book. I urge you to read it to the end and then share it."

—MARK LEVIN

"A Christian who disregards his connection to the land and people of Israel saws off the branch of the tree on which he sits. Jew or Christian, believer or unbeliever, the beauty of our Western way of life is inseparably linked to the God of Abraham, Isaac, and Jacob. Josh Hammer makes this case clearly and with a love of God and country that should inspire every defender of America to think twice before falling prey to the rising tides of anti-Semitism and anti-Zionism." —GLENN BECK

"The United States has one firm ally in the Middle East: Israel. Understanding this alliance and its role in the West's survival is paramount. Josh Hammer expertly explains the historical importance and future implications of this partnership and the impact it will have on future generations."

—DANA LOESCH

"Josh Hammer's *Israel and Civilization* is the best 'back to Judaism' book I've read in many years. With the failure of Enlightenment rationalism as his backdrop, Hammer tells the compelling story of his own return to God and Orthodox Jewish observance. En route, he shows how Torah and *mitzvot* are the key to a spiritually centered life for every Jew, whether in Israel or the Diaspora. But he also has a message for Christians—whose road to national restoration must bring them to a renewed encounter with the foundational texts of Judaism." —YORAM HAZONY

"Josh Hammer is one of the most brilliant people in the entire conservative movement." —LIZ WHEELER

ISRAEL

AND

CIVILIZATION

THE FATE of the
JEWISH NATION and the
DESTINY OF THE WEST

JOSH HAMMER

RADIUS BOOK GROUP
NEW YORK

Radius Book Group
A division of Diversion Publishing Corp.
www.radiusbookgroup.com

Radius Book Group and colophon are registered trademarks of
Diversion Publishing Corp.

For more information, email info@radiusbookgroup.com.

First Radius Books Edition: March 2025
Hardcover ISBN 978-1-63576-973-9
e-ISBN 978-1-63576-984-5

Printed in the United States of America
10 9 8 7 6 5 4 3

Radius books are available at special discounts for bulk purchases
in the US by corporations, institutions, and other organizations.
For more information, please contact admin@diversionbooks.com.

*To my daughter, Esther—may she be
a Maccabee of her own day.*

CONTENTS

1

OUR PERILOUS MOMENT

"Though I walk in the valley of the shadow of death, I will fear no evil, for You are with me; Your rod and Your staff—they will comfort me."

—PSALMS 23[1]

I'LL NEVER FORGET PULLING UP TO TREBLINKA. IT WAS MY FIRST time in Poland. We had driven up from Warsaw after a tour of the Warsaw Ghetto that same day. Treblinka is a tiny town, removed from the main highway and with a population of just a few hundred people. Other than a small green sign on the side of the road, easy to miss if you're not paying close attention, there is no indication that you have even entered a village where some of the most unspeakable evils in human history took place. But once we passed the sign and drove by the homes and farmhouses, I was overcome by the same thought, repeating itself ad nauseam: *These people knew—and they did nothing.*

We wound our way across the remote village, zigzagging tree-lined rural roads before arriving at our destination: the notorious Treblinka extermination camp. Almost one million Jews were murdered in this camp's gas chambers over its fifteen-month operational history from 1943 to 1944, making it the second-deadliest of all the Nazi camps after Auschwitz-Birkenau. I had been trying to steel myself for the tide of emotions that I knew would swirl to the surface once we arrived. But such mental and emotional preparation proved futile.

We were alone there that day—just me and two friends, the heavens above, and the memories of all those who perished in this hellish place during the most systematic genocide in human history. By the time we reached the parallel concrete blocks marking the old railway of death from the Warsaw Ghetto, my eyes were welling up with tears. We slowly advanced across the Treblinka killing field, with one of my friends, a man who has led countless tours of the camps for visiting foreign delegations, telling us stories of some of those murdered there by the Nazis.

Eventually, I reached the memorial for the Nazis' cremation pits. I tried to say a prayer for the deceased, but I could barely do so through the tears. I took a rock from a pathway and took it home with me. To this day, that rock sits next to me in my office—right beside a slightly larger rock, which was given to me some years ago in Jerusalem by a rabbi who said he smuggled it out of the Auschwitz crematorium. Some people tell me they think it's weird that I work every day with those rocks right on my desk, but they ground me and remind me who I am.

My time at Treblinka felt like an out-of-body experience. I was physically there but was weighed down by the most searing anger and acute sadness I had ever experienced in my life. We stopped at a gas station convenience store along the Polish highway on the way back to Warsaw. The two friends I was with bantered to try to lighten the mood, lighting up cigarettes to further decompress. I had no words to contribute and I'm not a smoker either, so instead I allowed myself to get lost in my own rapidly racing thoughts. *How did this happen? How did the world allow it to happen?*

Do young people today know about what happened here? Most important, do they even care?

It would be a few years until I felt precisely that same combustible mix of emotions—disbelief, abandonment, debilitating forlornness, righteous indignation—and found myself asking the same painful questions all over again. That time, I wasn't in the former extermination camp of Treblinka, Poland; I was in the former kibbutz of Kfar Aza, Israel, three months after the deadliest single day for the Jewish people since the Holocaust.

Kfar Aza was actually our group's third stop on January 9, 2024. We had stopped earlier that day in Ofakim and Sderot, cities that had been savagely attacked by Hamas jihadists during the pogrom that changed the world on October 7, 2023. My brother-in-law, who lives in nearby Netivot, met me that morning in Sderot. Since Hamas had won a bloody Palestinian–Arab civil war over Fatah in 2007 and established its iron fist rule in the Gaza Strip, it is likely that no Israeli town has suffered more than Sderot. Located less than a mile from Gaza, Sderot has endured incessant rocket fire from Hamas and its chief Islamist rival in the Strip, Palestinian Islamic Jihad. On October 7, Sderot was the site of a ferocious firefight against Hamas at the local police station.

Netivot, which was remarkably spared by Hamas's barbaric jihad on October 7, is only about six miles from Sderot. My brother-in-law is thus accustomed to hearing regular thunderous noises and watching Israel's miraculous Iron Dome missile defense system intercept indiscriminately fired Hamas rockets in midair—and then having to explain it all to his four young children. "The Arabs are putting on a firework show for us," he will sometimes quip. No one can deny the Jewish people's finely honed sense of gallows humor.

My brother-in-law is a religious man, so he does not struggle with the question of theodicy; like most great religions, Judaism has its own clear answers to the ever-lurking conundrum of why bad things happen to good and innocent people. But when I saw him that morning in Sderot and told him that my group was next going to Kfar Aza, my brother-in-law looked back at me blankly. I knew exactly what he was thinking: *Why? Are you prepared for the toll this is going to take on your "neshama"—your soul?*

I thought I was. But I was wrong. I had never seen anything like Kfar Aza in my life. The kibbutz, which is situated on the physical border fence with Gaza, was one of the hardest hit communities during the Simchat Torah Massacre of 2023. As in numerous other towns in the broader Gaza Envelope, dozens and dozens of Israelis in Kfar Aza were slaughtered on that fateful day by infiltrating Hamas jihadists in the most gruesome, sadistic, Nazi-esque ways imaginable.

Walking around the kibbutz barely three months later, one could practically still smell the haunting stench of death. Entire rows of homes looked like they had been blown up with bombs. There were stray bullet holes everywhere. Mattresses, doorframes, kitchen utensils, and children's toys were strewn about all over. The Israel Defense Forces had marked the homes according to who was either murdered or taken hostage. The accompanying photos of the young men and women—as with those we saw later that day in Re'im, site of the ill-fated Nova music festival—stared back at me, piercing my soul. *These were young people—they had so much still to live for.*

The IDF permitted us to go into one home, with the permission of the relatives of the deceased. On the wall of the home, you could see where the army had wiped away the murdered couple's blood; posted nearby was a large printout of the couple's harrowing last-ever WhatsApp conversation. Bullet holes were everywhere; household items were all over the floor, the whole house left undisturbed by the IDF as an enduring memory and tribute.

As I neared the end of my time in Kfar Aza, I was as despondent as I could ever remember being—my heart shattered. I thought back to my time at Treblinka a few years prior, and the same troubling questions came back with a vengeance. *How did this happen? How did the world allow it to happen? Do young people today know about what happened here? Most important, do they even care?*

Out of nowhere, I was awakened from my stupor by a surprisingly mellifluous sound: men singing and playing guitar. I walked toward the sound, and lo and behold, there were two Haredi ("ultra-Orthodox," in the tendentious words of most Western media) Jewish men strumming along and singing cheery tunes. Perhaps even more impressive, they were *smiling* while doing so. Some people from our group, along with those from the other groups there, formed an impromptu circle, putting our arms around each other and singing while swaying side to side. There were many IDF soldiers touring Kfar Aza on that day, and some of them also came over and joined. It was an incredibly powerful and moving moment, and I was fighting back tears the whole time.

I'm not sure that I could have dreamed up a more perfect encapsulation of the Jewish people and the Jewish spirit. In that moment, I was reminded of the comforting words of Psalm 23: "Though I walk in the valley of the shadow of death, I will fear no evil, for You are with me; Your rod and Your staff—they will comfort me."[2] And above all, I thought of one of our people's refrains, three words that have defined our very essence amid countless oppressors' attempts to kill us throughout the generations: *Am Yisrael Chai—the people of Israel live.*[3]

It is difficult, perhaps impossible, to overstate the significance of the Simchat Torah Massacre of October 7, 2023. The gruesome and unbearable stories—babies decapitated in their cribs, Holocaust survivors shot execution-style in their homes, mass rapes and sexual crimes committed against women—shocked the Israeli public and the global Jewish Diaspora to their core. In total, roughly 1,200 Israelis were killed, many thousands more were wounded, and 247 were taken hostage back to Gaza. The IDF compiled a highly graphic forty-seven-minute video that documents some of the worst Hamas atrocities committed on that most horrifying of days. I still have not watched it. I saw all I needed to see in Kfar Aza and Re'im. And too many rabbis have said that the urge to watch the video must be resisted, lest the viewer risk permanent damage to his soul.

The Simchat Torah Massacre of October 7, 2023, shattered many illusions in Israel. It exposed the tragic, fatal conceit of those in the Israeli military, security, and intelligence establishments who believed that Hamas had somehow moderated since its 1988 organizational charter, which explicitly states that "our struggle against the Jews is very great and very serious" and that Hamas "should be supported by more and more squadrons from this vast Arab and Islamic world, until the enemy is vanquished and Allah's victory is realized."[4] (It turns out Hamas really does have no higher purpose than slaughtering Jews.) October 7 also laid bare the foolishness of those who thought peace could be purchased with economic inducements, such as monthly payments to Gaza from Qatar and work permits granted to Gazans by Israel. (It turns out that money just made Hamas rich, and that Gazans used the permits to scope out where to massacre.) And it revealed that Israel's highly touted intelligence capabilities are not anywhere near as good as many had thought.

October 7 also exposed, most fundamentally, the overarching failure of the State of Israel to fulfill its preeminent task: keep Jews safe and ensure "Never Again" actually means *Never Again*. As former Israeli ambassador to the US Michael Oren put it two weeks later, "In every essential area the state [of Israel] fell short" during the Simchat Torah Massacre.[5] Many questioned the viability of Zionism itself in ways that few had done since the Yom Kippur War of 1973—the last major surprise Arab incursion into Israel, occurring almost exactly a half-century earlier and on a different Jewish holiday. Seventy-five years after David

Ben-Gurion declared Israel's independence, had it really come to this?

But however horrific the details of the Simchat Torah Massacre were, and despite all the existential soul-searching that went on in Israel, it was the apathetic—and sometimes outright hostile—immediate reaction of the "civilized" world to the pogrom that rocked Jews living all over the globe. The catastrophic event did not merely shock and destabilize the modern State of Israel, but it also shocked and destabilized all of global Jewry—*Am Yisrael*, the Jewish people and collective Jewish nation, or simply "Israel" as that term will sometimes be used throughout this book.

Almost immediately, the corridors of high society and elite power discounted the atrocities of October 7, throwing the Jews under the bus and sometimes even blaming them for their own rapes and murders. There was the infamous statement from thirty-four Harvard University student groups "hold[ing] the Israeli regime entirely responsible for all unfolding violence."[6] There were the chants on the steps of the Sydney Opera House to "gas the Jews."[7] There were the Jewish students at prestigious Cooper Union in New York City who were literally locked into a school library while pro-Palestinian agitators chanted and banged on the doors outside.[8] There was the Jewish man tragically killed by a Palestinian supporter at dueling rallies in California.[9] There were the countless examples of Jews being verbally abused or physically assaulted *for no other reason whatsoever other than the fact that they were Jewish.*

There was the time in November 2023 when I was personally shouted down by a pro-Hamas mob for about forty minutes at the University of Michigan[10]—all while university administrators and campus police stood on the sidelines doing nothing, in violation of my First Amendment rights.[11] There was the time in October 2024 when I was protested by another student jihadi mob at Loyola University Chicago School of Law and needed two plainclothes officers and a squad car for safe evacuation—from an event about constitutional law, having nothing to do with Israel.[12] And there was the infamous congressional hearing in early December 2023 wherein the presidents of Harvard University, the University of Pennsylvania, and the Massachusetts Institute of Technology refused to plainly condemn calls for the genocide of the Jewish people on their university campuses.[13] Instead, the "elite" university presidents infamously testified that the moral or legal permissibility of calls for Jewish genocide was situational— that it "depends on the context." The Jewish people, the single most persecuted people in human history, are ironically the only ones for whom the appropriateness of genocide incitement "depends on the context."

There was America's national day of pro-Hamas anarchic rage on April 15, 2024, during which terrorism supporters and sympathizers shut down the Golden Gate Bridge, blocked the entrance to Chicago's O'Hare International Airport, and wreaked havoc elsewhere from coast to coast.[14] That same week, which also saw the president of Columbia University called before Congress to answer for the fact that her school is regularly ranked as one of the most anti-Semitic institutions of higher education in America,[15] terrifying pro-Hamas/anti-Jewish demonstrations rocked Columbia's New York City campus, leading to hundreds of arrests, violent occupations of academic buildings, and even standoffs with police in riot gear.[16] Sadly, none of the arrested young jihadists were ultimately prosecuted.

These so-called "protesters" were not advocating for a "two-state solution" and the establishment of an independent Arab state in Judea and Samaria; they were openly clamoring for Tel Aviv to be "burned to the ground"[17] and taunting pro-Israel counter-protesters as "al-Qassam's next targets."[18] The al-Qassam Brigades are among Hamas's most notorious military forces and are functionally indistinguishable from ISIS or al-Qaeda. At Princeton University, the top-ranked national university most years in *U.S. News & World Report*'s influential annual rankings, guitar-strumming students unfurled the flag of the Iranian proxy Shiite jihadist outfit Hezbollah.[19] (That would be the same Hezbollah, incidentally, that murdered twelve Druze children in cold blood while they were playing recreational soccer in Israel's Golan Heights on July 27, 2024.) At the University of California, Los Angeles, many Jewish students were blocked from entering campus by a frothing pro-Hamas student mob because they would not denounce their own religion—something a federal judge would describe, a few months later, as "unimaginable" and "abhorrent to our constitutional guarantee of religious freedom."[20]

Speaking of Los Angeles, on June 23, 2024, the well-known predominantly Jewish neighborhood of Pico-Robertson suffered an actual anti-Jewish pogrom. Hamas supporters and other apologists for murderous jihad swarmed Adas Torah, a popular Orthodox synagogue in the area, in order to block congregants (and the general public) from entering to hear a speaker who was visiting that day to discuss potential residential property sales in Israel. As the Hamasniks blocked both car and foot traffic, chanting the typical Nazi-esque exterminationist slogans of "from the river to the sea, Palestine shall be free" and "long live intifada," congregants and other curious Angelenos were forced to use the synagogue's back entrance. Both concurrently and after the event's conclusion, Hamas supporters went block by block, looting local Jewish-owned businesses and instigating violent altercations with local Jews and Israel supporters. At least one bystander holding an Israeli flag was brutally beaten and bloodied.

The June 2024 Pico-Robertson pogrom followed the November 2023 murder, in nearby Ventura County, California, of Jewish pro-Israel advocate Paul Kessler at the hands of a pro-Palestinian rioter. Yet again, no perpetrator in either instance (Kessler's murder and the 2024 pogrom) was arrested and prosecuted to the fullest extent of the law. If there is one lesson to take away, as tragic (though historically familiar) as it may be, it is that

Jewish blood is cheap. And it is perhaps doubly cheap when the underlying anti-Semitic conduct occurs in a far-left jurisdiction, where there is a reflexive disinclination to prosecute the scoundrels the media sanitizes as mere "protesters."[21] Anti-Semitic rioters know they all too often get a pass from today's "progressive" prosecutors, who, at the federal and local level alike, conform their actions (and non-actions) to prevailing woke orthodoxies.[22] This is tragic for the rule of law, and especially tragic for American Jews.

On July 24, 2024, the same day that Israeli prime minister Benjamin Netanyahu gave a stirring address to a joint session of Congress in which he argued to an American audience that "our enemies are your enemies, our fight is your fight, and our victory will be your victory," keffiyeh-clad pro-Hamas mobs swarmed and ransacked America's capital by the thousands.[23] Congregating in large part outside Washington, DC's Union Station train depot, the radicals burned American flags while chanting "Allahu Akbar," tore down other American flags and replaced them with the terrorist flag of the Palestine Liberation Organization (PLO), flew the flags of Foreign Terrorist Organizations (Hamas and Hezbollah), assaulted innocent bystanders and police officers (including those who sought to protect the desecrated American flags), vandalized public monuments by spray-painting "Hamas is comin'," outright called at times for the genocide of the Jews, and assaulted US Park Police. Later that same week, we learned that all charges against the pro-Hamas rioters who assaulted police during the Union Station riot were dropped. Just as in California, in New York City, and elsewhere, anti-Jewish incitement and Jewish blood alike were proven cheap.

These dutiful Western foot soldiers for murderous Islamism bear a rather ghoulish resemblance to last century's Hitler Youth.[24] Those yearning for Hezbollah's jackboot and chanting "We are Hamas" and "Long live Hamas" just a few months after the single deadliest day for the Jewish people since the defeat of

Nazi Germany would have felt right at home in Berlin in 1938.[25] As we know from the Book of Ecclesiastes: "What has been is what will be, and what has been done is what will be done, and there is nothing new under the sun."[26] For the Jews, alas, it has always been thus. Today's Hamasniks are the modern-day incarnation of Hitler's Brownshirts; the terrorist flag of Yasser Arafat's PLO is the new Nazi swastika.

Overall, anti-Semitic incidents in the United States and throughout Europe massively surged in the months following October 7, 2023.[27] These incidents were perpetrated by "Iran's useful idiots," to again borrow from Netanyahu's July 24, 2024, speech to Congress.[28] The perpetrators' goal, moreover, was, and remains, not merely the destruction of the modern Jewish State of Israel or the Jewish people. As the ceaseless burnings of the American flag and defacing of historic American statues has demonstrated, the goal was, and remains, nothing less than the end of America and the destruction of Western civilization itself.

Those trying months following the October 7 pogrom shone the brightest possible spotlight on the truly radical state of American higher education—especially at its so-called "leading" or most "prestigious" institutions. The drift of American colleges and universities away from a pedagogical emphasis on traditional Western values has been a very long time in the making. William F. Buckley Jr. documented this transformation in the Ivy League way back in 1951,[29] and the metastasis was certainly well underway by the time of the 1960s-era campus radicals and the concomitant rise in influence of many leading Frankfurt School intellectuals.[30] By now, in the 2020s, it is shockingly obvious that something—truly, *many* things—has gone very, very wrong in American higher education.

Overall, the pro-Hamas campus insanity of 2023–2024 can best be understood as the chickens of a uniquely toxic stew finally coming home to roost: decades of academic and pedagogical radicalism peddling pseudoscientific piffle under the veneer of "critical theory," disastrous neoliberal immigration policy that has invariably treated human beings from incompatible foreign cultures as mere widgets in an economic marketplace, discriminatory and racist affirmative action policies in higher education admissions, and a broader crisis of meaning and increased nihilism in America's younger generations.

And it is all in support of a cause, the so-called "Palestinian" cause,[31] that first emerged in its modern form in the mid-twentieth century as a Kremlin information operation aiming to destabilize American interests on the geopolitical chessboard, and whose entire raison d'être is subjugationist anti-Jewish annihilationism in the Jewish people's ancestral and eternal homeland. Indeed, Hamas's misanthropic supporters throughout Western urban enclaves are correct about at least one thing: The atrocities of October 7, 2023—beheading Jewish babies, shooting Jewish Holocaust survivors execution-style, raping Jewish women, and so forth—were an authentic representation of what the "Palestinian cause" looks like in practice. Give the "We are Hamas" crowd credit for honesty: Unlike those who pathetically insist that Hamas "does not represent the Palestinian people," such as President Joe Biden,[32] the open Hamas supporters at least recognize that there is no real daylight between the savage butchers of Hamas and the "Palestinian" cause as it has existed for a century.[33]

Nor has the problem of ascendant Jew-hatred and the concomitant flirtation with jihadist evil, sadly, been limited to the cloistered ivory tower professoriate and impressionable young left-wing radicals always on the hunt for a new faux-moralistic crusade to fill the spiritual void. The American Right, which for most of my lifetime had been a reliable wellspring of philo-Semitic and pro-Israel sentiment, also emerged from the ashes of the October 7 pogrom deeply divided about the proper role of the Jewish people and the Jewish state within the broader right-of-center fold—and, by extension, within Western civilization itself.

De-Christianized younger conservatives, some of whom trafficked in the neo-Nietzschean fare of the popular pseudonymous writer "Bronze Age Pervert," took to asking about the "Jewish question" in the far corners of social media discourse. Many leading right-of-center commentators, such as Candace Owens and Tucker Carlson, immediately took hostile positions toward the Jewish state's post–October 7 military incursion in Gaza. Owens, before she was fired from the *Daily Wire*, "liked" a social media post endorsing the classic medieval blood libel—the libel that led to countless anti-Jewish pogroms in the heart of Europe. In the months following her firing, she doubled down repeatedly by dabbling in the most sordid and crass strands of Jew-hatred imaginable—including peddling 9/11 "truther" conspiracy theories alleging Israeli complicity and smearing the late, internationally renowned, and widely beloved leader of the Chabad-Lubavitch movement, Rabbi Menachem Mendel Schneerson, as a "racist" and "Jewish supremacist."

Some of Owens's like-minded confrères, including Carlson, fanned the flames of anti-Semitism in the aftermath of the Simchat Torah Massacre by openly questioning the American patriotism of those political commentators (such as the conspicuously Jewish Ben Shapiro) who made a habit of frequently discussing and analyzing the war against Hamas.[34] Later in 2024, Carlson platformed on his show an amateurish pseudo-historian, whom he lauded as the "best and most honest popular historian in the United States," who nonchalantly described *Winston Churchill* as the "arch-villain" of World War II for Carlson's large audience. Indeed, that same so-called "historian," Darryl Cooper, has previously speculated that Adolf Hitler, who apparently merely sought "an acceptable solution to the Jewish problem," is in heaven. Such talk is obviously repulsive and condemnable, but it is representative of a growing strain of thought on the nominal Right.

The cumulative effect of the Western response to the Simchat Torah Massacre of October 7, 2023, and the ensuing war in Gaza was nothing less than mind-blowing. As no less prominent a Jewish American than comedian Jerry Seinfeld told *GQ*, "Every Jewish person I know was surprised by how hostile the reaction was."[35] Virtually every Jew I know, and with whom I have spoken about such matters, would broadly agree with that sentiment. One close Jewish friend described those difficult months following the Simchat Torah Massacre as a situation where "we can feel the tectonic plates shifting under our feet but are powerless to stop it."

Although it took some time for the grim reality to set in, the ubiquity, variety, and volume of the anti-Semitic eruptions during those dark months after October 7 made clear that the decades-long "Golden Age of American Jews" was all but over.[36] The era of knee-jerk, reflexive American (and Western) support for Jewish civil rights in the Diaspora and Jewish nationalism in the Jewish people's ancestral homeland, which had emerged from those same ashes of the Holocaust that brought me to tears in Treblinka, had come to a crashing halt. *Am Yisrael*, the global Jewish nation inside and outside *Eretz Yisrael*, the Land of Israel, found itself fighting for acceptance and legitimacy in the eyes of the "civilized" world yet again.

Less than a century after the most industrialized and systematic genocide in recorded human history, and seventy-five years after the miraculous rebirth of Jewish sovereignty in the Land of Israel (following nearly two millennia of exile), Jews were once again forced to endure a tide of the world's oldest and most intractable form of bigotry. The words of the Haggadah, which Jews read every year during the Passover Seder, are perhaps a source of comfort and succor during such times: "This is what has stood by our fathers and us! For not just one alone has risen against us to destroy us, but in every generation they rise against us to destroy us; and the Holy One, blessed be He, saves us from their hand!"[37] And so it has been ever since God's first promises to Abraham in the Book of Genesis.[38]

But taking intellectual and theological comfort in the eternal nature of this truth—even *knowing* with every fiber of one's being and every morsel of one's *emunah*[39] that God loves His nation Israel and will never abandon it—is not the same as feeling personally secure or content on any given day. For my generation of Jews, who came of age during the "Golden Age" of American Jewish life,[40] our perilous new reality has been difficult to process and accept—both in the abstract and in the practical realities of everyday life.

The truth is that the explosion of anti-Semitism in the aftermath of the Simchat Torah Massacre actually says very little about the Jewish people and the Jewish State of Israel. But it says a lot, on the other hand, about the ailing, sordid state of America and the broader West. Outbursts of anti-Semitism, from time immemorial, are not about the Jews themselves. Rather, such outbursts are invariably symptomatic of a more sweeping and debilitating societal rot. That is not, of course, to suggest that no Jew anywhere has ever done anything that is wrong and deserving of rebuke. Such a suggestion would be ludicrous, and I know this from ample personal experience. When I debated the well-known Jewish leftist Peter Beinart on the Israeli–Palestinian conflict in 2021, to give but one example, I certainly witnessed firsthand a lot that was very wrong and deserving of strong rebuke![41]

But this is missing the point. Individual Jews, just like individuals of any subgroup, have of course done any number of bad things over the course of recorded history. The Jews, however, are a tiny nation: roughly 0.2 percent of the global population. Even in the United States, which has by far the largest Jewish population in the world outside the State of Israel, Jews comprise *at most* 2 to 2.5 percent of the adult population.[42] (There is, in fact, ample reason for believing the percentage may be considerably smaller than even this: Non-Orthodox American Jews, tragically, have skyrocketing rates of intermarriage, and pollsters must necessarily rely on respondents' subjective attestations that they are "Jewish," notwithstanding the fact they may not actually be Jewish under Jewish law.)

The simple mathematical reality is that, outside of the various historical iterations of sovereign Jewish states in the Land of Israel (including the modern State of Israel), the Jews have probably never comprised a statistically significant enough proportion of any national population to be able to alter a society's trajectory on their own. And this, of course, even assumes that the Jews in a certain area magically all agreed on a given pressing issue—something even a cursory familiarity with the great rabbinical debates of the Talmud or an awareness of the well-known "two Jews, three opinions" meme would reveal as assuredly impossible.

Instead, what history has shown us time and again is that when things start to go south in a given society, the Jews are typically the first scapegoats. Anti-Semitism is the shape-shifting chameleon of bigotries, constantly warping and transmuting to fit the malady of the day. And in American and Western society after the pogrom of October 7, 2023, the explosive rise of Jew-hatred has had extraordinarily little to do with Israel's righteous and restrained prosecution of its defensive war in Gaza against genocidal Hamas terrorists. John Spencer, chair of urban warfare studies at the Modern War Institute at West Point, described Israel's post–October 7 war in Gaza as establishing a "historically low" 1:1.5 combatant-to-civilian death ratio for "modern urban warfare"—well below the already-exemplary 1:2.5 ratio the United States itself attained during the 2016–2017 Battle of Mosul.[43]

Rather, the reemergence of the world's oldest hatred is a crass manifestation of pent-up rage stemming from a toxic brew of factors collectively wreaking havoc upon the Millennial and Gen Z generations: the decreased authority of religious institutions and declining church/synagogue attendance and membership; the supply-side suffusion of lethal drugs and increased demand for them due to collapsing families and shoddy parenting; personal and civilizational self-hatred due to decades of indoctrination at the hands of morally bankrupt pedagogy; massively destabilizing long-term immigration trends and the willful importation of foreigners from adversarial or hostile cultures who do not share traditional Western values; the offshoring of American manufacturing and the willful sacrifice of large swaths of American industry; the metastasis of Big Tech and its suffocating and addiction-inducing algorithms; and the rise in depression and suicidal ideation that tragically spawn from all of this.

This ghastly stew, and not any specific tactical frustration with the Israel Defense Forces' prosecution of its war effort against the Hamas jihadist outfit in Gaza following October 7, 2023, is what is to blame for the historical outbursts of anti-Semitism that followed that dark day throughout America and much of the developed Western world. The so-called "protesters" are not ultimately concerned about Israel. Their ultimate frustration, and their ultimate enemy, is the United States of America and Western civilization itself. Sometimes they even let the mask slip and make this point explicitly. Pamphleteers at the University of Michigan distributed literature saying that "Freedom for Palestine means death to America," for instance, and aspiring jihadists at Columbia University called to "eradicate America as we know it."[44]

Perhaps most evocative, George Washington University's own on-campus Gaza "encampment" projected flames onto a large American flag with text reading, "GAZA LIGHTS THE SPARK THAT WILL SET THE EMPIRE ABLAZE."[45] As the ever-perceptive activist and author Christopher F. Rufo commented, "This is the point: the radical Left sees Israel as the small oppressor and America as the great oppressor. The protestors are not Islamists, but, rather, see Islamism as a useful accelerant in their campaign to 'set the empire ablaze.'"[46]

Give the anti-American, anti–Western civilization jackals some credit for their candor, no matter how morbid such candor may be. It is ultimately up to the American people and our fellow citizens of the West to use our ears to hear and our eyes to see what is now so clearly right before us—and, even more importantly, to formulate an appropriate response to our hostile civilizational takeover.

At this point, let's pause and take a step back.

This book is about far more than the October 7, 2023, Hamas massacre in Israel. It is about far more than modern Islamism's sprawling war on the West through all its menacing tentacles— the Islamic Republic of Iran, the Muslim Brotherhood, the Islamic State, and so forth.

The unfortunate reality is that the Simchat Torah Massacre struck the State of Israel and global anti-Semitism skyrocketed at a time when Western civilization was tragically ill-informed and unsure of what exactly it even stands for—and therefore uniquely ill-situated to muster the fortitude to man the ramparts (be they proverbial or literal) to defend our people and our way of life from those who seek to subjugate and destroy it. This book, in short, must necessarily be about far more than Islamism's war on Israel and the West because the twenty-first-century West's debilitating decadence and crushing lack of civilizational confidence (or even self-awareness) requires a much deeper and more profound level of introspection and sophistication.

Let us begin our journey here: Thus far, I have been assuming that the mass Hamas assault on Israeli civilians on October 7, 2023, *was* indeed evil. For that matter, one might suggest that the visceral emotional reaction I experienced at Treblinka arose from an assumption that the Holocaust itself was a profoundly, and uniquely, evil event. Perhaps this seems obvious—indeed, it should. But let us suppose, if only for the sake of argument, that it may *not* be obvious.

So, before venturing any further, it is important to set some basic moral parameters and ask: On what specific ethical, philosophical, and moral grounds do we know that murder—let alone mass murder—*is* wrong? On what specific basis *was* Hamas wrong to commit such atrocities on October 7, 2023, against the Jewish people and the Jewish State of Israel? On what basis, for that matter, *was* Hitler wrong to murder the vast majority of European Jewry? How can we claim to possess not merely natural intuition, but objective *knowledge* of the inherent wrongness of the anti-Semites' murderous actions against the modern State of Israel and the global Jewish nation of Israel?

The truth is that matters of right and wrong, and other closely related basic conceptions of Western morality, are often either taken for granted or lost upon us. There is at least one clear reason for this: We, as Americans and as Westerners more broadly, fail to recognize the novel and indispensable contributions of the Jewish people and the Jewish nation—the original People of the Book, the broader nation of Israel—that today remain the moral pillars, ethical frameworks, and legal foundation of the Judeo-Christian West. It is no mere coincidence that, as Western civilizational self-respect, cultural self-esteem, and Westerners' basic knowledge of their own heritage have all declined, the Jewish people have been increasingly abandoned—at times even anathematized. And where Jews are abandoned and anathematized by secularists, Islamists, and interlopers, Christians are never far behind.

It is imperative that contemporary young Americans—indeed, all contemporary young Westerners—fall in love with their own civilization again. A concrete society, culture, or civilization cannot long endure, after all, unless it first knows what exactly it is, knows what exactly it stands for, and knows why exactly that self-conception, identity, purpose, and mission is valuable, merited, and worth defending and preserving against those who seek to harm or destroy it. There is a sequential reasoning process that can only have one logical point of origin: What *is* "Western civilization," as we use the term today? When, where, how, and why did "Western civilization," as we now know it, begin?

The simple truth is that what we today call "Western civilization" is the broader Judeo-Christian order. And it all began at Mount Sinai, with God's revelation to the Israelites and the formation of Israel as the particular Jewish nation. One cannot comprehend anything about Western morality, ethics, or law without first coming to understand the earth-shattering, eternal significance of God's revelation to the incipient nation of Israel at Mount Sinai. For believers and nonbelievers alike, it is impossible to intuit the unadulterated evil of the Holocaust, the Simchat Torah Massacre, and all the deeply anti-Semitic destruction that followed that terrible pogrom without first understanding the very foundational pillars of the West.

It is therefore to the origins of Western civilization that I will next turn.

2

THE **PEOPLE** OF THE **BOOK** AND THE **WEST**

"And now, if you obey Me and keep My covenant, you shall be to Me a treasure out of all peoples, for Mine is the entire earth. And you shall be to Me a kingdom of princes and a holy nation."

—EXODUS 19:5–6[1]

LAW HAD, OF COURSE, EXISTED PRIOR TO GOD'S HISTORY-ALTERING revelation to the Israelites at Mount Sinai. Hammurabi's Code is perhaps the most famous of the ancient pagan bodies of law, but there were plenty of others, as well. The difference between these bodies of law and the Law of Moses, as revealed by God Himself to an estimated millions of newly emancipated Jews,[2] is that the giving of the Law of Moses and the concomitant formation of the nation of Israel take place in the context of Divine Revelation.

The Law of Moses would go on to become the undisputed bedrock of Western legal codes, Western ethics, and in many ways Western political theory,[3] as I will discuss further. But for present purposes, I will focus on the epistemological and teleological significance of the Divine Revelation at Sinai.

The very idea of a divinely ordained code of law, conduct, and morality—given by a monotheistic God to His chosen people—remains unprecedented in the entire history of mankind. In transmitting His Torah, His law, and His wisdom to the nascent Israelite nation, God solidified and reified one of the foundational claims of the Genesis story: namely, that God "created Man in His image; in the image of God He created him."[4] That the infinite God revealed Himself and His ways to finite, lowly mankind—and the Israelite nation, specifically—necessitates that He made man *capable* of understanding and implementing His laws and His ways in the first place.

Revelation at Sinai thus established the inherent Godliness and holiness of man. If man is capable of listening, processing, interpreting, and implementing God's eternal code, then man must by definition be special—indeed, unique within the animal kingdom. This, above all, is what is meant by "God creat[ing] Man in His image." Indeed, God has already made us holy. This is why, when Jews are about to perform a positive *mitzvah* (i.e., an affirmative commandment), we always begin our prayer with: "*Barukh ata Adonai Eloheinu, melekh ha'olam, asher kid'shanu b'mitzvotav v'tzivanu.*" That italicized phrase—*asher kid'shanu*—is the Jewish people's way of thanking God for having *made us holy* and instilling within us an innate *kedushah*, or holiness.

This belief in the inherent holiness of mankind, which flows naturally from God's revelation at Sinai and the establishment of a unique relationship between man and man's Creator high above, is a foundational, overarching principle for what we today call Western civilization. Pagan society necessarily worships the "rational" human mind and/or the hedonistic self-indulgences of the human ego, denying a higher authority and a transcendental calling. Godly Revelation at a national level, *en masse*, as opposed to a single individual—which, in the entire history of mankind, only ever occurred at Mount Sinai—fundamentally changed the game, in terms of man's worldly relationships with his fellow man, his eternal relationship with his Creator, and his ultimate destiny.

Following revelation, there *was* a higher calling, there *was* a purpose, and there was a *reason* to follow the Divine Law. As the First of the Ten Commandments states, after all: "I am the Lord, your God, Who took you out of the land of Egypt, out of the house of bondage."[5] Surely, that is reason enough to obey the law—and to help fulfill our God-given purpose of sanctifying His name in all that we do in this earthly realm. It cannot possibly be overstated that the entirety of normative Western ethics, and of Christendom and Judeo-Christian civilization more generally, flows from these rudimentary precepts—which is to say that it flows from God's revelation to the incipient Israelite nation congregated at Mount Sinai.

It may also be helpful to work our way backward, beginning with some more modern thinkers who have contributed their thoughts to this same general topic.

Consider the obscure early-twentieth-century polymath Alfred Korzybski, father of the discipline of general semantics. Korzybski asked several probing—and timeless—questions in his seminal 1921 work, *The Manhood of Humanity: The Science and Art of Human Engineering.* Those questions include: What is man? What is man's nature? What distinguishes humanity from the other classes of life—vegetative and animal alike? What is unique about man that throughout all time and all places, he creatively initiates and contributes toward a notion of *civilization?*

Korzybski's profound and oft-quoted insight was that "humanity is the time-binding class of life."[6] As articulated by one of Korzybski's contemporaries, mathematical philosopher Cassius Jackson Keyser, relative to animal life, man is endowed with a unique "energy that invents—that produces instruments, ideas, institutions, and doctrines; it is, moreover, the energy that, having invented, criticizes, then invents again and *better*, thus advancing in excellence from creation to creation endlessly."[7] This special energy to engage in introspection and to *criticize*, and thereafter to *improve*, is peculiar to mankind and accounts for what we might call "human progress"—a distinct concept from anything else that exists throughout the rest of vegetative and animal life.

Keyser illustrated this point well when, building off Korzybski's "time-binding" conception in a 1922 lecture, he compares the activity of beavers building a dam to that of men building a bridge.[8] Both construction projects require the elements of time, toil, and raw materials, and both physical achievements may endure for a long time. But what of subsequent generations? Whereas new generations of beavers may look upon the dams of their predecessors and find nothing to improve upon, man is guided by past achievements and drawn to invent, innovate, and enhance—to build upon what already is.

As Keyser put it: "[I]f this was a bridge, he makes a better bridge or invents a ship . . . if it was the art of printing, he invents a printing press; if it was the discovery of the laws of planetary motion, he finds the law of gravitation."[9] For a beaver, there is no intergenerational, let alone "societal" or "civilizational," advancement. Each successive generation of beaver begins and ends in the same life station as its preceding generation. Beavers, like the other beasts of the animal kingdom, fundamentally do not progress and advance in sync with the ticking clock of Father Time. They exist to eat, drink, sleep, reproduce, and fulfill other basic biological needs and urges. But there is *no higher calling or purpose* for the beaver's existence.

Why is man fundamentally different from beavers and other beasts of the animal kingdom, not only in degree, but also in kind? Keyser explained: "[I]n man's case, unlike the beaver's, the old-*time* factor is not merely present, it *works* . . . it is living capital bearing interest . . . perpetually compounded at an ever-increasing rate. And the interest is growing wealth—not merely physical conveniences, but instruments of power, under-standing, intelligence, knowledge, and skill, beautiful arts, science, philosophy, wisdom, freedom—in a word, civiliza-tion."[10] This is what Korzybski meant by stating that humanity is time-binding: "[T]he *time*-factor, embodied in things accomplished, perpetually reinforces more and more the achieving potency of the human mind[.]"[11]

Korzybski, like so many other philosophers, ethicists, and sci-entists before and after him, therefore rejected a strictly zoologi-cal conception of man as merely a more advanced or specialized animal. Korzybski's insights into man and civilization are helpful in establishing the framework for the ineffable revolution that was God's revelation to the Israelites at Mount Sinai—and the inescapable consequences for all of humanity that have followed ever since.

The implications are clear. Humans are social creatures; we are all members of a family, and our families are typically mem-bers of a broader tribe. Humans are born into and raised in affil-iations with others, with complex and overlapping mutual bonds of interdependent loyalty. And the families and tribes we are born into each have their own backstories—their own treasure troves of knowledge, culture, wisdom, customs, and traditions that not only orient the way in which we experience the world, but also act as accelerants to propel us forward toward our own destinies.

For each individual, this accumulated accomplishment, which bears "interest" over "time" (to again borrow from Keyser), also means that from the moment we are born, unlike animals, we possess an inherent responsibility toward our community mem-bers, our kin, our forebears, and our fellow men not to squander, destroy, or set back the goodness of the past that has accumulated to bring us to our own moment in time. Men are, after all, differ-ent from beavers.

Amidst this metaphysical backdrop, let us consider how the Jewish religion and the Jewish tradition sheds indispensable light on *why* mankind is here in this intergenerational "interest"-bearing journey, as well as *for which purpose* and *to which end* we humans are drawn to progress and continue the never-ending work of building civilization.

One way Jewish tradition identifies man as a unique and exalted category of creation is by considering one of the defining features of humankind: our ability to speak.

Speech, which is inextricably linked to man's advanced cognitive capacity, elevates man above the other beasts of the animal kingdom. Speech allows us to think and to structure our thoughts, to draw out distinctions and to differentiate coherently, to classify patterns and trends, to articulate opinions and justify behavior, to communicate with others beyond ourselves, and to command others. In short, speech is the distinguishing, essential feature of humanity, and enables man to exist in His image. The ability to formulate and articulate ideas in a linguistic code is the basis for human cognition and reason; rationality and wisdom cannot exist but for speech. Man's likeness to God is found in his ability to speak.

The Bible teaches that God spoke the world into being *ex nihilo.* That is, from utter nothingness He created a world and brought it into being—and He did so specifically via speech.[12] Observant Jews restate this truth every morning in the first lines of *baruch she'amar,* one of the opening blessings of the *pesukei dezmira* section of the morning *shacharit* prayer: "Blessed is He who spoke, and the world came into being, blessed is He."[13] This is an indispensable part of Judaism's morning liturgy.

Why does the Torah describe God as using the distinct faculty of *speech* as He goes about the process of creating the universe? Perhaps God, who is omnipotent, could have merely thought or willed the universe into existence—or otherwise acted to form it. But no; he *spoke* it into existence. Why might that be?

First, our thoughts are intimate, internal. Verbalized speech, by contrast, is externalized, and relevant only when there is an "other" party. Before God spoke, there was no existence other than Him. The act of speaking itself creates and externalizes a reality outside of Himself—meaning, the broader universe, animal and vegetative life, and man himself, all as described in the Genesis narrative.

Second, speech is organized, definitional, limiting, confining, structured, and differentiated. Prior to His creation of the universe, we might think of God as manifesting Himself through infinite endless light. To make room, so to speak, for created reality and a sustainable natural order to exist and prosper, God needed to constrain and hide Himself so that the creation should not be overwhelmed by His awesome presence.

Speech allows for this. When a person speaks, even when the most gifted and articulate of rhetoricians does so, his speech can never fully manifest the exact idea that he has clearly in his mind or the exact feeling he harbors deeply in his heart. There are ideas and emotions that words are simply too inadequate to express, and which fall short of the full human experience the person is attempting to describe. So, too, with God, speech provides some definition and limitation, order, and consistency from a source (God) that has no definition or limitation, and where nothing else exists other than His exalted infiniteness.

Third, the fact that speech conceals God's infiniteness is not simply part of the process of creation; it is one of creation's *goals*. Why does God decide to create tangible reality in the first place? Jewish tradition, in a famous Midrash, teaches that He desired to have a home in the lowest possible realm—"lowest" insofar as the natural order predominates, unlike in the heavens, where God predominates.[14] In precisely such a place, man, through his own free will and not coerced by overwhelming Divine Revelation and bliss, should choose to connect with Him by following His commandments and "partnering" with Him to tend the garden of His creation. The goal is that God wants man to feel at home in an opaque, coarse, materialistic world that is otherwise hostile to the sublime, undefined infiniteness that predates God's creation of the universe. This is accomplished by way of man's actions—by man asserting his free will to choose to fulfill His Will, without being compelled to do so by overpowering revealed Godliness.

When God spoke our earthly reality into existence, He employed the faculty of speech. But when He created Adam, the first man, He formed a composite being: from the dust of the earth, which had already been spoken into existence, and then He breathed a soul into His man's nostrils. Jewish mysticism teaches that the breath that emanates from speech is shallow and superficial, but when a person *breathes*, they do so from deep inside their lungs.[15] So, too, the soul that God imbued within Adam was from a deeper, more sublime place within God.

That the Bible teaches us man is made in the image of God means that we are both *of* this physical world, but not fully *beholden* to it. We are endowed by our Creator with a soul—an animating purpose that allows us to transcend the physical. Yet we are nevertheless physical beings, and we are also created to be present and fulfill a mission in this physical world. We possess an element of the sublime and holy that gives us unique dignity and purpose among all the created beings of the animal kingdom.

To be made in His likeness means that our conduct can and *should* comport with Godly conduct—in a manner in accordance with His Will. As we will see, the Bible's Divine Image imperative also has tangible ramifications for political theory; whoever claims that John Locke's *Second Treatise of Government* or Thomas Jefferson's Declaration of Independence gifted the world the concept of genuine human equality has apparently never read the Book of Genesis.

As an aside, there is a common misunderstanding about how anthropomorphic speech is used in the Bible to describe God. The reality is the other way around: The Bible used Godlike speech to describe man. We are made in God's image; not the other way around. The fact that we have "hands," or tools that we can extend into reality to manipulate nature and bend it according to our will, is because we are made in God's likeness and He has a true hand; ours is merely made of flesh and blood, susceptible to damage and destined for eventual disintegration.

So, too, with any other anthropomorphic descriptors: The fact that the biblical language used with respect to God often seems human-centered is because the Torah was given to us to enable us to understand and make sense of it on our terms. And we were created in God's likeness—so by better understanding ourselves, we can better understand Him.

Adam, the first man, intimately knew God, his Creator. How, then, is it possible that the grave sin of idolatry—the worship of false deities—developed and spread so quickly and pervasively that Abraham, the first Jew, had to stand against the entire pagan world and spread the monotheistic belief in one God? How is it that the Israelites, even so many generations after Abraham, committed the paradigmatic idolatrous sin of the golden calf?

Idolatry is perhaps the single greatest offense committed against God—the Second of the Ten Commandments, and the first hortatory one—because it denies His sovereignty over His own creation. Paganism, the opposite of the Bible's monotheism, evinces solipsistic self-worship and/or a misplaced trust in false gods. Praying to the sun to request a good harvest or saying thank you to the sea or the moon denies God His due as the sole Creator who ever was, is, and will be. Intermediaries—from the rivers and rains that provide irrigation for the wheat harvest to the sun that provides the harvest's light and warmth—have no independent power, agency, or purpose on their own. Rather, it is the Creator who runs His creation; everything else is merely a tool through which He dispenses His providence.[16]

But the paganism of old is alive and well today—just in an altered form.[17] The denial of God and the concomitant worship of self can only take root among those who foolishly and hubristically elevate "science" or "reason" to the Godly pedestal of Truth and Wisdom. If the modern-day pagans—from atheists to hedonists to evangelists of the woke ideology—properly understood what science *is* and *is not*, they would realize their own analytical and epistemological folly. Alas, they don't.

Science is descriptive, empirical, and *functional*; it represents humanity's collective best guesses as to how the natural world functions, given observed data and existing technology at any given moment in time. But science makes no claims whatsoever about truth, morality, or ethical considerations—about what is right and what is wrong, or about what one ought to do when facing a difficult scenario. The scientific method is an inquiry into empirical phenomena. If something is not observable, repeatable, and falsifiable, then it does not reside in the domain of science. When a consensus emerges around a particular hypothesis, we get a working theory that functionally explains something about the natural world. Certain time-honored principles may be understood as "laws of nature" that explain durable, consistent relationships. As a consensus in the scientific community changes, a "paradigm shift" might occur that alters our functional understanding of the world around us.

All of this is to say that science is useful, but it is limited. Science never purports to make any claims about truth; it only offers best guesses about the natural world, which are themselves susceptible to constant scrutiny and reevaluation. Some scientific theories endure, and others do not. And science decidedly does not provide answers as to *why* any given natural phenomenon *is* the way it is; it only offers the how, what, when, and where. "Scientism," the pagan's attempt to extend the limited domain of science into an all-encompassing "belief system," is a hopeless and fraudulent endeavor.

Religious belief in the Divine, by contrast, is decidedly *not* scientific. It violates all of the above rules: It is axiomatic, and though certain phenomena are at times readily observable, they are not necessarily repeatable. When trust in science veers into *belief*—and assumptions and conclusions are no longer questioned—then science is no longer "science," but the false deity of "scientism." If belief in the Divine is not axiomatic, then it is necessarily not belief—it is empiricism. Religion makes claims of truth; science does not. Properly considered, religion and science are perfectly complementary; there is no problem of mutual exclusivity.

In the same vein, human reason is often falsely elevated as something closely approximating the highest—and perhaps singular—virtue by far too many societal elites. As economist Oren Cass has observed, in the context of America's contemporary political debates: "A case supported by a faith-based argument [or from inherited tradition] is presumptively wrong, a concession that no colorable argument from reason is available. Reason must be on the other side. The person making the [faith- or tradition-based] argument must be unreliable as well, because the resort to faith indicates either an inability or an unwillingness to be reasonable."[18] Furthermore, "arguments from faith [or tradition] are not merely unpersuasive within the cult of reason that holds overwhelming power in our society. They are disqualifying."[19]

The American ruling class—and the Western ruling class at large—has long placed human reason on a lofty pedestal. But the worship of human *reason qua reason* is a foolish and dangerous delusion of the highest order: It is the egomaniacal indulgence of self. As finite beings, man's capacity to reason is inherently limited. Our experiences of the world and the conclusions we draw from those experiences are plagued by the problems of induction. We also deduce myriad logical fallacies, mistaking that which may be circumstantially valid for that which is permanent and true. The implications have tremendous moral consequence; man, for instance, can easily find reasons to rationally justify his intended, subjectively desired ends in the false name of "reason" or logical consistency.

Western civilization is sometimes described as being predicated upon a double helix of intertwining *reason* and *revelation*—Jerusalem and Athens, or the Bible and Greek philosophy, as Leo Strauss often formulated it—and that is true to an extent. The political theory of the American Founding is certainly one prominent example of how revelation-based religion and reason-based liberal political theory can, at least at times, work in unison toward mutual causes and goals. (I will expand on this in subsequent chapters.)

But to elevate reason *over* revelation, faith, and inherited tradition is to fall prey to a debilitating solipsism; it is to forsake the eternal and the transcendental for the vogue fetishization of the self and other mere temporal concerns. Many of history's greatest tyrants, from ancient times through the bloody genocides of the twentieth century, justified their atrocities on grounds of "reason" and other vague, self-aggrandizing abstractions—a most damning indictment of appeals to "reason," if there ever were one. There are countless such examples. Untrammeled "reason" often becomes self-serving: Consider, for example, the ancient pagan worshipers of "reason" who sacrificed children for bountiful health, the Greek men of "reason" who glorified pedophilia or pederasty, and the Nazis who "rationalized" the extermination of Jews and other "inferior races" as just and necessary.

German society in the interwar period was the most scientifically advanced in the entire world; Germans prided themselves on their pristine achievements of the human mind. Such "reason," tragically, culminated in the train tracks of Auschwitz. In the antebellum United States, furthermore, "reason" could have easily militated in favor of either slavery abolition or expanded slaveholding in the then-accumulating Western territories; the application of "reason" merely depended on a given individual's particular circumstances, milieu, and exogenous priors.

Purportedly "rational" societies have repeatedly proven themselves capable of perpetrating the greatest evils. In the absence of a higher authority that sets out truths and imposes defining moral guardrails, we are only able to grasp at what may or may not be true, correct, just, or righteous. History clearly demonstrates that we often fail miserably. There is thus no compelling argument to subordinate the Truth of authentic revelation to the false pseudo-deity of "reason." All major monotheistic religions believe that man is naturally susceptible to, and perhaps even inclined toward, sin. So why in the world would we want to rely upon those same individuals to decide, absent some sort of firmer underpinning that has at its core a sturdy intergenerational transmission of traditions, customs, practices, and folkways, what is and is not "reasonable"—and to then structure our laws, morality, and ethics accordingly?

There *is* a limited role for "reason" in our way of thinking, but only when it is contextualized within, and constrained by, a proper exogenous order and values system. The great medieval Jewish sage Maimonides sought to reconcile elements of Aristotelian thought in his famous codification of *Halacha* (Jewish law), *Mishneh Torah*; indeed, Maimonides's other *magnum opus*, *The Guide for the Perplexed*, is almost entirely dedicated to exploring the ways in which Judaism and ancient Greek philosophy can (and cannot) be harmonized. Maimonides offers great praise for Aristotle's philosophical achievements and agrees with many of his propositions concerning, for instance, metaphysics.

Crucially, however, Maimonides never allows philosophy to obscure the Torah. Maimonides departs substantially from Aristotle, for example, when it comes to creation and revelation—two of the most foundational elements of Jewish thought. Overall, we might say that Maimonides incorporated Aristotelian concepts, but he only utilized them within the acceptable confines of Jewish law and Jewish tradition. In short, he used many Aristotelian insights in un-Aristotelian ways. Maimonides thus demonstrates an acceptable use of unaided "reason" or "rationalism": as a means to enrich one's exogenous, already-formed ways of thinking about the world. This stands in stark contrast to modernity's exaltation of *reason qua reason* as intrinsically noble or valuable, and perhaps even an end unto itself.

The post-European Enlightenment West's overreliance on "reason" and "rationalism," furthermore, has also caused tremendous harm to the practice and transmission of Judaism itself. "Reason"- and "rationalism"-based approaches to Judaism, first emerging in earnest with the *Haskalah* (i.e., "Jewish Enlightenment") of the eighteenth and nineteenth centuries and culminating in the spread of theologically liberal offshoots of Judaism in Western Jewish Diaspora communities such as Reform Judaism and Reconstructionist Judaism, have done more to destroy the Jewish nationhood and peoplehood than any other internal threat in the entire history of our people. It is due to the siren song of "reason" that many Jews have deemed observance of *Halacha* to be merely optional, an inconvenient obstacle to somehow-greater fulfillment. It is due to "reason" that many Jews have deemed intermarriage to be perfectly acceptable, notwithstanding the fact that intermarriage in practice means raising religiously confused and/or outright non-Jewish children.

Judaism is not supposed to be "reasonable." Jewish law and its all-encompassing life commitment is not, and certainly never was, intended to be a purely logical exercise—the sort of thing one studies in preparation for taking the SAT or LSAT admission tests. Judaism's particularist glory, rather, is instead that it merely *is*—its claim that it was, is, and will forever be God's truth.

To assume that Judaism must be "reasonable" or "rational" is to entirely misunderstand the Jew's purpose on earth. Judaism does not afford greater favor for observance of its "reasonable" or morally intuitive commandments, such as the Decalogues' proscriptions against murder and adultery, than it does for its "unreasonable" commandments, such as *shatnez*, the prohibition against wearing both wool and linen fabrics in one garment. Both the former category (*mishpatim*, "reasonable") and the latter category (*chukim*, "unreasonable") of religious commandments must be obeyed so that the Jew can fulfill his purpose of sanctifying God's name in all that he does. As Scripture says: "In all the way which the Lord, your God, has commanded you, you shall go, in order that you may live and that it may be well with you."[20] Such an anachronistic emphasis on "reason" or intuition, moreover, does not merely misunderstand the purpose of Judaism and the leading of a Jewish life—it deprives Judaism of that which makes it unique, which is, among other things, its claim to God revealing His truth to His chosen people at Mount Sinai.

It is only through the intergenerational transmission of one's inherited tradition rather than recourse to solipsistic "reason," furthermore, that man can attain genuine purpose and live a truly content life. I will come back to this crucial theme throughout this book.

If recourse to "reason" is so inherently problematic, then it logically follows that something else must take precedence as the preeminent civilizational building block for knowledge, wisdom, and virtue. That "something else" is revelation, the Bible, and the Judeo-Christian order that we recognize today as Western civilization. This brings us back to Mount Sinai, where God first revealed Himself to the ancient Israelites—and, by extension, to the entirety of His creation, man.

Man is a finite being with an inherent "time-binding" inclination to build, criticize, and improve. But beyond that, what should man do to ascertain truth, emulate proper conduct, and understand the proper set of rights and responsibilities between man and fellow man, between man and beast, and between man and Creator?

As finite beings, we are definitionally unable to simply "know" or "reason" our way toward these answers. Our non-Sinaitic morals and ethics thus look more like a pseudo-science; they are poorly drawn inferences informed only by the limited empirical data of our lived experiences and communal myths and traditions, and are always vulnerable to the corrupting influence of our own desires, passions, and interests.

It is only through this understanding of man's structural limitations that we can begin to comprehend the magnitude of God's revelation to Moses and the ancient Israelites at Mount Sinai. The truth is that it is only through direct communication from God to man that we human beings can truly *know* moral behavior. Many intellectuals, philosophers, and sophists alike have challenged this extraordinarily basic epistemological premise over the millennia. They have all failed.

With an estimated three-million-plus Jews gathered at the foot of Mount Sinai after God miraculously took them out of Egypt and split for them the Sea of Reeds, He gave them (via Moses) the Ten Commandments and the entirety of the Written and Oral Torah (the Five Books of Moses and the Talmud). This was the only moment in human history in which a people became a nation and experienced in unison a revelation from God in which they received His word and His wisdom.

No other people in the history of the world has ever even made a claim to a national revelation. There are many individual prophets throughout history—some true and some false—who have claimed personal revelation from the Creator. But only the Jews have ever encountered Divine Revelation at a *national* level. The Jews codified these laws and teachings from the Lawgiver of all lawgivers, and they studied and retained them in precise manner in a direct and unbroken chain from generation to generation—despite persecution, Diaspora, and countless other tragedies. Jews as far apart as Yemen, Poland, Morocco, Lithuania, and France retained and practiced the exact same text and the exact same set of laws, differing only in customs and other subsidiary cultural traditions.

Just as God created the world through His faculty of speech with His utterances that spoke reality into being—which Jews recall daily in the *barukh she'amar* prayer—so, too, in a mirrored process that links creation with its ultimate intended goal, did He speak to the incipient Jewish nation ten primary, foundational commandments. For with this truth and wisdom now revealed from on High, the Jews, as God's chosen people, are able to live in accordance with His Will. Just as creative speech brought about the natural order of a world from a state of disorder, so, too, do His laws given to the Jewish people at Mount Sinai bring about civilizational order and help man fulfill his purpose in this mortal realm.

But Divine Revelation at Sinai was not, and is not, merely about the Jews. The Divine Revelation that took place at Mount Sinai was an earth-shattering event for *all* people.[21] Though the Jewish people were given 613 overt commandments and their many additional derivatives found throughout the Written and Oral Law, seven primary commandments and their many derivatives by which to live were specifically earmarked for the rest of mankind (i.e., Gentiles). They are known as the Seven Noahide Laws, because they were articulated (well before Divine Revelation at Sinai) to Noah and his progeny, from which the entire human race can trace back.

The Seven Noahide Laws were ultimately rearticulated for all of humanity when God spoke to the assembled Jews at Sinai, thus confirming their everlasting truth and authority. The Seven Noahide Laws were included in the revelation at Sinai for one additional reason: The Jewish people, as God's chosen representatives in this world, are commanded to be a "light unto the nations." A core tenet of the Jewish people's national directive is the obligation to share God's true ways with the Gentile nations of the world, so that they, too, can be just and righteous inhabitants of God's good earth and flourishing subjects of His splendid kingdom. As one exceptional post–October 7 essay put it, "We [Jews] need to look for standards from within our tradition to set a moral example for the whole world."[22]

The Seven Noahide Laws are foundational to human flourishing and civilizational progress.[23] They are indispensable for healthy relations between man and fellow man, between man and beast, and between man and Creator. The Seven Noahide Laws are:

1. The prohibition of idolatry

2. The prohibition of blasphemy

3. The prohibition of murder and injury

4. The prohibition of eating meat that was removed from a living animal

5. The prohibition of theft

6. The prohibition of specific forbidden sexual relations

7. The obligation to establish laws and courts of justice

These principles, which in some ways overlap with the Ten Commandments, constitute perhaps the most intuitive foundation of a "moral minimum for good government," as my Edmund Burke Foundation colleague Yoram Hazony embraces the term in his 2018 book, *The Virtue of Nationalism*.[24] (Hazony more specifically emphasizes the Ten Commandments, but the Seven Noahide Laws—which explicitly also apply to Gentiles, and not merely Jews—are perhaps even more apt.) The Noahide Laws are, in the words of Steven Grosby, a professor of religion at Clemson University, "universal laws independent of the Jewish [nation] that were understood to be the foundation for civil toleration within a state and among states."[25]

The Noahide Laws remain today, along with the Ten Commandments themselves, the barest minimum of an identifiable moral standard by which we can assess and judge any people, tribe, or nation throughout the globe. There are many worthy objections to the long-running Straussian criticism of biblically based political philosophy as somehow lacking a "universal" moral standard. These familiar Straussian arguments have been rebutted elsewhere, including by Hazony, and to attempt to thoroughly do so again here would be beyond the scope of this book. But for present purposes, it will suffice to say that perhaps the easiest, most straightforward, and most definitive response to such Straussian criticism is to simply note the existence and the enduring, eternal significance of the quintessentially "universal" Noahide Laws.

Christianity and Islam both derive their foundational moral principles and monotheistic beliefs from Judaism; it is on account of God's revelation at Sinai to the Israelite nation that Christians and Muslims can make any authoritative claims to the Truth of the one God, in the first instance. The fact that the majority of the world's population now believes in the Truth of the one God, and thus has been de-paganized by Judaism's sister Abrahamic religions, is a testament to the enduring strength of the Torah and its revelation from God at Mount Sinai.

Let's revisit Alfred Korzybski's insights into man, civilization, and human nature.

The pulsating impulse within man that leads us to civilize and build up civilization, in which the achievements of the past act as a "compounding interest" for forward human flourishing, which he famously termed man's "time-binding" nature, is very much aligned with a Jewish conception of man and of our purpose of being here. But we must offer one very important adjustment.

The exuberance in Cassius Jackson Keyser's 1922 lecture regarding Korzybski's conception of man is palpable. Both Korzybski's conception and Keyser's lecture were written and delivered in the period immediately following World War I (then simply known as the Great War), when the zeitgeist was—reflecting upon the recent callous destruction of so much human life—a bright and cheerful turn toward global peace and prosperity and an embrace of science and reason to advance human flourishing.

Keyser's lecture thus has strong utopian and messianic undertones. And yet barely a decade and a half later, Hitler invaded Poland and the world entered a heretofore inconceivable level of utter evil, darkness, and destruction—all perpetrated by a country, and a people, widely seen as the zenith of scientific achievement and rational embrace. It turns out that whig historiography, which portrays history as a linear progression from a benighted past to an ever-more-enlightened present and future, is oversimplified nonsense.

How, then, did Korzybski and Keyser err?

Korzybski's conception of man rightly rejects the "animal mind" of the brute, which acts against the civilizing force of man's "time-binding" nature. Crucially, however, Korzybski rejected the supernatural conception of man supported by the Bible: namely, that man is composed of both body and soul, and made in God's image. Instead, Korzybski embraced a conception of man that relies upon human reason and science to inform his fellow man of what ethics he should have to abide by, what is meant by virtue, what constitutes wisdom, and so forth. And herein lies the folly.

Only when mankind embraces the civilization-optimized code of divine ethics and laws gifted to us by our Creator at Mount Sinai can, to again borrow from Keyser, human achievement of past generations serve as "not only living capital bearing interest, but interest perpetually compounded at an ever-increasing rate."[26]

We are commanded in Genesis to "fill the earth and subdue it."[27] The intent behind our creation, and the intent behind God's revelation of truth and moral wisdom found within His structure of articulated law, is to elevate and refine the world and elevate and refine ourselves—while peacefully and harmoniously inhabiting it. The innate human impulse to build and improve, to civilize and progress, is precisely because the animating soul within each of us is drawn toward its Divine mission—and the fruits of the structure revealed at Sinai compound and propel us forward at an exponential pace. The end-goal of the collective human civilization that we are progressing toward is nothing less than the messianic: the ultimate perfection and wholesome manifestation of God in this world.

When man removes, denies, or veers too far away from the divinely gifted, civilizational-optimized code of ethics and laws given to us at Mount Sinai, then we deplete our treasure chest of interest-bearing wealth that is held in trust from one generation to the next, setting us back to dark places. We encounter civilizational regression. Whig historiography fails.

This lesson could not be more prescient than it is right now. We are standing at a civilizational inflection point. We have achieved so much and come so far at this juncture in human history. Will we regress to darkness, or will we progress forward to light? The story of the Jewish people and our unique mission in the world to be torchbearers—lights unto the nations—can help diagnose our challenges and inform our enlightened path forward. Indeed, the Jews must do so for the sake not merely of themselves, but of the broader Judeo-Christian West itself.

3

RIGHT vs. WRONG

Jewish Morality as the Bedrock of the Western Tradition

"And God created man in His image; in the image of God He created him; male and female He created them."

—GENESIS 1:27[1]

LIKE VIRTUALLY EVERY OTHER AMERICAN MILLENNIAL, I LEARNED in elementary school about the so-called "Golden Rule": the foundational imperative, which arguably binds together a given community or society more than any other norm, that one should treat other people as he himself wishes to be treated. The Golden Rule struck me, even in my youth, as intuitive and commonsensical. (Indeed, I would like to think that it positively affected my childhood-era behavior in the classroom and on the playground!) Looking back decades later, the Golden Rule still strikes me as intuitive and commonsensical today. Indeed, it is difficult to contemplate how either a modern twenty-first-century community or nation-state, reliant as it must necessarily be upon the resilience of its citizenry's bonds of loyalty, can possibly cohere and prosper absent widespread adoption of the Golden Rule.

What I certainly did *not* learn in my New York State public elementary school classroom was the distinctly *Jewish* and *biblical* roots of what is now taught to countless young American children, in an entirely secular and mundane context, as the Golden Rule. Consider the positive commandment found in Leviticus 19:18: "You shall neither take revenge from nor bear a grudge against the members of your people; you shall love your neighbor as yourself."[2] The Golden Rule as it exists and is universally taught today can only be understood as a modern adaptation of the famous Levitical injunction to "love your neighbor as yourself."[3] Without Leviticus, in other words, there would be no Golden Rule as I was taught it in school and as millions of other young Americans of all religious and political stripes learn it in their respective schools every year. The Golden Rule is thus one of Judaism's many enduring, if perhaps underappreciated, contributions to the modern Western world.

The Talmud, the foundational text of Rabbinic Judaism, actually takes the importance and centrality of the Levitical "Golden Rule" injunction considerably further. In Tractate *Shabbat*, the portion of the Talmud addressing the laws and practices regarding the Jewish Sabbath, the great sage Hillel is approached by a curious Gentile. The Gentile requests that Hillel convert him to Judaism, but only on the condition that Hillel is able to teach him the entirety of the Torah while the Gentile man is standing on one foot.

Hillel's famed Talmudic rival Shammai had physically shoved the inquisitive man aside when approached with the same conditional request, but Hillel chose to respectfully engage.[4] Hillel took to one foot and responded: "What is hateful to you, do not do to your neighbor. That is the whole Torah; the rest is the explanation of this—go and study it!"[5] The great Jewish sage Hillel, in other words, asserts that the Golden Rule—"what is hateful to you, do not do to your neighbor," in his particular phrasing—represents the entirety of the Torah! The rest of the Torah, according to

Hillel, is just support—God-given window dressing, essentially—for that one fundamental principle.

As anyone with even a cursory knowledge of the Talmud knows, furthermore, in any given dispute between the great Talmudic rivals Hillel and Shammai, the *Halacha* (Jewish law) almost always follows Hillel. There is no reason to conclude that the two sages' famous recorded debate in Tractate *Shabbat* over how to handle the inquisitive, conversion-seeking Gentile is any exception. There is a very strong argument, in other words, that Hillel is correct that the entirety of the Torah really *does* boil down to, "what is hateful to you, do not do to your neighbor." The very core and essence of Judaism, therefore, *is* the Golden Rule.

Insofar as its distinctly Jewish and biblical roots are concerned, the Golden Rule is not a one-off among today's dominant societal norms. The Golden Rule is not an exception—a dispensation from an alternative anchoring legal order or ethical system. Rather, the Golden Rule is emblematic of a very common, perhaps even general, societal norm—the distinct, if often somewhat concealed, *Jewishness* of so much of contemporary American and Western society. When the label "Judeo-Christian" is invoked in America today, as it often is in our fractious political and legal discourse, it is typically with this undeniable prevalence of our society's Jewish origins and bases in mind.

Indeed, it would be difficult—perhaps impossible—to overstate the extent to which Jewish morality, Jewish ethics, Jewish tradition, and Jewish law have been seminal and indispensable to the broader millennia-long development of what we today call Western civilization. Whether individual Westerners or Western societies at large are cognizant of it or not, the reality is that Western civilization as we recognize it today would never have emerged were it not for Judaism, the Hebrew Bible, Jewish thought, the Jewish people, and the broader Jewish tradition.

Of all the faddish ideologies, subversive cultural developments, and otherwise-debilitating social pathologies that permeate the modern Western world, virtually all can be objected to on authentically Jewish and biblical grounds. Put another way: Of all the present malaise and societal rot that may instinctually strike us as wrong, there is usually a specifically Jewish- or Torah-based reason that we are able to intuit such harm. Just as the Torah—for Christians, the Old Testament—was so instrumental in the development of what came to be Western morality, ethics, tradition, and law, so, too, is it useful today in clarifying and explicating why exactly troublingly large swaths of what passes as "morality," "ethics," or "law" today are so misguided and dangerous.

Yet far too often, and perhaps especially since the Simchat Torah Massacre of October 7, 203, the seminal Jewish role in the formation and development of Western civilization has been downplayed, shunned, or categorically denied. At worst, online anti-Semites and their fellow travelers criticize or lambaste this outsized Jewish role as somehow having a pernicious or sinister effect.

Perhaps such historical, moral, legal, and ethical whitewashing ought to be unsurprising. The Jew is, at his core, a testimony of God's existence and the fact that He has concrete behavioral expectations for man. Therefore, the intergenerational survival and preservation of Jewish life is an incessant nagging weight on the world's moral conscience. It follows that all profligate, decadent, and immoral societies—those that do not worship and fear God—would be better off if the Jewish people did not exist. This helps explain not merely the millennia-old endurance of genocidal Jew-hatred, going at least as far back as Amalek's barbaric assault on the Children of Israel following the Exodus from Egypt, but also its acute resurgence in recent years following a prolonged post–World War II period of relative dormancy. This may partially explain the deliberate attempts we now see from anti-Semites on the Left, Right, and everywhere in between, especially since the Simchat Torah Massacre, to rewrite Western history and minimize the great role played by Judaism and the Jewish people.

But the Hebrew Bible, the Jewish people, Jewish thought, Jewish morality, and Jewish law *have* all contributed immensely to the broader Western philosophical, ethical, legal, and political canon. Far from dismissing Jewish influence on the West as irrelevant, destabilizing, or even menacing, Westerners of all religious stripes should—if anything—feel a debt of gratitude for all that Hebrew Scripture, Judaism, the Jewish people, and the broader Jewish tradition have contributed to our collective civilization. Judaism and Jewish thought have directly affected everything from personal morality to interpersonal relations to the development of entire modern legal and political orders rooted in biblical morality, such as the English common law, the US Constitution, and the broader Anglo-American conservative political tradition.

Given the sheer volume of dubious, typically bigotry-laden misinformation to the contrary in our post–October 7 public discourse on all things Jewish- and State of Israel–related, it is imperative that these Jewish contributions to the moral, ethical, political, and legal core of modern Western civilization be explained at some considerable length.

The foundational ethical underpinning of the modern world, whether we realize it or not, is the assertion that man was created in God's image: *b'Tzelem Elohim* in Hebrew, or *Imago Dei* in Latin. Judaism finds this world-altering affirmation—which appears toward the very beginning of the Bible, in Genesis 1:27—crucial in understanding man's relationship with his fellow man, his broader role in the world, and his relationship with his Creator.

The statement that man is created in the image of God, as I also discussed in the previous chapter, means that every man is formed as a small reflection of our Creator's qualities and characteristics.[6] Fundamentally, this establishes a supreme individual mandate to live an ethical life—one within certain moral, behavioral, and legal parameters. Indeed, that man is created in God's image was traditionally understood, to the rabbis of the Talmud, as an obligation to cleave to God's countless awe-inspiring attributes. As Tractate *Sotah* of the Talmud says:

> Just as [God] clothes the naked [Adam and Eve in the Garden of Eden] . . . so too you should clothe the naked. Just as [God] visits the sick [Abraham after his circumcision] . . . so too should you visit the sick. Just as God consoles mourners [Isaac after the death of his father, Abraham] . . . so too you should console mourners. Just as God buried the dead [Moses, toward the very end of the Torah] . . . so too should you bury the dead.[7]

The logic is simple and straightforward. Man is created in the image of God; ergo, act like Him. This idea—that we can only attach ourselves to God by imitating His wondrous attributes and ways—is a core concept throughout all of Jewish law and morality. Any other understanding of man cleaving to God beyond imitating His ways risks some degree of either anthropomorphism or idolatry—both of which are anathematic to Jewish thought and Jewish law.[8]

Judaism provides a comprehensive legal, moral, and ethical framework in which moral relativism is emphatically rejected. Judaism sees morality as absolute, permanent, and unwilling to yield to the ephemeral temptations of the moment. Consider, for instance, human sexuality and the "transgender" social phenomenon.

The Divine Image of Genesis 1:27 could not possibly be any clearer on this point: "And God created man in His image; in the image of God He created him; male and female He created them." There is simply no other way to understand the phrase "male and female He created them" other than to establish, as

modern biology, genetics, and simple common sense also establish, that sexual dimorphism and male-female sexual complemen-
tarity are real and immutable features of the human experience.
The biblical worldview, and certainly Jewish thought, therefore
demand that we reject broader legitimization of the transgender
phenomenon, and also suggests rejection of biologically incorrect pronouns deployed to match someone's subjective "gender
identity."[9] That such a conclusion may be unfashionable in the
eyes of highly educated societal elites today does not mitigate its
salience or truth.

While the Divine Image obligation of Genesis 1:27 requires
that individuals act in correspondence with the Divine will and
in the manner of the Divine, the injunction was also given in a
specific context and through a specific historical and situational
prism. Traditional Jewish thought teaches that the purpose of
the Israelites' Exodus from bondage in Egypt was to ensure they
could stand before God and accept His Torah during the Divine
Revelation at Mount Sinai.

As Rav Avdimi bar Hama bar Hasa says in the Talmudic
Tractate *Shabbat* about the moment the Israelites congregated at
the base of Mount Sinai to receive the Torah: God "overturned
the mountain above the Jews like a tub, and said to them: 'If
you accept the Torah, excellent, and if not, there will be your
burial.'"[10] The Israelites' acceptance of the Torah was not merely
limited to a code of private worship; *Halacha*, as we will soon see,
posits an all-encompassing way of life. Failure to accept and obey
the revealed law would negate not only the Exodus, but also the
very purpose of mankind—hearkening back to the Divine Image
imperative of Genesis 1:27—to reflect God in all that we do.

In the twice-daily *Shema* prayer that is foundational to the
Jewish liturgy, Jews recite: "I am the Lord your God who brought
you out of the land of Egypt to be your God." God's purpose
in His leading the Israelites from bondage in the Exodus from
Egypt and revealing Himself at Mount Sinai was to create a

special relationship with the Jewish people. As Scripture says: "You will be My people, and I will be your God."[11] This was also the chief purpose of the ten plagues that struck pharaoh and the Egyptians: "So you will know that I am God."[12]

However, in order to *sustain* His relationship with the Israelite nation after the Exodus, God constructed a comprehensive system of objective laws and codes: the Torah. This code served a dual function, to sustain the God–man relationship and to fulfill the Divine Image mandate of Genesis 1:27. Consequently, the very first biblical command the Jewish people receive in the Torah is the obligation to record the new months through the lunar cycle.[13] As explained by Rabbi Samson Raphael Hirsch, "Just as [the lunar cycle] is bound by physical laws, and rejuvenates itself, so are you, but of your own free will, to create your own rejuvenations."[14] True human freedom, in this understanding, is not a negative freedom *from* restraint, as liberal Enlightenment theory suggests; it is a positive freedom *to* fulfill specific duties and obligations in service of collective holiness and sanctifying God.

This is the entry point for beginning to understand *Halacha*, Jewish law.

The Jewish Halachic system, rooted in the Torah, is a comprehensive framework of laws and codes designed to sustain and nourish the relationship between God and man that was first established at Mount Sinai. *Halacha* is necessarily oriented toward the fulfillment of the seminal mandate that man reflect the Divine Image in all that he does on earth. As Rabbi Hirsch explained, the lunar cycle symbolizes the concept of freedom within the Divine structure: a disciplined, affirmative freedom to actively engage in spiritual and ethical rejuvenation that nourishes the God–man relationship and lives out God's will.

Having established this as our baseline, we can now begin to see just how influential the Jewish Halachic system and Jewish morality have been in the Western political, legal, and moral tradition.

I am a lawyer by training, and I regularly write on, and speak about, legal issues. Among those issues is *stare decisis*—the doctrine, especially as it developed at English common law and is still followed in common law–based legal systems today, that a court should give significant force to, and perhaps be bound by, the judgments and rulings of similar previous cases.

Interestingly, the American constitutional order, which exalts the text of a physical written constitution as the "supreme law of the land," does operate a bit differently than a purer common law–based legal system, such as England's.[15] Regardless, heated debates over the role of *stare decisis* in constitutional and statutory interpretation continue today in American legal and political circles. What many of my fellow attorneys and legal scholars probably do not realize is that the entire notion of *stare decisis*, or judicial precedent, actually emanates from the Jewish tradition.

It is God's will that there exists a certain degree of uniformity in Jewish practice and the interpretation of Jewish law. As Scripture says: "There shall be one law and one ordinance for you."[16] The Jewish legal principle of Halachic precedent is paramount in elucidating law, adapting and applying it to mankind's ever-changing and evolving circumstances, and sustaining the intergenerational practicality and legitimacy of the Jewish tradition. Under Jewish law, earlier rabbinic rulings—called *responsa*—serve as precedents for later cases. These precedents, especially from authoritative rabbis, guide subsequent legal decisions. Rabbinic Judaism—the overwhelmingly dominant strand of Judaism since the seventh-century codification of the Babylonian Talmud—has therefore developed a body of case law and precedent, similar to the English common law system that it would later help influence.[17]

Over the past two millennia, many anti-Semites have sought to discredit this system of Rabbinic Judaism and its foundational text, the Talmud, for allegedly straying from the biblical text. For example, there was the infamous Disputation of Paris (otherwise known as the "Trial of the Talmud") in thirteenth-century France, wherein the Talmud itself was subjected to a sham trial in the court of King Louis IX, resulting in the mass public burning of sacred Jewish texts—estimated to be twenty-four wagonloads of books—in the streets of Paris. Unfortunately, in some of the darker corners of social media today, there continues to be a great deal of confusion, misinformation, and outright bigotry surrounding this matter. The traditional Jewish view is that Rabbinic Judaism is based in the biblical text and that it was also made practically necessary, following the destruction of the Second Temple, to preserve the Oral Law that God also transmitted to Moses at Mount Sinai.

Traditional Jewish thought roots the rabbinic tradition of Halachic precedent and judicial decision-making in Deuteronomy 17:11: "According to the law they instruct you and according to the judgment they say to you, you shall do; you shall not divert from the word they tell you, either right or left."[18] We also cannot ignore what ought to be intuitive: a general need for legal uniformity. It cannot possibly be God's will, to take but one example, that exactly what constitutes "work" for purposes of desecrating the Sabbath merely lies in the subjective eyes of the beholder. Such a patchwork system would be highly impractical and destabilizing. Indeed, as Rabbi Pesach Wolicki has argued, "The Torah is written in such a way as to assume that there will be an authoritative body that interprets and implements the laws."[19]

Following the Romans' destruction of the Second Temple, the eradication of the ancient Jewish biblical court known as the Great Sanhedrin, and the commencement of the Jewish exile, rabbinic authority and a system of legal precedent became necessary to preserve the Oral Law and ensure the continuance of Judaism as a viable religion and way of life. Consider also God's injunction to Aaron, Moses's brother and the first biblical high priest, in Leviticus 10:11, "to instruct the children of Israel regarding all the statutes which the Lord has spoken to them through Moses."[20] But how, exactly, are Aaron's descendants in the Jewish priesthood expected to accomplish this?

Because the Book of Deuteronomy itself foreshadows that the nation of Israel will be forced into exile and deprived of any kind of central legal authority in Jerusalem, it can be inferred from the biblical text that the exiled nation would one day be forced to codify the Oral Law and adopt a legal system that preserves and protects the entirety of *Halacha* from the threat of extinction. That legal system, as developed by Rabbinic Judaism, bears a strong similarity to common law systems in use today. All common law–based legal systems still in use today thus owe a debt to Rabbinic Judaism, *Halacha*, and the biblical tradition more generally.

As Rabbi Aryeh Kaplan has explained, because Rabbinic Judaism is alluded to in the very Torah that the nation of Israel accepted in full at Mount Sinai, and also because the Israelites congregated at the base of Mount Sinai accepted the revealed Oral Law no less than they accepted the revealed Written Law, the authority of the Talmud was also legitimized at the time of the Divine Revelation:

> Since all [the nation of] Israel accepted the Talmud [when it accepted the Torah], it is the final authority in all questions of Torah law. Since such universal acceptance is a manifestation of God's will, one who opposes the teachings of the Talmud is like one who opposes God and His Torah. All later codes and decisions are binding only insofar as they are derived from the Talmud.[21]

Halacha, as developed in the Talmud and codified in later post-Talmud foundational works of Rabbinic Judaism, such as Maimonides's *Mishneh Torah*, Joseph Karo's *Shulchan Aruch*, and

Rabbi Yisrael Meir Kagan's *Mishneh Berurah,* is intended to promote certain activities, inculcate certain moral behaviors, and
foster certain social relations.[22] These biblical commands include,
among many other things, mandatory tithing for the poor, forgiv-
ing debtors every seven years, constructing a minimal social safety
net, and maintaining an army with specific military doctrines to
wage war when necessary.[23]

There are also countless behavioral customs, moral guardrails, and political norms ubiquitous across Western civilization
today that can clearly be rooted the writings of the prophets of
the Hebrew Bible. Isaiah, for instance, yearns for an era of peace
and righteousness where "nation shall not lift the sword against
nation, neither shall they learn war anymore"; and Jeremiah
implores the exiled Jews to display civil loyalty regardless of a
native land's particular religious and social practices, and to
instead "seek the peace of the city where I have exiled you and
pray for it to the Lord."[24] It is not a tremendous logical leap to go
from Jeremiah's localist emphasis to the foundational American
constitutional concept of federalism, or to the closely related
Catholic social teaching principle of subsidiarity.

In Jewish thought, law and ethics are inextricable; one can
simply not be understood without the other. This is but one of
the many fundamental flaws of Reform Judaism, which has arro-
gantly assumed the ability to separate law from ethics when it
abandons the binding authority of law and, after doing so, purports to still find something cognizable as "ethics." This is pure
hubris. There is no such thing as a "Jewish ethics" that is not
rooted in Jewish law.

Halacha is designed to foster ethical behavior, and ethical
principles are often themselves embedded within Halachic legal
requirements. We might view *Halacha* as a permanently intertwining, DNA strand–like "double helix" of law and ethics. This
integration of law, morality, and ethics ensures that dutifully following *Halacha* leads one toward the good in a comprehensive

sense, covering every aspect of human life. And it is only when the nation of Israel as a whole follows *Halacha* that the common good and human flourishing of the Jewish people is realized.

Halacha, grounded in Divine Revelation, has both legitimate philosophical and legal underpinnings. It is rooted in the Hebrew Bible, the Talmud, and later Jewish legal writings. It is predicated on the belief that laws derived from God's revealed Will are inherently just, morally authoritative, and all-encompassing in providing a comprehensive guide for human behavior. And from the Golden Rule rooted in Leviticus and Hillel to the affirmation of human equality and sexual dimorphism rooted in the Divine Image injunction of Genesis to the development of a common law legal system of *stare decisis* to Jeremiah's plea to focus on the welfare of one's locality to so much else in between, *Halacha* has continuously shaped and influenced what Western civilization entails today.

The philosophical basis of *Halacha* contrasts sharply with the philosophical bases of numerous alternative schools of thought that either initially developed during the European Enlightenment or have attained greater prominence since then, such as utilitarianism, classical liberalism, libertarianism, socialism, and hedonism. Traditional Jewish thought correctly stands against all of these worldviews, instead offering a biblical path forward.

As a school of ethical philosophy, utilitarianism concentrates on the outcomes of a given action. Utilitarianism maintains that the morality of every human action can be calculated, or at least estimated, based on the quantity and quality of pleasure or pain that the action yields across a defined population.[25] This differs sharply from a Jewish approach to ethics, which is not necessarily concerned with finite, time-bound calculations, but with the complex tapestry of an individual's sustained human-to-human relationships, his special relationship with his Creator, and his own divinely ordained worth rooted in the Book of Genesis's Divine Image injunction.

The great medieval Jewish sage Maimonides, for example, argues in favor of an iterant virtue-based ethics, surmising that "moral excellences or defects cannot be acquired . . . except using the frequent repetition of acts resulting from these qualities, which, practiced during a long period, accustoms us to them."[26] Maimonides sharpens this approach in his commentary on the well-known Talmudic Tractate *Pirkei Avot* ("Ethics of the Fathers"): "[T]he virtues do not come to a man according to the quantity of the greatness of the deed, but rather according to the great number of good deeds. And this is that indeed the virtues arrive by repetition of the good deeds many times."[27]

If the goal is the development of certain virtues and the formation of moral character within a specific legal framework, then Maimonides instructs, for instance, that it is better to divide one's charitable giving among many different individuals than to give a single numerically equivalent large sum to one individual—not because of the ultimate quantified good realized in the outcome, but because it better shapes the ethics of the individual donor.[28] While a Jeremy Bentham– or John Stuart Mill–inspired utilitarian would approach the question of charity with limited resources from a perspective of what maximizes the net good, Jewish law instead focuses on the ethical and virtuous training of the *giver*—not the recipients.

Perhaps the single most explicit and emphatic rejection of the philosophical school of utilitarianism by the Jewish virtue ethics of *Halacha* can be found in the Talmudic Tractate *Sanhedrin*: "With regard to anyone who destroys one soul from the Jewish people, i.e., kills one Jew, . . . [his] blame [is] as if he destroyed an entire world. . . . And conversely, anyone who sustains one soul from the Jewish people, . . . [his] credit [is] as if he sustained an entire world."[29] As such, Jewish law forbids the intentional killing of one person in order to ostensibly save others. Utilitarianism, by contrast, demotes individual self-worth, vitiates the overarching civilizational imperative of *b'Tzelem Elohim* (*Imago Dei*), and rejects the premise that *every* human life is worth living and protecting as an intrinsic matter. The utilitarianism of Jeremy Bentham and John Stuart Mill is thus inherently anti-biblical.

B'Tzelem Elohim also provides a closely related, and absolute, axiological principle: No one individual's blood is any redder than the blood of his peers.[30] The timeless injunction that all of mankind is made in the Divine Image confers the obligation on every disparate society the world over, across the generations, to perceive, protect, and preserve the sanctity and purpose of the individual human self—rather than to base public policy on further-removed, more abstract speculations that may relativize human value.[31]

Many Anglo-American political theorists ascribe the political principle of genuine human equality—which, importantly, must be distinguished from various false and faddish modern notions of pseudo-egalitarianism—to influential Enlightenment-era classical liberals, such as John Locke and Thomas Jefferson. The reality is the notion that man is all created equal, so artfully put into prose by Jefferson in America's Declaration of Independence and ultimately codified in the Equal Protection Clause of the US Constitution's Fourteenth Amendment, must be traced back all the way to the Divine Image injunction in the Book of Genesis.

John Stuart Mill's famous "harm principle," which posits that individuals should be free to act however they wish provided that their actions do not inflict tangible harm upon others, is foundational to many modern liberal legal systems. One might be inclined to think that the "harm principle" is rooted in, or closely related to, the Divine Image mandate; but Jewish ethics and the Halachic tradition understand the concept of harm within a much broader framework that also considers moral, communal, and divine obligations. Those trained in economics might think of these less palpable, secondary, or tertiary obligations, which are central to Jewish ethics, as social or spiritual "externalities."

Mill's harm principle, in essence, "expresses the jurisdictional trigger for society to consider interference of any sort" to be harmful.[32] Within the societal framework, under this approach, individuals should be free to act however they wish unless their actions render discernible harm unto somebody else; it is only at that point, according to Mill, that a law implemented to regulate or circumscribe an individual's behavior can be considered morally legitimate.

But at a most basic level, Jewish law does not view the individual to be *free*—at least as modern liberal theory would understand the concept. Rather, our bodies and our souls exist at the mercy of our Creator; therefore, we are only "free" to fulfill His Will. *Halacha* thus codifies a disciplined approach to achieving true freedom—not a negative freedom *from* constraints, as liberalism understands it, but the more traditional positive freedom *to* actively engage in spiritual and ethical rejuvenation. Jewish law presents a binding system, with rules and regulations, that mandate the individual and society to act within certain parameters. Whether or not an individual's action "harms" another in an empirical or otherwise-measurable way is frankly beside the point. Even though such an action may "harm" no one but the individual undertaking it, one is still not "free" to desecrate his own body, become a glutton, lust for a woman who is not his wife, or even to deploy certain instances of harmful language.[33] Other examples abound.

Biblical ethics thus deviates from Mill's harm principle in incorporating not only the prevention of tangible physical and economic harms unto others, but also the prevention of moral and spiritual harm to individuals, communities, and nations. The traditional Jewish view indeed obligates an individual to attempt to proactively prevent harm from befalling others. As it says in the Talmudic Tractate *Shabbat*:

> Anyone who had the capability to effectively protest the sinful conduct of the members of his household and did not protest, he himself is apprehended for the sins of the members of his household and punished. If he is in a position to protest the sinful conduct of the people of his town, and he fails to do so, he is apprehended for the sins of the people of his town. If he is in a position to protest the sinful conduct of the whole world, and he fails to do so, he is apprehended for the sins of the whole world.[34]

Jewish law therefore places a strong emphasis on communal responsibility and the general welfare of the broader nation. Individuals, in the biblical worldview, are accountable not merely for their own actions, but also for preventing harm within their community and society. As the ancient Greek philosopher Aristotle might have put it, the *telos*—the overarching substantive regime orientation—of Jewish law is the community's collective welfare and the common good, not indulging the idiosyncratic individualism of its constituent parts.

The responsibility to prevent harm that affects the moral fabric of the community manifests in various laws and customs that encourage or require individuals to prophylactically intervene in cases where the community might suffer harm—whether through sin, injustice, or neglect. At its core, Judaism understands that individuals do not exist in a vacuum; the atomistic view of the human experience, popular among utilitarians, classical liberals, and modern libertarians alike, is emphatically rejected by *Halacha* and the biblical tradition. Rather, the Hebrew Bible understands that humans are responsible for the maintenance of civil societies and stable orders. As it says in the Book of Leviticus: "You shall not stand by [the shedding of] your fellow's blood."[35]

At the heart of classical liberalism and libertarianism as they have existed and developed since the European Enlightenment is the assertion that individuals should have maximum freedom to act according to their own idiosyncratic will, provided they do not somehow infringe upon the natural or otherwise-bestowed rights of others. In modern liberal political theory, this has been thought to include (among other rights) the freedoms of speech, religion, and the pursuit of happiness.[36] But Jewish law's strong emphasis on communal responsibility and collective holiness necessarily implies that many purportedly "private" actions of individuals *do* affect the welfare of the entire community. Individual freedom thus cannot possibly be absolute; rather, it must be circumscribed within appropriate moral guardrails and oriented toward the Halachic *telos* of the common good of the community.

Communal responsibility and collective holiness are the ends ultimately sought by Jewish law. Indeed, *Halacha* even affirms the collective responsibility of the Jewish people to ensure that all Jews observe the commandments. If one Jew sins, it is seen as a failure of the entire community. This reinforces the concept that all Jews are interconnected and accountable for each other's spiritual and moral well-being. As the Talmudic Tractate *Sanhedrin* puts it: "[When] the Jewish people shall stumble, one due to the iniquity of another, i.e., they are punished for each other's sins, which teaches that all Jews are considered guarantors, i.e., responsible, for one another."[37] Or, to paraphrase another well-known verse from the Book of Genesis that has entered the rhetorical bloodstream of secular society, we are all ultimately our brothers' keepers.

We thus see that in Jewish moral thought, an individual actually personally *bears* the punishment for the sins of his peers. This is one Halachic method of safeguarding the interdependent bonds of human loyalty without which no community or nation can cohere. Each member of the community has a direct stake in the moral conduct of his peers; the community as a whole bears responsibility for the discrete actions of its constituent parts. Millian utilitarianism and modern libertarianism alike are patently alien to, and irreconcilable with, the Halachic tradition and a biblical worldview.

The great twentieth-century Halachist Rabbi Aharon Lichtenstein argued that in order for the Halachic system to prevail, each individual adherent must emphasize the ethical and spiritual dimensions of law-binding societies that transcend mere pleasure-seeking or "utility" maximization.[38] For the Jew, there exist considerably higher social, personal, and spiritual goals than the licentiousness of unencumbered hedonism. As Rabbi Lichtenstein once put it:

> The question is not whether there is room in human life for a person to have a certain measure of pleasure. Rather, the question is what is his basic perspective? . . . Does he see himself as basically being born to enjoy or to work? . . . To some extent, this feeling has permeated our world: a whole culture of enjoyment has begun to take hold. This is something which is recent. . . . That whole culture advocates that man is born for pleasure, but unfortunately has to work if he wants to enjoy. In contrast, we have to know that "'*Adam le-amal yulad*,' Man is born to do labor" (Job 5:7).[39]

A life centered solely on the pursuit of pleasure or "utility" maximization lacks depth and fails to account for the broader moral and spiritual dimensions of human existence. Hedonism and licentiousness are superficial because they reduce the richness of the human experience to a single totalizing (and ultimately unfulfilling) dimension: the pursuit of pleasure. Hedonism and licentiousness, like utilitarianism and libertarianism, are therefore also fundamentally incompatible with any biblical worldview anchored in the overarching Divine Image imperative of *b'Tzelem Elohim* (*Imago Dei*).

Rabbi Noah Weinberg, founder of the well-known Aish HaTorah yeshiva and educational outreach organization, argued along similar lines to those of Rabbi Lichtenstein. According to Rabbi Weinberg, Judaism demands that its adherents be willing to extend themselves beyond their comfortable physical limitations: "The opposite of pain is 'no pain'—i.e., comfort. Confusing comfort with pleasure leads to decadence [and] a life filled with escaping and running away from the pain and effort required to live a fulfilling life."[40]

The Jewish tradition certainly does not negate the role of pleasure in human life, but it contextualizes pleasure within the necessary framework and guardrails of Jewish thought and moral behavior. Indeed, the Jewish legal system affirmatively recognizes the legitimacy of pleasure when it is experienced in the context of fulfilling God's commandments, or when it is a natural by-product of living a life aligned with biblical values. For instance, such pleasure might include a Jewish husband fulfilling his wife's sexual needs—a marital obligation rooted in both the Hebrew Bible and the Talmud. Furthermore, some of the most notable Jewish legal authorities, such as Maimonides, have dictated that each person be permitted to sleep up to eight hours a night, so that he may properly utilize his physical body for spiritual activities.[41]

Moreover, *Halacha* recognizes the importance of enjoying the fruits of one's personal labor, especially since those fruits must themselves be understood as ultimately emanating from God. As the Book of Ecclesiastes says: "Is it not good for a man that he eat and drink and show himself enjoyment in his toil? This too have I seen that it is from the hand of God."[42] Human pleasure is therefore a gift from God when it is experienced within the context of a life of work, duty, and honor. Pleasure is not inherently negative, but it must be placed within proper guardrails and channeled toward living a balanced, purposeful, and spiritually elevating life.

In fact, swaths of Jewish law mandate incorporating the physical dimension of the human experience as expressions of Divine will. The Talmud, for instance, relates that the positive biblical command of "rejoicing" on the prescribed festivals must entail eating meat and drinking wine.[43] The requirement to experience joy through eating and drinking on the biblical festivals, as well as on the weekly Sabbath, shows how pleasure is seamlessly integrated within the framework of the commandments. Far from abetting moral or spiritual decadence, such properly channeled pleasure can actually nourish and elevate the God–man relationship that is at the heart of the biblical worldview. But our rejoicing must be oriented toward just and proper ends, and we can never lose sight of *yir'at shamayim*—"fear of heaven." As the psalmist says: "Serve the Lord with fear, and rejoice with quaking."[44]

Consider also the opening verses of chapter 19 of the Book of Leviticus: "God spoke to Moses, saying: Speak to the entire congregation of the children of Israel, and say to them, You shall be holy, for I, the Lord, your God, am holy."[45] Some of the most famous Halachists in Jewish history, such as the medieval luminaries Rashi and Maimonides, read this as a directive aimed at the realization of collective holiness: specifically, that self-control and refraining from sensual gratification will lead to greater holiness, and that this should be a defining trait of every God-fearing Jew.[46]

Nachmanides, the thirteenth-century Halachic authority, deviates slightly from Rashi and Maimonides, holding that this Levitical directive "is meant to ensure that the spirit of the Torah's laws is to be maintained even when legal loopholes exist."[47] Nachmanides therefore argues that it is possible for a person to strictly follow the technical details of the Bible's commandments but still live in a manner that contradicts the Torah's overarching ethical and spiritual aims—its *telos*, to again invoke

Aristotelian thought. Nachmanides colorfully describes such a person as "a scoundrel with the permission of the Torah."[48] Ritual observances are undoubtedly important in Jewish thought, but even more important is that someone is, at his core, a *good person*—a *mensch*, to borrow the Yiddish loanword.

One is reminded of Hillel's famous response to the inquisitive, conversion-seeking Gentile, which we encountered earlier in this chapter: "What is hateful to you, do not do to your neighbor. That is the whole Torah; the rest is the explanation of this—go and study it!"[49] Simply acting in legalistically permissible but ethically or morally corrupt fashion is wholly unacceptable within a biblical moral framework—and certainly runs contrary to *Halacha*. For societies to function, adherence not merely to black-letter law, but to basic moral parameters, is paramount. John Adams, the second president of the United States, famously made a similar point in a very different context: "Our Constitution was made only for a moral and religious People. It is wholly inadequate to the government of any other."[50]

The tension between radical individualism on the one hand, and communal responsibility and collective holiness on the other hand, is a leitmotif throughout Jewish thought.[51] Jewish tradition, as reflected in the Hebrew Bible and the Talmud, balances the undeniable importance of individual dignity and self-worth—rooted in the Divine Image injunction—with a strong emphasis on one's obligations to his community's moral well-being and general welfare. This recurring tension and the stable equilibrium between individualism and communitarianism sought by *Halacha* serves to counter liberal and libertarian claims that an individual is simply an atomistic island unto himself, existing in isolation without the unchosen obligations, interpersonal and intergenerational duties, and interdependent bonds of civic loyalty without which no community or nation can form.

Crucially, this recurring tension that runs throughout *Halacha* and Jewish thought also serves to counter equally anti-biblical absolutist communitarian or authoritarian worldviews, such as socialism and Marxism. Socialism and Marxism violate the supreme anchoring principle of *b'Tzelem Elohim*, diminish the importance of individual self-worth, and discard the inherent dignity of human labor so powerfully captured by Rabbi Lichtenstein. Socialism and Marxism must also be emphatically rejected for the very simple and compelling reason that private property rights are explicitly contemplated by, and frequently discussed in, both the Bible and the Talmud. There are entire Talmudic Tractates, such as *Bava Metzia* and (especially) *Bava Batra*, that largely deal with individuals' rights and responsibilities in owning and managing private property. No worldview that abolishes private property or engenders covetousness, which is explicitly proscribed by the Tenth Commandment, can possibly be reconciled with a biblical worldview. It is a complete nonstarter.

In the biblical account of creation, all species in the animal kingdom are created in pairs.[52] But man is different. The Talmudic Tractate *Sanhedrin* relates that "Adam the first man was created alone" in order to teach that "anyone who destroys one soul from the Jewish people, i.e., kills one Jew, [it is] as if he destroyed an entire world, as Adam was one person, from whom the population of an entire world came forth."[53] Every person, in short, possesses unique value and dignity. We are all here for a specific reason and purpose, even if we may not know what that purpose is. Again, the overarching Divine Image imperative of *b'Tzelem Elohim* reigns supreme.

The Talmud also discusses a scenario where two individuals are stranded in the desert and only have enough water for one to survive. In such a scenario, Rabbi Akiva famously teaches that "your life takes precedence over the life of [an]other."[54] While creating a strong sense of shared obligation, Jewish law therefore also acknowledges the primary importance of self-preservation, rooted in respect for individual dignity and self-worth. But it does so within a context that recognizes the recurring tension between one's self-interest and the needs of the community. Ultimately, Jewish law affirms the importance of protecting one's own life above all else—the supreme Halachic principle of *pikuach nefesh*—but remains acutely aware of one's obligations to his community, tribe, and nation. In Western societies today, we see rulers, policymakers, and judges strive—and often struggle—in their own ways to achieve a similar balancing act.

In evaluating any integrated system of law, morality, and ethics, it is crucial that we ask some foundational, overarching questions—namely: To what ends? For what tasks? And for what purposes? This is the Aristotelian concept of a regime's *telos*—its substantive overarching orientation, which is discernible via the normative ends to which the system is necessarily oriented. More recently than the ancient Greeks, the great eighteenth-century English common lawyer Sir William Blackstone, who first codified the entire corpus of the English common law in his *Commentaries on the Laws of England*, would have referred to this same notion in the context of constitutional or statutory interpretation as the *ratio legis*, or "reason of the law."[55] It is only what an integrated legal, moral, and ethical order is oriented toward substantively righteous ends, and has a normatively just "*telos*" or "*ratio legis*," that it is worth respecting and upholding as law in the first instance. This is why, for example, the US Constitution is worth respecting and cherishing in a way the Constitution of the Soviet Union fundamentally was not.

Halacha, Judaism's integrated legal, moral, and ethical code, is oriented toward a quintessentially just and righteous cause—the fulfillment of the Divine Image mandate established toward the very beginning of the Hebrew Bible by sanctifying God in all that we do on earth. *Halacha*, as formulated in the Hebrew Bible and developed in the Talmud and subsequent works of Rabbinic Judaism, seeks this goal by, among other means, constantly trying to balance the inherent dignity of the individual with the needs and prerogatives of one's broader community. And *Halacha* has at its very core, according to no less an authority than Hillel, the Golden Rule that one ought to treat others as he himself wishes to be treated.

For all these reasons, the biblical worldview codified in Judaism's Halachic legal code ought to be held in higher esteem than other integrated legal, moral, and ethical worldviews that are neither rooted in nor oriented toward similarly just and righteous ends, such as utilitarianism, liberalism, libertarianism, hedonism, or socialism. And it is why, unlike those sundry fleeting and unworthy paradigms, Jewish morality and the broader Judeo-Christian biblical worldview still provides the proper moral, ethical, legal, and political foundation for Western civilization today.

It is this same biblically rooted balancing act between individual self-worth, on the one hand, and communal and national responsibilities, on the other hand, that has long also formed the very basis of Anglo-American conservatism and the broader Anglo-American political and legal tradition as it has existed for many hundreds of years. It is to this subject that this book will now turn.

4

POLITICAL HEBRAISM IN BRITAIN AND AMERICA

"Justice, justice shall you pursue, that you may live and possess the land the Lord, your God, is giving you."

—DEUTERONOMY 16:20[1]

AS I WILL DISCUSS AT SOME LENGTH IN A LATER CHAPTER OF THIS book, the household of my youth was very assimilated. It was broadly "spiritual but not religious," as it is often said, while also acknowledging and partaking in at least some of the major holidays' customs and rituals that are more popular with non-Orthodox American Jewry. I intend to raise my children quite differently, to put it mildly, but I do not fault my loving parents for raising me in the manner they did and according to what they thought was best.

In hindsight, furthermore, we arguably did have an ersatz "religion" in our household—and thankfully not wokeism, as is the case for so many young Americans today who grow up without biblical religion. Our household in suburban New York was, if nothing else, steeped in the civic religion of American patriotism.

One of my favorite childhood books, which I spent countless hours poring over with my mother and grandmother, was a sweeping, child-friendly survey of the highlights and lowlights of every American president. (As a child of the 1990s, the book stopped with the Bill Clinton presidency.) I remember being bewildered by William Henry Harrison, "Old Tippecanoe," who only lasted a month as president before succumbing to a fatal case of pneumonia—and I recall being fascinated by Grover Cleveland, the great "Bourbon Democrat," who served two non-consecutive terms in the late-nineteenth century. In my second-grade class, I was the only student to memorize the chronological order of every president to serve since George Washington; Mrs. Praino taught it to us in a hymn that borrowed the melody of the popular children's tune "Ten Little Indians." I could still recite it today to that very same tune.

On July Fourth every year, I would dress up in a red, white, and blue outfit, adorn my bicycle in matching ribbons and other decorations, and partake in the annual village parade—which conveniently started on our block. Mounted policemen would lead the high school band, which would play "Yankee Doodle" and other popular patriotic songs as everyone marched or biked along behind. The parade ended at a local sports field, where children would participate in a three-legged race, an egg toss, and other games. There was also the much-anticipated competition to see who could bake the best patriotic cake; my childhood best friend's diligent mother, may she rest in peace, took home the prize almost every year.

As a lifelong sports fan, I grew up cheering for the local college football team, which happened to be the most overtly patriotic football program in America: the Army Black Knights, representing the United States Military Academy at West Point. In the summer between sixth and seventh grade, a handful of my childhood friends and I spent a week at West Point for sleep-away baseball camp. I remember standing in awe of the Douglas MacArthur Monument; it was one of MacArthur's most famous quotations, "There is no substitute for victory," which famously hung in the home-team clubhouse of my childhood home away from home, Yankee Stadium in the Bronx. I remember waking up at the crack of dawn every morning to the sound of the bugler's reveille and cadets marching in lockstep outside our dormitory.

Then, the terrorist attacks of September 11, 2001, happened just about a month after I got home from West Point, leaving an indelible mark on me. The world was changed forever, and my already-strong sense of American patriotism was only further solidified.

One of the clearest and most commonly recurring leitmotifs of my life thus far is my passionate love of this country. That deep and abiding love has informed many of my career decisions to date, including my attending law school, my spending a year clerking for a federal appeals judge, and my conscientious decision following my judicial clerkship to devote my professional career to helping restore this great but fallen nation—the pinnacle and indispensable cog of Western civilization—to its former glory and grandeur.

And for my entire life, at every turn, I have admired Abraham Lincoln as my single favorite figure in American history. That admiration began at a young age: I was born on Lincoln's birthday, February 12. In fact, my childhood best friend was born on George Washington's birthday, February 22, and I recall friendly childhood arguments over who was the better of America's two most revered historical leaders. "Washington won the Revolutionary War and started the country!" my friend would say. "But Lincoln won the Civil War and preserved the Union!" I would retort.

There are more reasons to admire Lincoln than I could enumerate. He overcame the abject poverty of his youth, self-educated with a voracious reading appetite, and became a lawyer and one of the most gifted orators the English language has ever seen. Lincoln's moral intuitions and moral reasoning abilities were simply exceptional. His great 1858 Senate campaign trail debate rival, Stephen Douglas, could wax poetic about majoritarian "popular sovereignty" as a purported end unto itself, but as Lincoln had so neatly put it four years prior in his 1854 Peoria speech, the relevant question is instead not the procedural but the substantive one: "whether a negro is *not* or *is* a man." Despite his firm moral convictions on the "peculiar institution," however, Lincoln was not a political radical; he nurtured a careful sense of prudence, which Aristotle two thousand years before him had regarded as the queen of the virtues and the statesman's most important trait.[2]

Lincoln was a republican who despised the judicial despotism of Chief Justice Roger Taney's Supreme Court, going so far as to openly defy the court's infamous pro-slavery *Dred Scott* ruling by issuing passports to blacks in the western US territories.[3] He cherished the rationalistic Declaration of Independence but, as my Edmund Burke Foundation colleague Rafi Eis has put it, he was also a traditionalist who understood that "national memory is essential to anchoring the nation's principles in their appropriate context."[4] Above all, Lincoln sought to ennoble Americans and elevate them to their better angels during a time of unprecedented internecine strife. He ultimately gave his life to the cause of the Union's preservation, concluding one of his final public speeches with those stirring words in his Second Inaugural Address that still ring today: "With malice toward none, with charity for all, with firmness in the right as God gives us to see the right, let us strive on to finish the work we are in [and] to bind up the nation's wounds."[5]

As his religiously rooted call to action in his Second Inaugural Address indicates, Lincoln was a biblically literate Christian who frequently referenced Scripture in his public writings and private correspondences. And unlike many of his nineteenth-century contemporaries, he was a great friend and admirer of the Jewish people. Lincoln, echoing the Pilgrims of 1620 who set sail in the *Mayflower* and saw in themselves a reenactment of the ancient Israelites' Exodus from pharaoh's Egypt, famously referred to Americans in the vivid covenantal language of an "almost chosen people."[6] As president, he approved the first-ever Jewish military chaplain in American history (Jacob Frankel of Philadelphia) and countermanded General Ulysses S. Grant's discriminatory General Order No. 11, which attempted to expel all Jews from the Union war zone under Grant's control.[7] As retold by Jonathan Sarna and Benjamin Shapell in their 2015 book, *Lincoln and the Jews*, when Jewish expellee Cesar Kaskel met with the president to request the order's revocation, the conversation apparently took a starkly biblical turn:

> *Lincoln:* And so the children of Israel were driven from the happy land of Canaan?

> *Kaskel:* Yes, and that is why we have come unto Father Abraham's bosom, seeking protection.

> *Lincoln:* And this protection they shall have at once.[8]

Though Lincoln's lifelong philo-Semitism and affection for the political philosophy of the Hebrew Bible were not traits necessarily shared by most men of his era, his warmth toward the Jewish people and biblical Jewish wisdom were indeed shared by many of his fellow great men of destiny who, over the centuries, have contributed immensely to the Anglo-American political and legal tradition. The Hebrew Bible and Jewish legal and political traditions played foundational roles in shaping the Anglo-American political and legal systems, serving as key influences for both the English common law and the political theory of the American Founding.

Key English common law figures, such as the seventeenth-century jurist and Talmudic scholar John Selden, incorporated principles from Mosaic Law and Rabbinical Law into the development of common law, showcasing how Jewish jurisprudence materially contributed to the development of one of the greatest legal orders ever known to man. Similarly, many of the American Founders—including George Washington, Benjamin Franklin, John Adams, and Alexander Hamilton—demonstrated an admiration for Jewish history and the Hebrew Bible that influenced their vision for the nascent republic. Washington's famous 1790 letter to the Jews of Newport, Rhode Island, for instance, emphasized Jewish security and free exercise of religion, thus echoing biblical themes of justice and equal human dignity under God. Franklin proposed that the then-nascent American republic adopt a national seal of Moses parting the Red Sea—a symbol of liberation, also broadly adopted by the Pilgrims of Plymouth Colony a century and a half prior, that mirrored the American struggle for freedom and independence.

These well-known examples, along with many others, reflect a broader philo-Semitic trend among the American Founders, their English common law forebears, and their political and spiritual descendants—such as Abraham Lincoln, who quoted his well-thumbed Christian Bible's Old Testament far more frequently than its New Testament in his letters and speeches, and for whom the Jewish lawyer and politician Abraham Jonas was the only person he ever described as "one of my most valued friends."⁹ Over the course of many hundreds of years, Jewish thought and values became deeply intertwined with, and seamlessly integrated within, the development of the broader Anglo-American conservative political and legal tradition as we know it today.

It is worth our time to explore that political and legal tradition, and especially the role within that tradition played by Anglo-American philo-Semitism and what we might call "political Hebraism," at some greater length.

■ ■ ■

The English common law tradition, from the beginning and as it developed in the centuries following the Norman Conquest in 1066, was influenced by biblical ideas and Jewish law. As discussed in the last chapter, the *stare decisis* system of gradual, incrementalist change via judge-made case law and precedent, perhaps the single most readily identifiable hallmark of the English common law, was imported from the Talmudic tradition of Rabbinic Judaism. Indeed, the People of the Book's lasting influence on the common law had become so obvious over the course of the common law's centuries-long development that Lord Mansfield, the eighteenth-century lord chief justice of the King's Bench who was widely regarded as the most powerful British jurist of his time, held in the 1767 case of *Chamberlain of London v. Evans* that "the essential principles of revealed religion are part of the common law" itself.[10]

Lord Mansfield's sentiment echoed the great fifteenth-century English conservative common lawyer John Fortescue, also a former chief justice of the King's Bench, who once observed of his fellow judges that after a court session is adjourned, "they spend the rest of the day in the study of the laws [and] reading of the Holy Scriptures."[11] As my Edmund Burke Foundation colleagues Yoram Hazony and Ofir Haivry have observed, Fortescue's own description of the English constitution took pains to note that the power of the Crown is necessarily limited by traditional English national laws, just as "the powers of the Jewish king in the Mosaic constitution in Deuteronomy are limited by the traditional laws of the Israelite nation."[12] For Fortescue, it was crucial that the Crown, just as the monarchy established in Deuteronomy, is itself subject to the law and not in any way above the law.[13] In general, Fortescue, who is arguably the intellectual godfather of the conservative Anglo-American legal and political tradition as it was famously explicated by the eighteenth-century statesman

Edmund Burke and still exists today, drew frequently from the words and ideas of the Hebrew Bible.[14]

Throughout his jurisprudence and written works, Fortescue favorably contrasted the salutary impact of biblical, Judeo-Christian values on the development of the English constitution and the common law with the more pernicious influence of Roman law in the development of the civil law of continental Europe, which he harshly criticized in his book *De Laudibus Legum Angliae* (*In Praise of the Laws of England*) as authoritarian and inimical to flourishing. To Fortescue, it was as clear as day that the common law did not develop according to the traditions of Roman law; rather, it was the Bible itself that was the common law's chief influence.

As but one prominent example of biblical influence on the English common law and the broader Anglo-American legal and political tradition, consider the well-known legal principle "Blackstone's ratio"—Sir William Blackstone's proposition, popularized in his influential eighteenth-century treatise *Commentaries of the Laws of England*, that it is better for ten guilty persons to escape free than for one innocent to suffer wrongly. Blackstone's *Commentaries* were deeply influential on the American Founding, and Blackstone, alongside Montesquieu, was one of the most frequently cited men during the Founding-era debates over the ratification of the Constitution of 1787.[15] "Blackstone's ratio" has been internalized by America's collective civic conscience and constitutional culture as they still exist today; consider, for example, the 2020 US Supreme Court case of *Ramos v. Louisiana*, which held that the Sixth Amendment, as "incorporated" against the states by the Fourteenth Amendment, requires that state courts reach a unanimous jury verdict in order to convict a defendant of a serious crime. This is "Blackstone's ratio" at work.

In reality, Blackstone borrowed his eponymous ratio from Fortescue, who had posited it three centuries prior in *De Laudibus*—with an even higher ratio of twenty guilty men escaping instead of one innocent man condemned to death. And Fortescue, in turn, likely borrowed the broader concept of erring on the side of great caution in cases of capital punishment from the medieval Jewish sage Maimonides, who cautioned against arbitrary capital punishment in *Sefer HaMitzvot* by arguing that "we do not declare punishments based on strong appearances," and that "if we declare punishments based on appearances and conjecture, we would surely sometimes kill someone innocent."[16] Maimonides, in turn, was simply expounding the Book of Exodus: "Distance yourself from a false matter; and do not kill a truly innocent person or one who has been declared innocent, for I will not vindicate a guilty person."[17]

Many of the defining traits of the English common law as it developed in an incrementalist manner over the course of many centuries, and as it was subsequently adopted by every American state except Louisiana, can be traced to the Hebrew Bible. And some of those defining English common law principles that cannot be traced to the Mosaic Law itself can instead be traced to the Talmudic traditions of Rabbinic Judaism—as discussed last chapter, for instance, in the context of *stare decisis* (judicial precedent).

One notable English common lawyer who did perhaps more than any other figure to solidify the lasting influence of Jewish law—from the Torah and the Talmud alike—on the development of the English common law was the seventeenth-century Christian parliamentarian John Selden. Though underappreciated by many historians, Selden did more to establish the very core of Anglo-American political and legal conservatism—namely, a focus above all on historical empiricism and the intergenerational transmission of inherited and bequeathed tradition—than anyone other than perhaps Burke himself.

In 1621, Parliament, through Selden's urging, took up the question of the judicial authority of Parliament to evaluate the validity of certain patents. In his treatise *Book of Precedents*, Selden had criticized the then-widely accepted notion of binding royal prerogative in patent-granting, extolling, as Steven Grosby has written, the virtues of "evidence for custom or settled practice that would, as such, point to the law."[18] Such an endorsement of "evidence for custom or settled practice" reflects a general preference for the probative or binding authority of *stare decisis*, as well as the importance of intergenerational transmission of national tradition—concepts Selden greatly admired, along with the broader intellectual corpus of Rabbinic Judaism.[19] At one point, "Rabbi" Selden, who was not actually himself Jewish and was in fact a pious member of the Church of England, even mused that Parliament should be organized along the lines of the ancient Second Temple–era Sanhedrin.[20]

In 1628, Selden was instrumental in Parliament's passing the seminal Petition of Right, which sought to protect the traditional rights and liberties of English subjects, as identified in the English constitution, against threats emanating from both absolutist royal prerogative and universalist rationalism.[21] In the Petition of Right, we can identify antecedents of perhaps half the liberties subsequently enshrined in 1791 as the US Constitution's Bill of Rights, as well as the "great writ" of *habeas corpus*.[22] It is perhaps noteworthy that, in advocating for the inclusion of the foundational individual liberty protection of *habeas corpus* in the Petition of Right, Selden's legal objection to the sweeping authority of royal prerogative clashed with the Roman law approach, which, Grosby noted, would have suggested that "if *salus publica lex suprema est* (the welfare of the people is the supreme law), then *fiscus semper habet ius pignoris* (the state's fund always has the right of first pledge)."[23]

By 1629, Selden was imprisoned in the Tower of London, having been dubiously charged and convicted of conspiracy and sedition against King Charles I for his activities during the 1628–29 Parliament—including his work in drafting and passing the Petition of Right. Remarkably, Selden requested one book to accompany him during his lonely incarceration: an Aramaic copy of the Babylonian Talmud. As my Edmund Burke Foundation colleague Ofir Haivry has observed, "Despite likely having never met a Jew in his life, Selden . . . dedicated most of his spare hours [in prison] to studying this text."[24] Following his release from prison, Selden dedicated large swaths of the latter part of his prolific career to elaborating on the intricacies of Jewish law—and their enduring relevance to the English common law and to his own day and age, more generally.

Writing in 1631 in *De Successionibus in Bona Defuncti*, a book about the Jewish laws of inheritance, Selden argued that a Christian's exclusive scholarly focus on the New Testament or the Church Fathers will not result in a sufficient legal or intellectual understanding of the Bible.[25] Rather, Selden argued, mastery of the Talmud itself was also essential.[26] Though just as skeptical of unaided "reason" and liberal rationalism as he was of royal absolutism, Selden argued in his 1640 book, *De Jure Naturali et Gentium juxta Disciplinam Ebraeorum*, that the closest thing we can identify as a universally applicable, objective, "moral minimum"[27] natural law are the Seven Noahide Laws, which I discussed two chapters ago.[28] Rather than looking to Aristotelian or Lockean "reason" for a universal legal and moral baseline, Selden looked to the Talmud's explication of the Hebrew Bible.

Perhaps above all, Selden's attempt to identify a moderate sweet spot between the caprices of royal absolutism and the unboundedness of liberal rationalism mirrors, in a way, *Halacha*'s attempt to identify a moderate sweet spot between communitarian obligations and the concept of collective holiness, on the one hand, and the inherent individual dignity of every human being as rooted in the Divine Image injunction of Genesis 1:27, on the other hand. As Hazony and Haivry have written, "Selden thus turns, much as the Hebrew Bible does, to a form of pragmatism to explain what is meant when statesmen and jurists speak of *truth*."[29] One of the ways that such a moderate pragmatism manifests itself is through the incrementalism of *stare decisis*, a bedrock principle of both Rabbinic Judaism and the Anglo-American common law tradition. Although Selden would not live to see it, much of his prescribed moderation in Parliament–Crown relations was posthumously vindicated in the "Glorious Revolution" of 1688, which reaffirmed the rights and liberties of the English constitution he so cherished. In securing the rights of Britons against imperious abuse of royal power, the "Glorious Revolution" thus affirmed the Deuteronomistic roots of the Crown under the English constitution.

The phenomenon of erudite Christian Hebraists using their knowledge of the Torah, and the tradition of Rabbinic Judaism was certainly not limited to Britain. The Pilgrims who sailed across the Atlantic on the *Mayflower* and eventually established Plymouth Colony viewed their journey through the prism of the Hebrew Bible—namely, they viewed themselves as a "New Israel" crossing their own version of the Red Sea in hopes of better fulfilling God's laws. William Bradford, who was on the *Mayflower*, signed the Mayflower Compact, and later served as the second governor of Plymouth Colony, was himself partially literate in the Hebrew language—which he described as "that most ancient language, and holy tongue, in which the Law, and oracles of God were [written]."[30] In fact, Bradford believed that, after his death, he would then speak "the most ancient language," Hebrew, with God and the angels in the World to Come.[31]

Perhaps even more remarkably, there is reason to believe that the first modern Thanksgiving holiday, celebrated in Plymouth Colony in 1621, had its roots in the Jewish rite of *Birkat HaGomel*—the communal Jewish prayer of thanksgiving fittingly offered, among other occasions, when one has successfully crossed the ocean.[32] The Pilgrims of Plymouth Colony, including Bradford, were heavily influenced by the sixteenth–seventeenth century

English Christian Hebraist Henry Ainsworth. As Nick Bunker explained in his 2011 book, *Making Haste from Babylon*:

> Writing about the Mishnah, the Jewish code of laws, [Maimonides] said that the words of [Psalm 107] . . . gave birth to the Jewish rite of thanksgiving. The Talmud lists four occasions when the *Birkat HaGomel* was compulsory: the healing of a sickness, the release of a prisoner, the end of a voyage, and the arrival of travelers at their destination. Ainsworth listed them too, and described the form taken by the Jewish prayer. It was a public confession of the goodness and majesty of God, of exactly the kind the Pilgrims performed [upon the *Mayflower* first landing] at Provincetown [in 1620]. A year later, most likely in October 1621, after their first harvest, the colonists held the festivities commemorated by the modern Thanksgiving.[33]

Growing up, I often thought of the Thanksgiving holiday as the American civic analogue to the Jewish holiday of Passover—especially with the Passover Haggadah's well-known song of thanks, *"Dayenu"* ("it would have been enough"). Perhaps, in retrospect, I should have been thinking of *Birkat HaGomel* when we ate the Thanksgiving turkey!

There were no Jews aboard the *Mayflower* or in Plymouth Colony, and despite the Pilgrims' clear biblical intimacy and appreciation for both the Hebrew Bible and the Hebrew language, there is no reason to believe they were themselves personally philo-Semitic. But it is undeniable that the Mayflower Compact, the founding political charter of Plymouth Colony, closely—likely deliberately—mirrored the core Halachic concepts of collective holiness and intergenerational covenant, and it is plausible that the very first Thanksgiving ever held on American soil was modeled after a somewhat obscure Jewish communal prayer that many nonobservant Jews have probably never even heard of. For a group of exclusively non-Jews, that is quite a Jewish legacy to leave behind.

Nor were the Pilgrims and Plymouth Colony the final word on political Hebraism in the New World—far from it. A century and a half later, in the then–newly established United States, the nation's Founders displayed an intimate familiarity with the Hebrew Bible and its attendant political and legal traditions. That familiarity and intellectual curiosity greatly shaped their worldview and affected the trajectory of the nascent American republic.

By 1790, the United States had won its independence from Britain and ratified, following the failure of the Articles of Confederation, the Constitution of 1787. The formation of the new nation brought with it fierce debates about the nature of freedom, republican self-governance, and the common good— many of which were aired during the Constitutional Convention, and many more of which subsequently appeared in *The Federalist Papers* and the *Anti-Federalist Papers*. One indispensable facet of the emerging American political identity was the principle of religious liberty, which was enumerated in 1791 as the nation's very first explicitly secured liberty in the First Amendment to the Constitution. The First Amendment, along with the other nine amendments of the Bill of Rights, was ratified one year after President George Washington famously addressed the largest Jewish community in the United States at that time—in Newport, Rhode Island—then numbering roughly twenty-five families.[34]

While the early United States was founded by men—such as the Pilgrims—fleeing religious intolerance in the Old World, the notion of *full* equality for all religious minorities was still controversial. Many states had laws that restricted political participation to Protestants, and in some instances to Christians more generally. Jews, Catholics, and other religious minorities often faced various types of legal and social discrimination. In this context, the Jewish community's address to Washington upon his visit to Newport in 1790 expressed hope that the fledgling American regime would uphold the core principles of liberty and equality that had been enunciated in the Founding documents, including the Declaration of Independence of 1776. Washington's response to the Hebrew Congregation of Newport, on August 18, 1790, was just the reassurance that the Jews of Newport had requested.

Washington made clear that America's self-proclaimed core principles do indeed extend to all religious groups. The modern ahistorical misnomer of "separation of church and state" notwithstanding,[35] the first president's letter to the Jews of Newport was a clarion call that the free exercise of religion would abound in the United States. President Washington, in four crisp but memorable paragraphs, lauded religious liberty, as opposed to merely religious tolerance, and emphasized the concept of freedom of conscience as foundational to all mankind.[36] Perhaps most fundamentally, Washington assured American Jewry that the United States "gives to bigotry no sanction [and] to persecution no assistance."[37] The "children of the stock of Abraham," like all their fellow Americans, would be equal parts of the government, and "every one shall sit in safety under his own vine and fig tree, and there shall be none to make him afraid."[38] These fateful words forever altered the course of American history, helping to lay the groundwork for a Christianity that has always been far more hospitable to the Jewish people (and other religious minorities) than historically it has been elsewhere.

Washington, like many of the Founders, evinced a deep-rooted— and perhaps anachronistic—philo-Semitism, which led him to champion the free religious exercise and general flourishing of American Jewry.[39] Nor was Washington's philo-Semitism limited to his magnanimous response to the Jews of Newport, Rhode Island. Prior to his presidency, Washington had presided over the Constitutional Convention in Philadelphia, wherein he had permitted a German-born Jewish immigrant named Jonas Phillips to address the body in opposition to a proposal for a Christian religious test for federal officeholders. Phillips's petition was successful; the No Religious Test Clause in Article VI of the Constitution still affirms today that "no religious Test shall ever be required as a Qualification to any Office or public Trust under the United States."[40]

Washington was also known to be personally friendly with Haym Salomon, a Polish-born Jewish merchant best known as a leading financier of both the Continental Congress and the American Revolutionary War—including the dispositive Battle of Yorktown, which saw the surrender of British general Charles Cornwallis and the end of the war. Though it has never been confirmed, many have long believed that, in designing the Great Seal of the United States, Washington arranged the thirteen stars (which represent the original thirteen colonies) in the shape of the Star of David in order to commemorate Salomon's contributions to American independence. As the popular myth goes, Washington is said to have asked Salomon what he desired as compensation for his generous financing of the war effort, and Salomon responded, "I want nothing for myself, rather something for my people."[41]

George Washington's philo-Semitism was shared by many of America's other well-known Founders. There is perhaps no starker additional example of Founding-era American philo-Semitism than Benjamin Franklin's desire to make the national seal of the United States a depiction of Moses parting the Red Sea—a fascinating example of how the Founders frequently drew on biblical imagery to symbolize the new nation's asserted ideals.

This proposal, which Franklin made in July of 1776 as part of his duties for a Continental Congress committee tasked with designing the national seal, reflected his view of the American Revolution as a profound and righteous struggle for national liberation and self-determination—akin to the biblical Exodus story. As John Adams, who was assigned to the same committee by the Continental Congress, recounted in a letter to his wife, Abigail, one month later, Franklin proposed an image for the young republic's national seal of "Moses lifting up his wand, and dividing the Red Sea, and Pharaoh, in his chariot overwhelmed with the waters," along with the motto, "Rebellion to tyrants is obedience to God."[42]

The parallels with William Bradford and Plymouth Colony are unmistakable. As Yale professor Philip Gorski, author of the 2017 book *American Covenant: A History of Civil Religion from the Puritans to the Present,* has said, Franklin's proposal "shows how powerful, how influential the Exodus narrative was, and remained, during the revolutionary era."[43] Many of the Founders viewed their struggle for political emancipation as similar to the ancient Israelites' escape from Egyptian bondage.

Franklin, like Bradford and the Pilgrims before him, saw America as a fundamentally covenantal political project. Franklin, though personally a deist who questioned traditional Judeo-Christian religious doctrine, nonetheless believed in the idea of Divine Providence guiding human affairs. His choice of the Exodus story was consistent with his view that the American Revolution had a higher moral, and perhaps even transcendental, purpose. In the same way that God had aided the Israelites in their quest for freedom, Franklin saw divine favor in America's struggle for independence. By invoking this biblical imagery, Franklin appealed to the belief that America had a special role in the world—a belief echoed nearly a century later by Abraham Lincoln in his Trenton, New Jersey, speech of February 1861, when he referred to Americans as an "almost chosen people."[44] Truly, many of the Founders saw themselves as quasi–"New Israelites," with the American Revolution framed in terms of biblical stories of deliverance and covenant.[45] Many of the colonists saw themselves as forging a new covenant with God in the form of a republican government rooted in liberty, justice, and human flourishing.[46]

Fascinatingly, there were also those in the Founding era who advocated that Hebrew, not English, become the national language of the republic. While the notion of Hebrew as either the *lingua franca* or official language of the United States never materialized, figures as politically and intellectually diverse as Alexander Hamilton, Thomas Jefferson, John Adams, Benjamin Franklin, and others all apparently spoke of it approvingly.[47] Marquis de Chastellux, a French general who served alongside General George Washington during the American Revolution, observed in 1780 that Americans "have seriously proposed to introduce a new language; and some, for the public convenience, would have the Hebrew substituted to the English, taught in the schools, and used in all public acts."[48] The Frenchman additionally noted that during the Continental Congress, "certain members of Congress proposed that the use of English be formally prohibited in the United States, and Hebrew substituted for it."[49]

The admiration of the Hebrew language seeped, in many instances, into outright admiration of the Hebrew people; many of the Founders were deeply philo-Semitic, admiring Jewish culture, history, perseverance, and Judaism's legal traditions and moral teachings. For example, in an 1809 letter to François Adriaan van der Kemp, John Adams famously wrote in glowing terms about the Jewish people, going so far as to describe the original People of the Book as "the most essential Instrument for civilizing the Nations":

> I will insist that the Hebrews have done more to civilize Men than any other Nation. If I were an Atheist and believed in blind eternal Fate, I should Still believe that Fate had ordained the Jews to be the most essential Instrument for civilizing the Nations. If I were an Atheist of the other Sect, who believe or pretend to believe that all is ordered by Chance, I Should believe that Chance had ordered the Jews to preserve and

propagate, to all Mankind the Doctrine of a Supreme intelligent wise, almighty Sovereign of the Universe, which I believe to be the great essential Principle of all Morality and consequently of all Civilization.[50]

It is difficult to imagine a more stirring example of passionate philo-Semitism than that. Crucially, Adams, like John Selden almost two centuries before him in England, was a philosophical conservative of a distinctly Anglo-American bent. Adams's three-volume *Defence of the Constitutions of Government of the United States of America* staunchly defended the Anglo-American constitutional tradition against the criticisms of liberal rationalists and Enlightenment philosophers,[51] and as president in 1798 he offered one of his most famous conservative dicta: "Our Constitution was made only for a moral and religious people. It is wholly inadequate to the government of any other."[52] And for President Adams, there was no doubt as to the identity of the ultimate wellspring and enduring guardian of such a "moral and religious people": the original People of the Book, the Jews.

Alexander Hamilton, like Adams a conservative in the distinct Anglo-American mold, viewed the Jewish people similarly—which is to say, very warmly. Thought by some historians to actually *be* Jewish himself, Hamilton was at minimum surrounded by Jewish friends and colleagues since his boyhood days in the West Indies. He was tutored in grammar school by a Jewish headmistress, and he memorized the Ten Commandments in the original Hebrew at a young age. Later in life as a lawyer in New York City, Hamilton "ardently" defended many Jewish clients[53] and befriended Gershom Seixas, a Jewish man who was also involved in the governance of Columbia University, Hamilton's alma mater.[54] Seixas would become the first American-born *chazzan* (Jewish cantor) anywhere in the colonies—something he achieved at Mikveh Israel in Philadelphia, which was also the home synagogue for Haym Salomon and Jonas Phillips.

Overall, historian Ron Chernow—whose biography of Alexander Hamilton inspired the popular Broadly musical *Hamilton*—described Hamilton's deep admiration for the Jewish people as a "lifelong reverence."[55] As Hamilton once wrote, that the Jewish people were still alive in his time—and today—is itself proof of God's existence:

> The state and progress of the Jews, from their earliest history to the present time, has been so entirely out of the ordinary course of human affairs, is it not then a fair conclusion, that the cause also is an extraordinary one—in other words, that it is the effect of some great providential plan? The man who will draw this conclusion, will look for the solution in the Bible. He who will not draw it ought to give us another fair solution.[56]

Unsurprisingly, Hamilton was also a vociferous proponent of the No Religious Test Clause's inclusion in the Constitution, which Jonas Phillips had spoken out in favor of during the heated debates of the Constitutional Convention of 1787. Hamilton's ardent opposition was broadly considered one of the reasons no Christian religious test for federal officeholders was ever adopted.

While Hebrew never became America's national language, the fact that it was apparently considered for such an honor—during the colonial era by Bradford and the Puritans, and then again during the Founding era by men such as Adams and Hamilton—reflects the deep respect the Founders and their forebears had for the Hebrew Bible and/or Judaism's legal and moral traditions.[57] The Founders saw in the Hebrew Bible a powerful model for justice, ordered liberty, and self-governance—ideals they sought to embed in the fabric of American republicanism. Through their symbolic gestures and didactic practices, the Founders underscored the importance of biblical morality in the creation of the United States.

My own personal hero in American history, Abraham Lincoln, was, as we have already seen, nothing less than an ardent devotee of political Hebraism and a tremendous friend of the Jewish people in his own time. In fact, there was at least one Jewish man who shrewdly picked up on Lincoln's philo-Semitism and epochal stature even before his presidential inauguration in March of 1861. Rabbi Meir Soloveichik has explained:

> In February of 1861, President-elect Abraham Lincoln, still in Springfield, Illinois, received a gift from a Jew named Abraham Kohn. A fierce abolitionist, Kohn was convinced, as his daughter later wrote, that Lincoln "was the destined Moses of the slaves and the saviour of his country." The gift was a framed painting of an American flag, and on the stripes of that flag, Kohn had inscribed Hebrew verses from Joshua: "As I was with Moses, so I will be with thee; . . . the Lord thy God is with thee whithersoever thou goest."[58]

Kohn's gift to the president-elect was uncanny—perhaps even prophetic. As the Civil War soon raged, Lincoln began to merge "allusions to Israel with America" in his speeches and correspondences.[59] In February 1861, Lincoln spoke on nationalism and peoplehood in Trenton, New Jersey:

> I am exceedingly anxious that this Union, the Constitution, and the liberties of the people shall be perpetuated in accordance with the original idea for which that struggle was made and I shall be most happy indeed if I shall be an humble instrument in the hands of the Almighty, and of this, his almost chosen people, for perpetuating the object of that great struggle.[60]

Like the ancient Israelites, America, in this dispensation, had—and perhaps has—a special covenant or destiny to fulfill. But while America, for Lincoln, was founded in nobleness and destined for greatness, it still had a long way to go to realize its Founding ideals and purpose.

For Jewish Americans, Lincoln's reference to America as an "almost chosen people" surely resonated at the time—and ought to still resonate today. Traditional Jewish thought has long understood the concept of national chosenness as a call to uphold God's Word, fulfill the dictates of the Mosaic Law, and be a "light unto the nations" despite so much historical persecution and suffering. Lincoln's use of similar language in 1861 would have felt familiar and comforting to contemporaneous Jewish Americans, who were just beginning to see themselves as an earnest part of the American experiment. Many Jewish Americans likely saw Lincoln's words as an affirmation that America, like ancient Israel, was a nation with a moral purpose that aligned with the Jewish values of justice, ordered liberty, and collective holiness.[61]

Lincoln's frequent use of biblical language and allegory contributed to the broader notion of an "American civic religion," where religious imagery and moral concepts—often drawn from the Hebrew Bible—have long been used to frame national identity and political discourse. As a people associated with the theological concept of chosenness, Jewish Americans were perhaps uniquely positioned to understand and engage with the moral implications of Lincoln's vision for the nation.[62] But so, too, for that matter, were all biblically literate American Christians who, like Lincoln himself, were intimately familiar not merely with their Bible's New Testament, but also with its Old Testament.

In a 2024 essay for *Modern Age Journal,* Joseph Prudhomme asked, "How would the American Founders have responded to the creation of Israel?"[63] Based on the pervasive philo-Semitic attitudes prevalent in early America, Prudhomme concluded in the positive: "It seems clear that a great many of the American founders would have disagreed, and disagreed strongly, with the claim that support for Israel as a Jewish state is, to any appreciable degree, un-American."[64]

The American Founders' deep admiration for Judaism and its moral teachings, along with their recognition of the Hebrew Bible's timeless teachings on political statesmanship and just governance, would have led them to view the establishment of the State of Israel in 1948 as a fulfillment of the very values they held dear. Their philo-Semitism, demonstrated through George Washington's embrace of Jewish citizens, Benjamin Franklin's proposal for Moses parting the Red Sea as the national seal, and John Adams's and Alexander Hamilton's speaking of the Jews in as warm and stirring language as they did, evinced a profound respect for Jewish history, Jewish culture, and Jewish morality.

John Adams, for his part, was even more explicit on the issue of Zionism, writing in an 1819 letter to American Jewish lay leader Mordechai Manuel Noah (a grandson of Jonas Phillips): "I really wish the Jews again [to have] in Judea an independent nation."[65] John Adams's own presidential son, John Quincy Adams, agreed, offering his support for the "rebuilding of Judea as an independent nation."[66] Nor were the Adams family sentiments anomalous in American history. About a century later, in 1922, Congress passed, and President Warren G. Harding signed, the Lodge–Fish Resolution—a joint resolution of both houses of Congress endorsing, as Britain's Balfour Declaration had done five years prior, Jewish sovereignty in the Holy Land. In the words of the Lodge–Fish Resolution, "The United States of America favors the establishment in Palestine of a national home for the Jewish people."[67]

It is difficult not to directly connect the philo-Semitism of the Founders and Lincoln to the ultimate success of the Lodge–Fish Resolution in 1922—as well as to President Harry Truman's near-instantaneous recognition of the State of Israel upon David

Ben-Gurion's monumental independence declaration in May of 1948.

The Founders saw the legal and moral frameworks of Judaism as foundational to the biblical and English common law traditions that, perhaps more than any other political and intellectual inheritances, shaped the burgeoning American republic. This admiration naturally extended to the idea, far-fetched though it would have been in the late-eighteenth century, that an independent Jewish state in the Land of Israel would represent a legitimate and morally sound endeavor.

Many of the American Founders, as we see most clearly in the case of John Adams, were, in short, proto-Zionists. And it is to this subject—the legitimacy and grandeur of Zionism, or Jewish nationalism in the Land of Israel—that this book now turns.

5

THE CASE FOR JEWISH NATIONALISM

"And I will make you into a great nation, and I will bless you, and I will aggrandize your name, and [you shall] be a blessing."

—GENESIS 12:2[1]

ONE OF MY VERY FAVORITE PLACES IN ALL OF ISRAEL IS THE CITY OF David in Jerusalem.[2] A remarkable archaeological site that brings the Bible to life for countless visitors every year, Israel's City of David National Park is located just a stone's throw away from the Western Wall, barely outside what is now referred to as the Old City of Jerusalem.

Interestingly, what is now called the Old City is not actually the oldest settlement in Jerusalem. That distinction belongs to the City of David, which was where King David settled after leaving Hebron to unite the Kingdom of Israel. The City of David, which includes the Gihon Spring and the ancient Pool of Siloam, predates the building of Solomon's Temple on nearby Mount Moriah.

The contemporary archaeological excavations led by the City of David Foundation are mesmerizing—not merely for religious Jews and Christians, but for any student of history or anyone curious about the physical origins of Western civilization. I have been to the City of David multiple times, most recently on my post–October 7, 2023, trip to Israel, when I visited two days after our searing visit to Kfar Aza and four days after an inspirational day trip to the holy city of Hebron. (Incidentally, in Hebron we saw firsthand ancient roadways that *predate* King David and were perhaps even used by the biblical patriarch Abraham's contemporaries.[3])

The City of David's excavations are remarkable: The worlds of the ancient Jewish prophets and kings come to life in the most tangible ways imaginable. On my last trip, our tour guide quoted a line from Scripture and then physically showed us an engraving on a nearby column, from the era of King Hezekiah, that depicted exactly what had been described by the underlying verse he had just read in the Book of Jeremiah. How can someone experience something like that and *not* believe in the authenticity of the Hebrew Bible?

Our group also descended the famous "stepped street," which is part of an extraordinary in-progress City of David excavation that, once completed, will reconnect the Pool of Siloam to the Temple Mount. While making our way down toward the pool, we passed around and held a bit of paper that was charred with ash—the very ash from the Romans' burning of Herod's Temple in the year 70 CE. I actually have a small bottle of some of that very ash—it was gifted to me by someone who works at City of David, and it sits on my desk right next to the rocks I have from Auschwitz and Treblinka.

In 2024, the Israeli Antiquities Authority released their findings of a 2019 excavation in Zanoah, a city mentioned twice in the Book of Joshua—in which the Israelites finally cross the river Jordan and enter the Promised Land—as helping define the boundaries of the tribal allotment of Judah. The findings reveal stone walls, pottery, jugs, bowls, iron tools, and other artifacts that date back more than 3,200 years—which corroborates the biblical narrative that Joshua led the Israelites into the Land of Israel around 1407 to 1406 BCE.[4] Speaking of King Hezekiah, in the Zanoah excavation, "preserved pottery was also pulled from the ground, with one featuring a stamp on the handle that read 'of the King,' which was to honor King Hezekiah's reign in Judah."[5] Overall, about a fifth of the discovered pottery fragments in Zanoah date to the time immediately following the Israelite arrival in the Promised Land.[6]

The Jewish people have a real, millennia-old historical record in the Land of Israel. These are verifiable facts. As Yair Netanyahu, the son of Israeli prime minister Benjamin Netanyahu, wrote in a 2022 op-ed for *Newsweek* that I solicited and edited while serving as the publication's opinion editor: "These truths, drawn from ancient and modern history, archaeology, and even international and US law, do not simply disprove the Palestinian propaganda depiction of Jewish usurpers who swooped in a century ago to steal Arab land. These truths demonstrate that the Jewish people have a long-standing and exclusive right to the Land of Israel. Countless archaeological artifacts have been discovered confirming the Bible's descriptions of the ancient Kingdoms of Judea and Israel."[7]

Indeed, they have.

The Jewish people have had an uninterrupted presence in the Land of Israel ever since the Joshua-led conquest of Canaan that followed the death of Moses. Even after the destruction of Herod's Temple in 70 CE and the beginning of the Jewish Diaspora, Jewish communities remained scattered throughout the Land of Israel. The town of Yavneh, for instance, thrived in ensuing centuries as a Talmudic center under the leadership of Yochanan ben Zakkai and Rabban Gamliel II. Maimonides, perhaps the single greatest medieval Jewish sage, briefly lived in the Land of Israel and likely prayed at the Temple Mount in Jerusalem.[8] The *Shulchan Aruch*, Joseph Karo's sixteenth-century codification of Jewish law that has today reached near-universal acceptance among observant Jews, was composed in the holy city of Safed. All throughout the many centuries of Ottoman control of the Land of Israel and the pre-1948 era of British-controlled Mandatory Palestine, there continually existed the *yishuv*—Jews living in the Land of Israel.

Austro-Hungarian Jewish journalist Theodor Herzl is typically hailed as the father of modern Zionism. And Herzl undoubtedly deserves a great deal of credit for his organizational prowess and prophetic vision, the latter of which he most clearly demonstrated in his 1896 work *Der Judenstaat* (*The Jewish State*). Indeed, I have paid my respects to Herzl numerous times at his tomb, located in the eponymous Mount Herzl in Jerusalem. But at the same time, it has always seemed to me something of a historical misnomer to claim that Herzl "invented" Zionism. What does that even mean, exactly? Surely, he got this idea from *somewhere*.

The Land of Israel has been the Jewish people's promised land since time immemorial—at least since God first "formed a covenant" with the biblical patriarch Abraham, "saying, 'To your seed I have given this land, from the river of Egypt until the great river, the Euphrates river.'"[9] Observant Jews pray for the restoration of Jerusalem three times every single day during the Amidah prayer, the central prayer in the Jewish liturgy. We end our Passover Seders every year with the aspirational cry, "Next year in Jerusalem!" The holy city of Jerusalem, and by extension the entire Land of Israel, is hardwired into our very beings—our very *souls*. No matter what the modern-day *kapos* of vile self-hating organizations such as Jewish Voice for Peace and IfNotNow might claim, support for the Land of Israel—and by logical extension, necessarily also the modern State of Israel—is an absolute "pillar" of Judaism.[10] The psalmist is clear on this point: "If I forget you, O Jerusalem, may my right hand forget."[11]

As much as the fools of the United Nations Educational, Scientific, and Cultural Organization (UNESCO) might try to whitewash the Holy Land so as to Islamicize and de-Judaize it,[12] there is demonstrable, undeniable archaeological evidence that the Jews inhabited the Land of Israel for millennia before the prophet Muhammad roamed the earth. To the extent that Zionism can be defined as a national liberation movement seeking to unite (or reunite) a scattered nation with the physical land that the nation was promised and where it first emerged in concrete form, furthermore, God Himself is the first "Zionist."

It is all foretold in the Book of Deuteronomy: "The Lord, your God, will bring back your exiles, and . . . He will once again gather you from all the nations, where the Lord, your God, had dispersed you. . . . And the Lord, your God, will bring you to the land which your forefathers possessed, and you [too] will take possession of it, and He will do good to you."[13] That is precisely what has, in fact, happened. How perfectly prescient is our Creator?

It is often said that there are three primary ways for a nation-state to attain legitimacy under customary international law: indigeneity, international resolution, and victory in war. The modern State of Israel has separately and independently attained legitimacy on all three grounds.

As discussed, the Jews are the world's last remaining indigenous people to the Land of Israel. It is true that there *were* other people who were indigenous to the land prior to the Joshua-led conquest of Canaan, but none of them still exist today. As but one example, the Philistines, another ancient people whom the Bible also takes repeated note of, were conquered by the Assyrians centuries before the Babylonians destroyed Solomon's Temple.[14] Countless other examples abound of since-vanquished or -vanished peoples who once inhabited the broader Levant. Scripture, for instance, also mentions (among other ancient nations and peoples) the Canaanites, Hittites, Amorites, Perizzites, Jebusites, Girgashites, Moabites, Rephaites, Anakim, Horites, Ammonites, Caphtorites, Sidonians, Geshurites, and the Maachathites.[15] But the upshot is that the Jews are the sole remaining people today who are actually indigenous to the Land of Israel. And it is worth reemphasizing: We know this not merely from Scripture or history books, but from the irrefutable archaeological evidence. This basic, rudimentary fact simply cannot be debated, no matter how shrill the shrieks of hysteria may be from misbegotten critical race theory–inspired "anti-colonialist" or "anti-imperialist" activists.

The Philistines, incidentally, are sometimes said to be the progenitors of today's Palestinian-Arabs. Nothing could be further from the truth. A 2019 DNA study of exhumed Philistine skeletons in coastal Israel found that the Philistines came from a "southern European gene pool," and thus bear no relation to the Palestinian-Arabs of today.[16] That makes sense, because old Palestine Liberation Organization (PLO) officials themselves have confirmed that today's Palestinian-Arabs are ethnically indistinguishable from any other Arabs.

As top PLO official Zuhair Muhsin candidly confessed in a 1977 interview:

> There are no differences between Jordanians, Palestinians, Syrians, and Lebanese. We are all part of one nation. It is only for political reasons that we carefully underline our Palestinian identity. . . . Yes, the existence of a separate Palestinian identity serves only tactical purposes. The founding of a Palestinian state is a new tool in the continuing battle against Israel.[17]

The original use of the term "Palestine" in the Land of Israel by the Jews' Roman oppressors was an attempt to de-Judaize the land. The Roman term "Palestine," which has had a longer shelf life than the Romans could have possibly predicted, has absolutely nothing to do with *either* the ancient Philistines or the Palestinian-Arabs of today.

The modern State of Israel is also legitimate because of international resolution and concomitant rudimentary principles of international law. It is worth recounting some relevant history here in detail.[18]

Following the Romans' destruction of Herod's Temple in 70 CE, the Land of Israel frequently changed legal hands for nearly two millennia. For centuries leading up to World War I, the land was part of the Ottoman Empire. The Balfour Declaration of 1917, thirteen years after Herzl's death, was the first modern expression of Zionist support by a major political power (Britain). The Balfour Declaration helped lead to the Mandate for Palestine, based on Article XXII of the Covenant of the League of Nations and assigned to Britain at the San Remo Conference of 1920. This was the instrument of international law that effectuated the Declaration's call for a "national home for the Jewish people."[19] The Mandate for Palestine was but one of many "mandates" in the aftermath of German and Ottoman defeat in World War I. Crucially, all other mandate successor states follow the borders of each state's preexisting mandate.

Britain was chosen to administer the Mandate for Palestine, whose territory included all of the modern-day states of Israel and Jordan. Under the terms of the Mandate, the territory was further subdivided between Mandatory Palestine and the Emirate of Transjordan; the Mandate's "Jewish home" provisions were suspensible in the latter, implicitly paving the way for contiguous Jewish and Arab states. The borders of the former coincided with the borders of the Land of Israel, and the borders of the latter corresponded with the borders of the modern Hashemite Kingdom of Jordan. The border between Mandatory Palestine and the Emirate of Transjordan was the Jordan River and a line extending south toward the Dead Sea, into which the Jordan River empties.[20]

The Mandate got its final approval in 1922, at which time Mandatory Palestine and the Emirate of Transjordan were formally severed. Britain, under the terms of the Mandate, was charged with reconstituting the Jews' "national home" in the Land of Israel: "An appropriate Jewish agency shall be recogni[z]ed as a public body for the purpose of advising and co-operating with the Administration of Palestine in such economic, social, and other matters as may affect the establishment of the Jewish national home and the interests of the Jewish population in Palestine."[21] Eventually, the Hashemite Kingdom of Transjordan declared independence in 1946. The new Kingdom assumed the same borders as the Emirate of Transjordan, in accordance with the well-known international law principle of *uti possidetis juris* ("may you continue to possess such as you do possess"),[22] according to which a new state acquires sovereignty with the same borders bequeathed it by the area's last sovereign entity.[23]

Similarly, *uti possidetis juris* took effect the very moment founding Israeli prime minister David Ben-Gurion declared the independence of a new Jewish state in the Land of Israel on May 15, 1948. Just as Transjordan, which declared independence two years earlier, assumed the preexisting borders of the Mandate's Emirate of Transjordan, so, too, did the State of Israel assume the preexisting border of Mandatory Palestine. Israel, upon its independence on May 14, 1948, inherited all of Judea and Samaria (as well as the Gaza Strip).[24] *This* is the original "two-state solution" to the so-called "Israeli–Palestinian conflict." Jordan was, and remains, the actual "Palestinian–Arab" state under the original partition plan. Judea and Samaria, the Jews' ancestral and biblical homeland that is today usually called the "West Bank," was *never* supposed to be under anything but Jewish control.

Naturally, the modern "from the river to the sea, Palestine will be free!" crowd is grossly ignorant about real history.

Finally, in addition to Jewish indigeneity in the Land of Israel and international resolutions and concomitant international law principles, the modern State of Israel is also legitimate due to its military victories. Israel has won three absolute military victories over Arab invaders who sought to annihilate the Jewish state and wipe away any taint of Jewish territorial sovereignty in the Levant.

First, after Ben-Gurion declared independence in May 1948, the surrounding militaries of Egypt, Lebanon, Transjordan, and Syria immediately invaded the fledgling Jewish state. The resultant war, which culminated in a miraculous Israeli victory against all odds, dragged on for nearly a year. Between February and July of 1949, Israel reached successive armistice agreements with each of the Arab countries.[25] Under the temporary ceasefire lines of 1949, Jordan fully occupied Judea and Samaria (what the international community generally refers to as the "West Bank"), the eastern portions of Jerusalem, and the Old City of Jerusalem in a dubiously legal fashion.

Notably, the text of the armistice agreements was explicit— as insisted upon not by Israel, but by the defeated Arab would-be conquerors themselves—that the ceasefire lines did not represent a final settlement of any contested territory.[26] As the Israeli–Transjordanian armistice agreement said, in language mirroring its sister accords, "The [a]rmistice [d]emarcation [l]ines defined in articles V and VI of this [a]greement are agreed upon by the [p]arties without prejudice to future territorial settlements or boundary lines or to claims of either [p]arty relating thereto."[27] Nothing therefore changed under customary international law.

In the Six-Day War of 1967, Israel's Arab neighbors again attempted to annihilate it and cleanse the Holy Land of any Jewish taint. Israel's victory in this defensive war was astonishing, and the Jewish state regained territorial possession of Judea and Samaria, the Gaza Strip, the Sinai Peninsula (which Israel subsequently ceded to Egypt in 1979 in exchange for peace), and the

Golan Heights. But once again, nothing changed under international law: *uti possidetis juris* continued to apply after the Six-Day War, just as it did in 1948, tracing back to the Mandate.[28] And so it was, yet again, after the grueling Israeli victory in the Yom Kippur War of 1973—radical Arabs' most recent wide-scale attempt, prior to the Hamas-orchestrated Simchat Torah Massacre of October 7, 2023, to commit genocide against the Jews of Israel and render the Levant *Judenrein* on a major Jewish holiday.[29]

The modern State of Israel is indisputably legitimate, its myriad zealous critics notwithstanding, according to all the various ways that a nation-state can attain international legitimacy under the rules of the modern Westphalian nation-state order.

Perhaps that would be enough. (As Jews say at our Passover Seders, "Dayenu!"—"it would have been enough!") But the grotesque lies of the "Boycott, Divestment, and Sanctions" (BDS) movement and other vile but widely disseminated anti-Israel agitprop notwithstanding, the modern State of Israel is not merely legitimate the same way that any regular country in Europe or the Americas is legitimate. Israel may well be, as Liel Leibovitz of *Tablet* magazine argued in a 2021 essay, "the most legitimate state on Earth, and therefore the pillar on which the legitimacy of the global order of nation-states rests."[30]

The notion of a defined physical territory for the ancient Israelites—"from the river of Egypt until the great river, the Euphrates river"—is something that goes back as far as God's promise to the patriarch Abraham itself.[31] There is no extant nation-state on earth that has as deep historical ties to the physical land on which that nation rests. But the nation-state roots of Israel comprise many additional layers beyond Scripture.

As a purely historical matter, it was ancient Israel, under the United Kingdom of King David, that truly first laid the foundation for what would become, following the seventeenth-century

Peace of Westphalia thousands of years later, the modern nation-state. David P. Goldman expounded on this point in a 2018 *Tablet* essay:

> One does not have to accept the biblical account to recognize that Israel set a precedent for all the states that followed. It united a group of tribes around a common religion and priesthood with a universal God, eschewing the worship of family or clan gods that otherwise was universal in the ancient world. . . . No other nation like the biblical Israel arose in the ancient world with a unified monarchy, a unified legal system, and unified religion.[32]

It was ancient Israel that first exemplified how to unify and concretize a nation out of disparate families and tribes, as Yoram Hazony persuasively explained in his 2018 book, *The Virtue of Nationalism*.[33] At the time, the biblical nation-state model stood in stark contrast to other contemporaneous geopolitical orders, such as the pagan empires—such as Rome—that dominated classical antiquity. These competing road maps for how to best structure society, humble nationalism on the one hand and hegemonic globalism on the other hand, continue to stand athwart one another today.

The modern post-1948 State of Israel, and modern post–Theodor Herzl political Zionism more generally, is nothing less than an indigenous people's righteous movement to return to their ancestral homeland, as that homeland was established according to everything from Scripture to incontestable empirical and archaeological evidence. The national restoration of the Hebrew language as a Jewish *lingua franca*, itself no small miracle two millennia after the onset of the Jewish Diaspora, is microcosmic of the direct national trajectory—with all the authenticity and legitimacy such a remarkable trajectory entails—from King

David's United Kingdom of Israel, which existed one millennium before Christ, to Ben-Gurion's fateful proclamation establishing the modern state on May 14, 1948.

In modern Israel, Jews who look nothing whatsoever like one another, and who come from far-flung lands such as Poland, Spain, Morocco, Yemen, and Ethiopia, have come home because they are all members of the same broader family—the same Jewish people and nation of Israel, *Am Yisrael*. Cultural differences notwithstanding, they speak the same language and adhere to the same religion of their forefathers. To again quote Leibovitz, "Everything in Israel springs naturally from its people's way of life, which is a product of a national culture shaped by a collective narrative and shared traditions."[34]

It is notable that during Israel's raucous judicial reform debate of 2023, protesters on the Israeli Left—who I strongly opposed on the underlying merits[35]—waved the Israeli flag in the streets. (Counter-protesters on the Israeli Right, naturally, did the same thing.) The left-wing activists were misguided in opposing the proposals to rein in Israel's imperious national judiciary, but at least they made their points while draped in the flag. That is a considerable contrast from similar left-wing protests in the streets of the United States, where protesters are more likely to echo the Iranian regime's call for the *death* of America than to proudly fly the American flag. To wit, when is the last time the PLO flag has been seen at a public demonstration alongside the American flag? It is almost inconceivable; the underlying cognitive dissonance is overwhelming.

Nationalism and pride in one's homeland, which is also shaped and bolstered by the State of Israel's general rule of mandatory society-wide conscription into the Israel Defense Forces, is typically not a partisan or "political" issue in the Jewish state. Nor is it a class issue: Even Israel's upper crust is still, for the most part, broadly Zionist and not yet truly "post-Zionist." In these respects, the State of Israel is a noble outlier among its fellow Western nations.

The fact that the legitimacy and purity of the modern Israeli nation-state is so strong, and that nothing less than the Bible and some of the oldest archaeological excavations on the earth are profound historical supporting sources, goes far in explaining why so many on the globalist Left harbor such a dripping, intense hatred for the Jewish state. Simple, old-fashioned anti-Semitism, as previously discussed, obviously plays a large role here, as well. But the multifront assault against the Jewish people and the Jewish state is more complicated than that.

Intrinsic in the very concept of the nation-state, crucially, is a certain degree of epistemological humility and restraint. It is perhaps human nature, if a peoplehood or a nationhood is confident in its convictions and beliefs, to attempt to forcibly export its teachings and practices unto the broader world. Indeed, this is what empires and expansionist tyrannies have done since time immemorial. The Roman Empire is a particularly noteworthy example from classical antiquity, and its zeal for forceful evangelism and subjugation can be juxtaposed with the biblical nation-state model as an alternative framework of ordered global affairs.[36] The biblical ideal—and the notion of the nation of Israel as a "chosen people"—is predicated not upon overt evangelism, but in more humbly serving as a source of inspiration for the broader world (hence, a "light unto the nations"). As I have previously discussed, many "Christian Hebraists" of the past millennium, such as the great English common lawyer John Selden, English political theorist James Harrington, and German mathematician Wilhelm Sickard, thus "looked past ancient Greece and Rome to ancient Israel for a model of the ideal government."[37]

Looking back millennia later, the restraint of the biblical United Kingdom of Israel is made all the more impressive by the fact that the ancient Israelites were a covenantal people who had witnessed incredible miracles, such as the splitting of the Red Sea during the Exodus from Egypt. One might be tempted to think that if any historical people would be forgiven for harboring imperialist or hegemonic ambitions, it might be the ancient Israelites! But with steadfast soberness, they lacked any such ambitions. They were humble, restrained nationalists.

And therein lies the rub. If there is one thing that the contemporary Western progressive Left is *not*, it is "humble" or "restrained." Modern progressivism, which is distinct from the classical "live and let live" / John Stuart Mill–style liberalism of a bygone era, is predicated upon forcibly exporting its idiosyncratic catechism unto the masses.

Don't approve of redefining the definition of marriage as it had existed throughout every major global culture and religion for millennia in order to accommodate the personal romantic desires of same-sex couples? *Homophobe!* Don't approve of allowing high school–age biological males with male sexual organs still intact to change in women's locker rooms? *Transphobe!* Don't approve of "Diversity, Equity, and Inclusion" bureaucracies on university campuses that amount, in practice, to something closely approximating *de jure* anti-white, anti-Asian, and anti-Jewish racism? *Racist* (paradoxically)!

And on and on it goes. To the modern woke Left, "tolerance" is only permissible for someone else if that individual conscientiously toes the line and imbibes the tenets of the prevailing woke orthodoxy. Ultimately, dissenters will bend the knee and be homogenized into the left-wing blob. As radio host Erick Erickson memorably put it in a prescient 2013 blog post[38] and subsequent book of the same name,[39] *"you will be made to care."* In practice, "you will be made to care" amounts to nothing less than intellectual and lifestyle totalitarianism—perhaps a "softer" totalitarianism than the Soviet Union's jackboot or the Islamist despotism of Hamas, for instance, but a form of totalitarianism nonetheless. The European Union, the United Nations, and the global neoliberal "Great Reset" of the World Economic Forum are all real-world examples of this. Contemporary progressivism, globalism/universalism, and forcible intellectual homogeneity are all sides of the same noxious coin.

It logically follows, then, that for the ardent progressive or aspiring globalist, the particularist, fiercely nationalist, and distinctly Jewish State of Israel is a bête noire. If one's sociopolitical goal is to erode all the distinctions that make us human in the first instance, dismantle the Westphalian nation-state system, and immanentize a borderless, universalist eschaton à la "The Great Reset," it makes sense to focus disproportionately on the world's only Jewish state. It is the only state in the Middle East, after all, stubbornly preventing region-wide imperial Islamic rule. What's more, if one's goal is to dismantle contemporary Western Christendom, it makes sense to begin with the religion that helped birth Christianity—Judaism—in the very land where Christianity itself began.

But the Jewish State of Israel will *not*, to again invoke Erickson, "be made to care." It will *not* bend the knee. Israel's pride, to borrow from *National Review* founder William F. Buckley Jr., is that it "stands athwart history, yelling Stop, at a time when no one is inclined to do so."[40] It is Israel's witness to Jewish particularism and nationalism—its defiance in being, symbolically and quite literally, the "Jew of the nations"—that engenders so much of the modern left-wing ire against it. "The Jews formed the first nation-state, that is, the first polity defined by common language and religion," as David P. Goldman put it in a 2024 essay for the Claremont Institute's *American Mind* online journal.[41] And so today, over three thousand years later, the Jewish state continues to serve as the paradigmatic modern nation-state—with all the glory, and on occasion all the embitterment, that such a status necessarily entails.

■ ■ ■

At a concrete and empirical level, the modern State of Israel has also been, based on any relevant socioeconomic or other important societal metric, a smashing national success story.

As of 2024, Israel's economy ranked twentieth globally in terms of GDP per capita, according to the International Monetary Fund—one spot ahead of the United Kingdom, and just behind its Abraham Accords peace partner, the United Arab Emirates.[42] For a country initially founded as a near-socialist state, and one that did not meaningfully embrace free-market economic principles until the 1990s, this is nothing less than extraordinary. Today, Israel's high-tech sector is the world's envy, and the Tel Aviv area routinely ranks as a top-five global tech hub.[43] Many Israeli tech startups, such as the navigation app Waze, have gone on to achieve widespread use and worldwide recognition.

Militarily, Israel has won all of its existential wars of survival, and it is a designated Major Non-NATO Ally under US federal law and a frequent military training partner of the US and other aligned Western nations. Israel's military and intelligence prowess were world-famous and universally respected (or perhaps feared) for many decades—at least until the debilitating effect that the Simchat Torah Massacre of October 7, 2023, had on its reputation and perception. Perhaps most important, the State of Israel is widely understood—if not technically corroborated, per long-standing Israeli policy—to be a nuclear power, making it one of only nine nuclear states in the world. Israel's presumed nuclear capabilities provide a powerful deterrent to nettlesome actors—hardly sufficient, but necessary in such a tough region.

The Israel Defense Forces' national military conscription policy, combined with the Jewish state being a nuclear-armed power, reify Zionism's post-Holocaust commitment of "Never Again." The modern State of Israel was not founded in direct response to the Holocaust—Herzl wrote his influential book *Der Judenstaat* on 1896, for instance—but the 1948 timing of Ben-Gurion's independence declaration nonetheless transpired in the unmistakable shadow and aftermath of the most methodical genocide in human history. Simply put, there is no more important guarantor of prolonged Jewish existence on earth than the modern State of Israel. The state's famous Law of Return, which accords any Jew in the Diaspora the legal right to immigrate to Israel and attain Israeli citizenship, is not merely philosophically consistent with the eternal Jewish yearning for Zion—it has also never been more practically necessary, amid the rising tide of noxious Jew-hatred the world over. If "Never Again" is to mean anything whatsoever, it requires a strong State of Israel.

Perhaps most important, Israel, despite its myriad challenges and near-constant security concerns, is a happy country filled with happy people. According to the 2024 World Happiness Report, Israel ranked as the fifth-happiest country in the world—and the very happiest non-Nordic country in the world.[44] For a country that exists under such an intense microscope, in which its government's every move is criticized and in which its citizens go on with their daily lives knowing that revanchist Islamic foes on all fronts wish for nothing less than the nation's destruction, this is simply remarkable.

Those Jews living in Israel today are happy for one very simple, but also profound, reason: Reattaining Jewish sovereignty in the Land of Israel is exactly what Jews dreamed about and prayed for on a daily basis throughout millennia of exile. For our generation of Jews living both in Israel and in the global Diaspora, it is imperative not to take this for granted. How many of our ancestors prayed toward Jerusalem, wishing to be there to celebrate holidays and cherish Jewish holy sites despite the fact that the land was governed by foreign colonizers such as the Ottomans or the British? How incredibly lucky are we to be alive today to see this extraordinary rebirth of full Jewish sovereignty in the Holy Land? If only our forefathers had lived to see this!

Crucially, even if they are not intuitive Zionists or supporters of contemporary Jewish nationalism for all the foregoing reasons, Christians around the world should also support the modern State of Israel for one very simple reason, which I will elaborate on in the next chapter: Jewish custody of Christian holy sites is necessary in order to physically maintain the sites and ensure equal access to them. Arab Muslims governing throughout the broader area, be they Hamas, the Palestinian Authority, or otherwise, have proven to be entirely untrustworthy and unreliable custodians of Christian holy sites in the Levant—and of Christians themselves throughout the Middle East.

Beleaguered Coptic Christians in Egypt live in perpetual fear of a lethal Islamist terror attack. Christians in Lebanon, who now live under Hezbollah's jackboot, are increasingly endangered, as well; this, notwithstanding the long and rich history of Christianity in that part of the Levant. In Jesus's birth city of Bethlehem, which is now controlled by the Palestinian Authority, a 2020 survey showed that the Christian population had declined from 84 percent of the city's population in 1922 to 22 percent of the city's population in 2007.[45] In total, Christians now comprise less than 1 percent of the population of the Gaza Strip and the so-called "West Bank," having dropped by almost half over the past century.[46]

For all the false and malicious slandering of Israel as a purported "apartheid state," it is Arab Muslims who are ethnically and religiously cleansing the region. And their attempt to Islamicize the region has not been strictly limited to de-Judaizing. Islamization of the Levant has certainly entailed a lot of de-Judaizing, but local Muslims have also been de-Christianizing the region the best they can. This should be obvious to anyone who has reviewed the region's demographics, or even so much as studied a map.

■ ■ ■

The modern State of Israel is not merely ground zero of the fight between Western civilization and the forces of darkness that seek to exterminate it: wokeism, Islamism, and global neoliberalism. To be clear, it certainly *is* exactly that. But it is also much more than that. True to its heritage and stature as the first ancient civilization to unify a concrete nation out of disparate tribes, modern Israel is now also ground zero of the fight for the nation-state concept itself. If one is a nationalist—meaning, to borrow from Hazony, that one believes the world is best governed by a patchwork of independent nations that are given great (if not quite limitless) leeway to determine their own courses of discrete action according to their own national customs, traditions, and principles—then one simply must support the modern State of Israel.

The modern Jewish State of Israel is the proverbial canary in the coal mine, much like the broader Jewish nation of Israel—*Am Yisrael*—has been on countless occasions throughout human history. It is the tip of the spear of the broader grassroots pushback against the three menacing hegemonies of our time: Islamism, wokeism, and global neoliberalism. The battle for Jewish nationalism is thus only partially about the Jews. It is really a battle for the soul, and broader fate, of the West.

6

THE STATE OF ISRAEL

The Western World's
Indispensable Bulwark

"He will not allow your foot to falter; Your Guardian will not slumber. Behold the Guardian of Israel will neither slumber nor sleep."

—PSALMS 121:3–4[1]

MANY AMERICANS SUPPORT VARIOUS PUBLIC POLICIES AND arrive at their political conclusions, more generally, through the first-order analytical prism of faith. Some of my closest friends in the world are evangelical Protestants or devout Catholics, and this is certainly true of them. If someone is raised in a religious setting and views his faith as the most important facet of his life, then this is only natural. And this is not an exclusively Christian phenomenon, of course; it is also true for many traditional and Orthodox Jews, as well as religious individuals from other faith traditions. It is simply logical for someone to deduce second-order inferences from the starting place of a more foundational overarching worldview. Indeed, this happens all the time.

But as I will explain in greater detail in a few chapters, I essentially did this in reverse. I was not raised in a particularly religious home, but I did come to embrace strong conservative political views by the time I was in junior high. In many ways, my childhood innocence and naivete died on September 11, 2001. I was twelve years old, and in seventh grade in suburban New York at the time. The tragic events of that day and the ineluctable corresponding reality that both good and evil exist—and that only the former can contain, or defeat, the latter—launched me on the path that I am still on today.

It was only later on, at various points along that winding path, that I came to embrace and cherish the three central pillars of modern Jewish life: Torah, *Am Yisrael* (the people, or nation, of Israel), and *Eretz Yisrael* (the Land of Israel, which necessarily entails the modern, post-1948 State of Israel). I still have a long way to go (God-willing) on my Jewish journey, but I would like to think I am on the right track.

The first time I intuited the importance and necessity of the modern State of Israel came, as one might expect, on my first visit there. I was twenty-one years old, and I was there on a Taglit-Birthright trip. (Many American Jews who were raised in a more religiously traditional and/or activist Zionist household than I was actually visit Israel for the first time at a much younger age.) My whole Birthright trip was illuminating. It had a tremendous impact on me, and I recall it fondly to this day.

I remember being blown away by the serenity and holiness of the Old City of Jerusalem, as sundown approached on Friday evening and the Jewish Sabbath beckoned. I also immediately fell in love with the northern Israeli city of Safed, which is the highest-elevation city in the country and a centuries-long hub for Kabbalah (Jewish mysticism). For years now, I have worn a thin gold chain with two pendants, one of which is a gold *Magen David* (Star of David) that I bought in Safed. (The other pendant is a *Shaddai* symbol, modeled after the Hebrew letter "shin," that was owned by my wife's late grandfather and subsequently passed on to me.)

But in terms of geopolitics, the single most important moment of my initial Birthright trip to Israel occurred in the infamously rocket-pummeled border town of Sderot, located less than a mile from Hamas-controlled Gaza.

My Birthright trip was in August 2010, so just a few years after the beginning of the catastrophic Israeli experiment in disengagement from Gaza. In 2003, then-Israeli prime minister Ariel Sharon, who had made his bones for nearly a half-century as a hero of multiple existential wars, a brilliant military tactician and field commander, a national security hawk, and an esteemed leader of the Israeli Right, destroyed his hard-earned reputation in his dotage by proposing the full and unilateral Israeli withdrawal from the Gaza Strip. The fateful plan was completed in September 2005, just four months before Sharon suffered a devastating stroke that left him in a vegetative state until his death in 2014.

At the time of the Israeli disengagement from Gaza, roughly eight thousand Jews lived in the coastal enclave, spread across twenty-one villages. (Media outlets typically use the term "settlement" to describe Jewish residences in far-flung parts of the Land of Israel, which I reject for moral tendentiousness and incorrectness under long-standing principles of international law.) Many of the eight thousand Jews living in Gaza accepted government-provided compensation packages to "voluntarily" vacate their homes and relocate, but many did not. Ultimately, Israeli security forces evicted Jewish holdouts, destroyed their residences and synagogues, and even dismantled Jewish cemeteries. The entire boneheaded plan amounted to a giant exercise in performative self-flagellation, intended to persuade an unpersuadable "international community" that Israel was not the obstacle to peace.

Even before the tragic events that would soon follow, Israel's unilateral withdrawal and forcible expulsion of the Gush

Katif "settlement" bloc in Gaza was highly controversial on the Israeli Right. Former and then-future prime minister Benjamin Netanyahu resigned from Sharon's government over the disengagement plan and Sharon was soon forced out of the Likud, Israel's major right-of-center political party, where he had been a prized member for decades.

Following Israel's withdrawal, Hamas, a Sunni Islamist outfit that self-identifies as the Palestinian-Arab offshoot of the international Muslim Brotherhood and whose 1988 founding organizational charter explicitly calls for the annihilation of the State of Israel and the death of global Jewry,[2] was elected to govern Gaza. Fighting immediately erupted between Hamas and Ramallah-based Fatah, the so-called "moderate" Palestinian-Arab faction led by Holocaust-denier Mahmoud Abbas, whose murderous thugs later participated in the Hamas-orchestrated Simchat Torah Massacre of October 7, 2023.[3] Hamas ultimately prevailed in a bloody 2007 Palestinian-Arab civil war that saw at least 161 slain and more than 700 additional wounded.

By the time of my Birthright trip in 2010, as I stood on the outlook point in Sderot surveying Gaza, Israel had already been forced to fight one war against Hamas: Operation Cast Lead, as the Israel Defense Forces dubbed it, lasted about three weeks from December 2008 to January 2009. Israel has, of course, been forced to fight multiple additional wars against Hamas in Gaza since then, including Operation Protective Edge in the summer of 2014 and Operation Iron Swords in the aftermath of the Simchat Torah Massacre. (I was a law clerk on Capitol Hill in 2014 during Operation Protective Edge, and I referenced the conflict in my first-ever piece of political commentary, which I published the day I concluded my internship.[4])

Overall, tens of thousands of Hamas's rockets have been indiscriminately launched at Israeli civilians since the group gained control of Gaza. Israel's Iron Dome short-range rocket interception system, which debuted in 2011, has been a merciful lifesaver, but it is far from perfect. Iron Dome is extremely expensive to replenish, has been rumored to expose operating soldiers to radiation and thereby cause cancer,[5] and has an interception failure rate of roughly 10 percent. Iron Dome, in short, is just a Band-Aid—and a highly flawed one, at that.

Accordingly, bomb shelters remain a ubiquitous fact of life throughout much of Israel. Most Israeli houses and apartments, especially those close to Gaza or Lebanon—due to Hezbollah, the Iranian-sponsored Shiite jihadist outfit that controls large swaths of Lebanon—have their own "bomb-proof" safe rooms. Hezbollah, which possessed roughly 150,000 missiles and rockets on the eve of the Simchat Torah Massacre, also began indiscriminately firing into Israel within hours of the Hamas assault. The media focused on Hamas and the war in Gaza in those trying post–October 7 months, but tens of thousands of Israeli civilians living in the country's north were also displaced from their homes, having been made refugees in their own country. Israel finally responded in the second half of 2024 with targeted assassinations of Hezbollah leadership, innovative spycraft such as a mass-exploding pager operation, and the IDF's first full-fledged ground invasion of Lebanon since 2006.

I was overwhelmed at the Sderot lookout point on my 2010 Birthright trip. We had a clear view, and I could see multiple Palestinian-Arab towns in the distance, past the demilitarized neutral zone. This was before Israel had Iron Dome, and my heart rate accelerated; our group had already seen the bomb shelters and numerous damaged buildings in Sderot, and I felt exposed. But above all, standing there on that hot summertime day, the reality finally hit me: *Israel's fight is our fight.* America and Israel are two nations, each derived from the same Judeo-Christian heritage and each committed to defending Western civilization from the forces of tyrannical barbarism. The fundamentalist Sunni jihadists of Hamas, who perpetrate their monstrous deeds in the name of "liberation" from "colonialism," are indistinguishable

from the fundamentalist Sunni jihadists of al-Qaeda, who perpetrated the 9/11 attacks in the name of opposing American and
Western "subjugation."

I have been a staunch, unwavering Zionist ever since.

Years later, I had the opportunity to advocate in front of an
Israeli audience for the undoing of Ariel Sharon's tragic 2005
Gaza withdrawal and for reestablishing the Gush Katif "settle-
ment" bloc: I spoke at the Sovereignty Movement's January 11,
2024, conference at the Bible Lands Museum in Jerusalem titled,
"Wake-Up Call from Gaza: Putting an End to the Two-State
Paradigm."[6] While it is unlikely that Israel resettles Jews in Gaza
any time soon, one can always hope.

I am hardly the only one to have had the realization that Israel is
a natural outpost and bulwark of Western civilization, engaged
in the same righteous fight against many of the same baleful enemies as is America and our other close Western allies. In general,
American public polling moved in a strongly pro-Israel direction
in the aftermath of the devastating 9/11 terrorist attacks. As law
professor David E. Bernstein put it in a 2015 blog post, 9/11:

> Made Americans more sensitive to Israel's terrorism-
> related security concerns, and [former Palestine
> Liberation Organization Chairman Yasser] Arafat's
> decision to continue and accelerate the terrorist
> Second Intifada, replete with bus, café, and synagogue
> bombings, was hardly likely to endear the Palestinian
> cause to Americans after 9/11.[7]

This makes a great deal of sense, of course. It is foundational
to human nature that shared traits and shared lived experience
tend to instill warm, positive feelings among otherwise distinctive individuals, tribes, or nations. Yet, when I speak on college

campuses or to other groups of young graduates on topics pertaining to foreign policy, Islamic extremism, or Israel, I am perpetually struck by the reality that most of my Gen Z audience was *not even born yet* when 9/11 happened.

That most of Gen Z was not alive at the time of 9/11 also likely explains why I usually get some pushback at college talks for taking a strong pro-Israel position. At minimum, I get more pushback for being pro-Israel than a campus speaker presenting to a generally conservative student audience probably would have encountered a decade ago. If (God forbid) another mass-casualty terrorist attack were to occur on US soil, as seems increasingly likely due to the reckless immigration policies of recent years, would that wake people up anew?

Our failed neoconservative, regime-change wars in Afghanistan and Iraq are also to blame for younger Americans' apathy and antagonism toward Israel. These Americans grew up in the shadows of those wars, and they associate US support for Israel with the failed foreign policy of swashbuckling, moralistic nation-building crusades. But this exercise in foreign policy reasoning by tenuous association is deeply misguided, as I will explain at length in the next chapter.

One question that I commonly hear from Israel-skeptical college students and young graduates is a variation of this: "Israel is a small country and it clearly gains a great deal from its longstanding close ties with and military aid from America, but what does *America* gain from the US–Israel relationship?" I hear some variation of this question asked frequently enough that it is worth addressing head-on.

America benefits in many ways from its close relationship with Israel, and perhaps the most obvious way is in enhanced national security and deterrence on the world stage.

The vast majority of Israel's most infamous Islamist enemies throughout the Middle East—including Lebanon-based Shiite Iranian proxy Hezbollah, the Palestinian-Arab Muslim

Brotherhood offshoot Hamas, Gaza-based rival Islamist faction and Sunni Iranian proxy Palestinian Islamic Jihad, the Marxist-Leninist Popular Front for the Liberation of Palestine, Iraq-based and Iran-backed Kata'ib Hezbollah, and the Islamic Republic of Iran's infamous Islamic Revolutionary Guard Corps—are US State Department–recognized Foreign Terrorist Organizations.[8] (The Yemen-based Houthis, another Iran-backed Shiite militia, were a State Department–recognized Foreign Terrorist Organization before the Biden administration, in a myopic act of unrequited Iranian appeasement, removed them from the list; in the months following October 7, 2023, the Biden administration re-added the Houthis as a lesser Specially Designated Global Terrorist entity.[9])

That fact alone speaks volumes. Israel's enemies are America's enemies. Nor is this merely an abstract hypothetical or thought experiment. Time and again, we see Israel take military or covert action against enemies of not merely Israel, but of America itself. Often, these mutual enemies have American blood directly on their hands.

Consider, as but one example, the American tragedy at the remote Tower 22 military outpost, located in the far northeastern corner of Jordan near the tripoint with Syria and Iraq. On January 28, 2024, Iran-backed terrorist militias in Iraq launched a drone assault at Tower 22; one attack drone evaded the outpost's aerial defenses, striking the base and killing three US soldiers while injuring forty-seven more. The soldiers' deaths were needless but all-too-predictable, coming as they did after the Biden administration deliberately refused to respond for months to more than 160 separate Iran-backed attacks on US military bases in the Middle East in the aftermath of the Simchat Torah Massacre.

On April 1, 2024, the Israel Defense Forces eliminated a top Islamic Revolutionary Guard Corps commander, Mohammad Reza Zahedi, in a targeted strike on an auxiliary building adjoining the Iranian embassy in Damascus, Syria. It is impossible to know if Zahedi was the man who personally ordered the fateful attack drone launched from Iraq that killed the three American soldiers at Tower 22, but it is entirely plausible that he was. And even if he was not the one who literally ordered that precise fateful drone launch, the deterrent effect against Iran-backed Islamist thugs seeking to maim and kill American military assets overseas was the same.

Truthfully, this same dynamic holds *every* time Israel takes out an Iranian military or intelligence asset. Iran is directly responsible for the deaths of hundreds and hundreds of American soldiers and Marines via its infamous roadside improvised explosive devices (IEDs) deployed during the Iraq War. And even more so than the myriad IED deaths during the Iraq War, Iran and its Lebanese proxy Hezbollah were directly and unequivocally culpable for the April 1983 US embassy bombing in Beirut and the October 1983 Beirut barracks bombings that killed 63 innocent civilians and 241 US Marine Corps personnel, respectively. Other than al-Qaeda and perhaps the Iranian regime itself, no terrorist organization has more American blood on its hands than Hezbollah.

On July 30, 2024, the Israel Defense Forces eliminated top-ranking Hezbollah military commander Fuad Shukr in Beirut. Shukr was not merely responsible for the mass murder of twelve Druze (Israeli-Arab) children playing soccer in the Golan Heights the weekend prior; he was also one of the top-ranking Hezbollah officials directly culpable for the Beirut barracks mass slaughter of US Marines back in 1983. The United States State Department had long labeled Fuad Shukr a "Specially Designated Global Terrorist" and put a $5 million bounty on his head after the Marine barracks bombing.[10] Decades of inaction followed; but the IDF delivered the goods on July 30, 2024, sending an arch-terrorist with American blood on his hands to the ash heap of history. (President Joe Biden was nonetheless enraged by the

Shukr assassination, apparently chiding Prime Minister Benjamin Netanyahu, "Bibi, what the f***?")[11]

History repeated itself less than two months later when the IDF finally decided to escalate meaningfully its military campaign against Hezbollah in Lebanon after nearly a year of rocket fire that had systematically depopulated the Israeli north. On September 20, 2024, another Israeli airstrike in Beirut eliminated senior Hezbollah commander Ibrahim Aqil. Aqil, like Shukr, had long been designated by the US State Department as a "Specially Designated Global Terrorist" due to his instrumental role in the lethal 1983 truck bombing at the US embassy in Beirut; Aqil's bounty, in fact, was two million dollars higher than Shukr's.[12]

One week later, the IDF delivered the Hezbollah grand prize: Hassan Nasrallah, who had led the outfit for more than three decades as its secretary-general, was eliminated in a massive Beirut blast just minutes after Prime Minister Benjamin Netanyahu finished a fiery speech at the United Nations in New York City. The Nasrallah strike, in turn, came on the heels of a daring, sophisticated, and brilliant Mossad operation carried out against Hezbollah commandos in Lebanon and Syria: mass Israeli-orchestrated explosions of Hezbollah-held personal pagers, walkie-talkies, and other handheld devices. As one former CIA analyst told me at the time, the Mossad's exploding pager operation was so innovative and exceptional that spy agencies around the world will still be studying it decades from now. Overall, Israel decimated nearly the entirety of Hezbollah's organizational leadership in a matter of weeks in September 2024.

In righteously eliminating so many high-ranking Hezbollah leaders in such a short span, the IDF performed a remarkable public service for the United States military and the American people—a just retribution for the terrible deeds of murderous arch-jihadists with tremendous American blood on their hands, decades in the making on all counts. Nor was the IDF, during this crucial 2024 stretch, preoccupied with Hezbollah to the exclusion of other jihadist outfits: In a stunning but largely unrelated targeted assassination that followed the Fuad Shukr assassination in Beirut less than twelve hours later, Israel also eliminated Hamas political chief Ismail Haniyeh, one of the masterminds of the October 7, 2023, massacre, in Tehran. Israel did it again on October 16, 2024, eliminating Yahya Sinwar—the chief architect of the Simchat Torah Massacre and the longtime organizational leader of Hamas in the Gaza Strip—during a chance encounter in Rafah, Hamas's southernmost stronghold in the Gaza Strip. Notably, Israel would not have been able to hunt down Sinwar if Prime Minister Netanyahu had listened to those weak-minded Western leaders, such as President Biden, who adamantly opposed an IDF incursion into Rafah.

The overall message sent by Israel from all these high-profile 2024 strikes could not have been clearer: We can, and we will, come after you—no matter where you try to hide. The combined effect was a remarkable demonstration of Israeli—and Western—defiance against the Islamic Republic of Iran and its sprawling regional network of terrorist proxies. Pure, unadulterated power is the lingua franca of Middle East geopolitics—a point often lost on many Americans and other holier-than-thou Westerners, but rarely lost on hardheaded Israelis.

Indeed, considering all the IDF's various tactical strikes against leading jihadists throughout 2024, it might not be possible to come up with clearer—and more remarkable—examples of Israel, as the regional actor on the ground and proverbial canary in the coal mine, doing some of America's (and the broader West's) most pressing counterterrorism dirty work for it. More generally, every single time the Israeli military eliminates a Hezbollah commando or a top Hamas official, destroys a Palestinian Islamic Jihad launch site, degrades a Yemen-based Houthi weapons cache, or blows up an Iran/Islamic Revolutionary Guard Corps–sponsored materiel convoy in Iraq or Syria, it is not merely Israel that stands to benefit. *America's tangible national interest and security interests benefit, as well.* Israel is quite literally doing America's—and the West's—dirty work for it. All it requests in return is not to be excoriated for doing so.

At this time, the State of Israel only has one truly existential enemy state actor in the Middle East: the Iranian regime. (Recep Tayyip Erdoğan's Turkey has rapidly emerged as a formidable strategic threat to Israel, but it is thankfully not yet an existential threat.) It was not always this way. Prior to the Islamic Revolution in 1979, during an era when Arab countries such as Egypt, Syria, Jordan, and Saudi Arabia were violently opposed to the then-nascent Jewish state, Israel and Iran had friendly relations. Everything changed with the Islamic Revolution in 1979. For the past few decades, and especially since Saudi Arabia began cracking down internally on Wahhabism and radical Islamist clerics in the years following 9/11, Iran has been the uncontested "head of the snake" of jihad and destruction throughout the Middle East.

The terrorist mullahcracy in Tehran is the world's single largest exporter of state-sponsored jihad, and Iran funds and foments a dastardly multi-front assault on Israel: Iran-backed Houthis fire on Israel from Yemen, Iran-backed Hamas and Palestinian Islamic Jihadists fire on Israel from Gaza, Iran-backed groups launch attacks against Israeli Jews from Judea and Samaria (what the media typically refers to as the "West Bank"), Iran-backed Hezbollah rains drones and missiles on Israel from Lebanon, and myriad Iran-backed groups scattered across both Syria and Iraq also attack Israel with incoming fire.

As if that were not bad enough, in an astonishing escalation by the Iranian regime—in response to the Zahedi death in Damascus—on April 13, 2024, Iran directly attacked Israel by launching 170 drones, over 30 cruise missiles, and more than 120 ballistic missiles from its own territory. This unprecedented fusillade marked the first time Iran had ever attacked Israel from its own territory, as opposed to doing so via one of its regional proxies. The Iranian regime's attack against the Jewish state was a tactical failure in which 99 percent of Iran's projectiles were—thank God—successfully intercepted by the Israel Defense Forces and a US-led multinational coalition that included both European and (notably) Arab countries. Iran later tried again, launching nearly 200 ballistic missiles at Israel on October 1, 2024, seemingly in response to the Nasrallah and Haniyeh assassinations. A similar multinational coalition once again repelled the enormous Iranian missile barrage; miraculously, the only fatality was a Palestinian–Arab man who was killed by falling debris near the Palestinian Authority–governed city of Jericho.

But the two Iranian attacks were highly revealing, nonetheless. After the April 2024 and October 2024 missile assaults against Israel launched from sovereign Iranian territory itself, no one could plausibly deny the Iranian regime's genocidal intentions and desire to perpetrate a second Holocaust against the Jewish people. It turns out that when they chant "Death to Israel" in the streets of Tehran or inside the Iranian legislature, they actually really mean it.[13] Israel is ultimately going to have to figure out a way to decisively deal with the Iranian threat and, above all, work with its Abraham Accords peace partners to deny the mullahs the nuclear weaponry they have long sought.

But in the Islamic Republic of Iran's twisted worldview, the United States is despised just as much as, and perhaps, even *more* than, the State of Israel. When regime acolytes clamor "Death to Israel," they are almost always quick to add "Death to America." Iranian regime ideology, furthermore, holds out Israel as the "Little Satan" and the United States as the "Great Satan." These terms have been ubiquitous throughout Iranian regime propaganda ever since fanatical Islamists overthrew Shah Mohammad Reza Pahlavi and seized power in 1979.[14]

When I spoke at a Young America's Foundation college student conference in Washington, DC, in 2024, one attendee approached after my speech to tell me that he was born in Tehran and lived there until he was sixteen years old. The student told me that when he was in school in Tehran, teachers would begin each school day by requiring all pupils to solemnly vow to do everything in their power to destroy the "Little Satan" of Israel and the "Great Satan" of America. This is apparently the Iranian regime's version of a Pledge of Allegiance!

Does anyone sincerely doubt whether a nuclear-armed Iran in possession of intercontinental ballistic missiles (ICBMs) on which to attach nuclear warheads would not merely seek the annihilation of the State of Israel and a second Holocaust perpetrated against its Jews, but also the destruction of as much of the United States as possible? At a bare minimum, the risk alone is not worth taking. The doctrine of "mutually assured destruction" prevented nuclear catastrophe during the Cold War between the United States and the Soviet Union, but such a doctrine was premised upon cold, calculating, rational agents—not psychopathic Shiite radicals ready and perhaps eager to embrace their seventy-two purported virgins in heaven.

An emboldened State of Israel remains the West's most straightforward means to deter Iranian hegemony, forestall Iran's menacing quest for a nuclear weapon, and to contain jihadist expansionism more generally throughout the region and around the globe. This means robust, unequivocal American and Western support for Israel's various overt and covert Iran-containment operations—from the Israel Defense Forces' devastation of Hezbollah arsenals in southern Lebanon to the IDF's destruction of key Iranian nuclear assets, to Mossad's orchestrated Hezbollah pager explosions and assassinations of Iran's prized nuclear scientists, and everything in between. No foreign soldier should ever, ever be asked to fight for Israel; indeed, long-standing Israeli policy affirmatively forbids it. But Western leaders and diplomats still must have Israel's back when it does the world a favor by doing what needs to be done.

Of all the Middle East states, it is only the State of Israel that can reliably be trusted to fulfill this crucial role. It is only Israel that can truly be said to be the Western world's man on the spot—its proverbial eyes and ears on the ground in a uniquely troubled region of the world, a nation-state whose national self-interest in such a combustible corner of the globe more or less perfectly mirrors the West's broader civilizational self-interest to secure itself against the forces of Islamist subjugation.

A number of Arab states hold themselves out as steadfast Western partners when it comes to fending off Islamism, crushing jihadist revanchism, and more generally securing that most coveted of Western interests in the Middle East: stability. At best, these states are unreliable and highly fickle. The current regimes in Saudi Arabia and the United Arab Emirates, for example, are both anti-Islamist and anti–Muslim Brotherhood, but in the post–October 7, 2023, months they still frequently put out appalling foreign ministry statements blaming Israel for the conflict in Gaza and failing to lay any blame at the feet of the Hamas militants who launched the Simchat Torah Massacre. Even worse, both countries recently reestablished formal diplomatic ties with Iran. Such a move is perhaps sound realpolitik for Riyadh and Abu Dhabi, but it does not redound to the American national interest.

The most sinister of the Arab countries that holds itself out as a close American ally is Qatar. The tiny, extravagantly wealthy emirate looks the other way when the US launches strategic operations, such as the January 2020 assassination of Iranian arch-terrorist Qasem Soleimani, from Qatar-based Al Udeid Air Base, America's largest military base in the Middle East. The fact that Al Udeid is shockingly close to the Doha penthouses where Hamas leadership physically lives seems not to bother top US military brass. On the contrary, Qatar's cynical loaning of Al Udeid has been so successful in duping Americans that the Biden administration even formally designated Qatar a "major non-NATO ally of the United States" in March 2022.[15]

Considering Qatar's funding and housing of Hamas leadership, its providing of aid and comfort to myriad other Islamist outfits, and its global dissemination of Islamist propaganda via its state-owned Al Jazeera network, America's coziness with Qatar is absolutely absurd. Far from being a "major non-NATO ally" of the United States, Qatar is much worthier of a notorious US State Department label currently only claimed by Cuba, North Korea, Iran, and Syria: State Sponsor of Terrorism.[16]

In the aftermath of the 9/11 terrorist attacks, it became fashionable for American policymakers from both major political parties to offer some version of this refrain: "We must fight the terrorists overseas so that we don't have to fight them here." This sentiment always was, and still remains, baseless drivel. On the American home front, avoiding having to fight the terrorists here means tightening our immigration policies, securing our borders, drastically tightening asylum eligibility, and implementing biometric visa tracking—all things our shambolic federal government has failed to do since the *Final Report of the National Commission on Terrorist Attacks Upon the United States* recommended such prophylactic actions over two decades ago. And on the foreign front, avoiding having to fight the terrorists here at home does not necessarily mean sending our own troops into harm's way, but rather relying upon regional allies—and especially our one uniquely trustworthy and dependable Middle East ally—on the ground to "mow the lawn" and contain the Islamist problem there so that it does not bother us here.

Specifically, all of this necessitates a closer alliance with and a greater dependence on the modern State of Israel, the Western world's singular indispensable bulwark against barbaric Islamism, to secure its own national self-interests against our common civilizational foes.

In 2016, I was one of four student leaders who organized, planned, and led the University of Chicago Law School's inaugural mass spring break trip to Israel. Organized by a secular organization called iTrek, which describes its mission as "intro-duc[ing] tomorrow's leaders in business, law, policy, and STEM to Israel," we had roughly forty-five law students join.[17] The vast majority of our participants were not Jews, but Christians—some of whom remain among my very closest friends in the world. Many of the Christian participants wanted to visit cherished Christian holy sites, to walk the streets that Jesus walked, and so forth. Some secular participants simply wanted to experience Israel for them-selves, and to get a close-up view of one of the world's most intrac-table geopolitical and civilizational conflicts—between Israel and the Palestinian-Arabs.

I have now been to Israel a number of times, and it is not obvi-ous why this particular trip—one that lacked any religious Jewish *kiruv* (outreach), and which was led by a liberal tour guide who proudly supported the disastrous Oslo Accords with the Palestine Liberation Organization as a young left-wing peace activist during the 1990s—might still stand out in my memory. But in hindsight, my 2016 spring break trip ended up being one of my *most* memorable trips to the Jewish state to date.

I have been passionate about Jewish–Christian relations for my entire life. My best friend from childhood was a religious Christian, and his mother would occasionally even invite my (Jewish) mother to her church group's Bible study group. (My mother politely declined the offers.) After I graduated from col-lege and became more deeply involved in conservative political and legal circles, I naturally became closer friends with some of the religious Christians who disproportionately dominate American conservatism. To this day, many of my very favorite people—genuinely warm, decent, kindhearted individuals—are religious Christians. And most of them are not merely neutral toward the Jewish people and the Jewish state—they are positively disposed toward both, and often deeply so.

My many warm personal experiences aside, public polls consis-tently show that the younger generation of evangelical Christians in America is not as readily supportive of the State of Israel as previous generations have been.[18] This ought to be a five-alarm fire for *all* American supporters of Israel, be they Jewish, Christian, secular, or otherwise. Some liberal and secular Jews wince at staunch evangelical Christian support for Israel for patently silly reasons: They mistakenly view such support as motivated by theological dispensationalism, which they perceive to be gauche, despite the fact that evangelical support for the Jewish people and the Jewish state is truthfully based in God's promises made in the Book of Genesis.[19] Indeed, I have had to personally talk a number of liberal and secular Jews out of harboring such ludicrous Christophobic delusions.

The basic empirical reality is this: Jews constitute a very small percentage of the United States' population. While the exact number fluctuates, it is typically around 2 percent. And demographic trends are less than fully comforting: Traditional and Orthodox American Jews have higher birth rates and bigger families, while liberal and secular American Jews have a high intermarriage rate (72 percent for non-Orthodox Jews, per a 2021 study[20]), and it is dubious at best whether most of them will raise proudly Jewish children.

There are, of course, many more millions of religious Christians in America than there are Jews of all religious and cultural stripes combined. Christians United for Israel, a self-explanatory advocacy and lobbying organization with a large membership and an extensive presence on Capitol Hill, is much more authentically Zionist than any similarly situated and nominally Jewish pro-Israel outfit, such as American Israel Public Affairs Committee (AIPAC). A newer and more nimble group called Keep God's Land, which sprung up in the aftermath of the Simchat Torah Massacre, is also promising: The organization is a Jewish–Christian alliance, involving 150 or so of the top Christian leaders in the United States, and explicitly oriented toward opposing an independent new Palestinian-Arab state and defending Israeli sovereignty in the Jewish biblical heartland of Judea and Samaria.[21]

The empirical reality is actually quite simple. As former Israeli ambassador to the United States and current Israeli minister of strategic affairs Ron Dermer correctly remarked in 2021 comments that were considered "controversial" at the time, "People have to understand that the backbone of Israel's support in the United States is the evangelical Christians. It's true because of numbers and also because of their passionate and unequivocal support for Israel."[22] The fact that younger evangelicals do not necessarily share the ubiquitous pro-Israel sentiments of the 1980s-era Moral Majority is not a reason to give up; it is a reason to *double down*.

It was with this broader context in mind that I planned and co-led our 2016 University of Chicago Law School iTrek trip. Every time I have been with fellow Jews to the Kotel (Western Wall) in Jerusalem, the Cave of the Patriarchs in Hebron, or any number of Jewish holy sites and tombs of prominent rabbis scattered throughout Israel, I am delighted to see my coreligionists' faces light up. Indeed, in January 2024, I was at the Kotel with a close Jewish friend on his long-overdue maiden trip to Israel and watched him break down in tears during Kabbalat Shabbat (the welcoming of the Jewish Sabbath). But seeing my Christian friends' and classmates' faces light up from visiting their own holy sites—such as the Church of the Annunciation in Nazareth and the Church of the Holy Sepulchre in Jerusalem—and having their own spiritually intimate experiences during our 2016 law school trip was an extraordinarily rewarding experience as well.

Notably, our 2016 iTrek group was unable to visit one highly prominent Christian holy site: the Church of the Nativity in Bethlehem. There is a simple reason for that: Bethlehem, despite being merely five and a half miles from Jerusalem, is in Palestinian Authority–controlled territory under the terms of the

1990s-era Oslo Accords. That means the Church of the Nativity is verboten for Jews, who risk death or serious bodily injury for so much as visiting. Israeli Jews are explicitly forbidden from visiting. Indeed, it turns out that "apartheid" in the Land of Israel is actually very real; it just cuts in the *opposite* direction than the corporate media and gullible news consumers might think.[23] Arguably even worse, as I mentioned in the last chapter, the ruling Arabs have ethnically cleansed Bethlehem of its Christians; they have fallen from 84 percent of the city's population in 1922 to 22 percent of its population in 2007.[24]

I recall chatting with a Christian lay leader outside the Church of the Annunciation in Nazareth about how the State of Israel secures Christians' religious liberty, freedom of conscience, and access to Christian holy sites. Suffice it to say, this Christian lay leader was less optimistic about safeguarded religious pluralism, conscience protection, and holy site access in the alternative scenario—that of Muslim control over the Land of Israel. All one needs to do is look at the tragedy that is contemporary Bethlehem.

The Arabs of the Palestinian Authority make no effort whatsoever to secure religious pluralism access to the holy sites under their jurisdiction. Indeed, that is a profound understatement. In ancient Jericho, where the Book of Joshua recounts that the Jews fought to enter the Land of Israel they had been promised, the Palestinian Authority has deliberately paved over local synagogues, ritual baths, and ancient Jewish palaces. The Ramallah-based Palestinian Authority kleptocrats have also greenlit the establishment of a new suburban development atop Joshua's Altar in Samaria.[25] These acts of rank historical revisionism are part of a broader Palestinian Authority attempt to whitewash the Jews out of their very own homeland—an effort wholly supported by the United Nations Educational, Scientific, and Cultural Organization (UNESCO), the deeply anti-Semitic United Nations agency tasked with maintenance of international heritage sites.[26]

The fact that Christian access to the Church of the Nativity in Bethlehem and Jewish access to Judaism's single holiest site, the Temple Mount in Jerusalem, are so limited and contentious points toward an inescapable reality: Arabs have no interest in safeguarding the holy sites for all three major monotheistic faiths. For those Jews and Christians who want to preserve free, religiously pluralistic, and equal access to as many historical and holy sites as possible in the Land of Israel, there is only one viable option: Support the State of Israel's control of *all* sites to the widest extent possible.

Only under Israeli control can holy and historical sites be properly protected, guarded, and made available and accessible to all. Only under Israeli control can Western civilization's heritage in the Holy Land be safeguarded and preserved from crusading Islamism and the pernicious forces of Muslim historical revisionism, more generally. For religious Christians— Protestants, Catholics, and Eastern Orthodox alike—this ought to be reason *alone* to support maximal Israeli sovereignty and jurisdiction throughout as much of the Holy Land as feasible.

If the men and women who run the State of Israel's public diplomacy efforts were not so utterly foolish, they would realize that Christians comprise Israel's natural base of support and that arguments along these lines should therefore find broad appeal. Perhaps one day, Israeli public diplomacy will retire the trite and tired braggadocio about Tel Aviv being the world's gayest city and learn the right lesson: Naturally sympathetic Christians, not unappeasable progressives, are the Jewish state's best friends in the world.

At a time of declining religiosity throughout the broader West and a vanishing Christian church in Europe, in particular, the State of Israel's religious backbone stands out and ought to serve as inspiration—indeed, as a possible model of governance.

The State of Israel is not governed by *Halacha* (Jewish law), but Jewish law, custom, tradition, and culture nonetheless permeate Israeli social and public life. The Hebrew Bible is taught in Israeli elementary schools; in fact, Israeli schools devote three times as many hours to teaching religious subjects as do European schools, according to at least one study.[27] Israeli public schools take field trips not only to places of national or historical importance, but also to places of biblical or religious importance. The workweek is structured to prioritize the Jewish Sabbath, running Sunday through Thursday instead of Monday through Friday. The entire country comes to a somber standstill on Yom HaShoah, Israel's Holocaust Remembrance Day. The biblical exhortation to "be fruitful and multiply"[28] is certainly widely heeded: Israel's birth rate, which is roughly three children per woman, is almost double that of the United States.[29]

In my view, the modern State of Israel can, and should, go much further in incorporating Halachic principles as binding civil law. The ease with which one can find treif (non-kosher) food such as pork or shellfish in Tel Aviv restaurants, for example, is abhorrent. But even as things currently stand, Israel is considerably more predicated upon its unique religious heritage than is any other Western country today.

There is of course full religious pluralism in the State of Israel; Israel's Christian community is the only Christian population in the Middle East that is growing, and its Arabs serve in the national parliament (the Knesset), the Supreme Court, and the highest echelons of Israeli society. But there is still no mistaking that the State of Israel is a *Jewish* nationalist project. Though there are laudable exceptions, such as Prime Minister Viktor Orbán's Hungary, most Western states are now failing to do anything meaningful to uphold their unique religious and national traditions. They should follow Israel's lead and, to the extent possible, prudent, and permitted by law, un-"separate" church and state in public life while still robustly protecting private religious minority rights. I will have much more to say on this point in this book's final chapter.

The State of Israel's unapologetic nationalism should also serve as an inspiration and model for other Western countries.

Mandatory service in the Israeli Defense Forces, with long-standing controversial dispensations for Haredim ("Ultra-Orthodox" Jews), is a core component of modern Israeli life. Society-wide conscription into the Israel Defense Forces helps shape and unify Israeli society, ensuring a baseline level of shared experiences for each rising generation that helps to bridge festering differences and foster commonality and the interdependent mutual bonds of loyalty that alone can sustain a coherent nation-state. Israel's national day of remembrance for fallen soldiers, Yom HaZikaron, is a deeply solemn affair that famously includes a minute-long siren heard throughout the entire country. Israelis stop everything they are doing; videos go viral every year—footage of traffic coming to a standstill even on the busiest highways, as motorists stop and step out of their cars in order to honor the state's fallen heroes.

If the modern Western nation-state order is going to survive the onslaught from the three hegemonic forces of wokeism, Islamism, and global neoliberalism that seek to subjugate it, it is the nation-state itself that must serve as a beachhead. The modern State of Israel, like any other nation, is far from perfect. But in crucial ways, it embodies the best that a nation-state can offer, and has historically offered, to both its own citizens and the world at large—going all the way back to the original ancient Israelite nation itself. At a bare minimum, the modern State of Israel is worthy of respect, gratitude, and enthusiastic support from its fellow defenders of the West.

7

REALIST FOREIGN POLICY
AND THE US–ISRAEL ALLIANCE

"And I will bless those who bless you, and the one who curses you I will curse, and all the families of the earth shall be blessed in you."

—GENESIS 12:3[1]

I HAD JUST STARTED SEVENTH GRADE WHEN AL-QAEDA STRUCK THE Pentagon and brought down the Twin Towers. I vividly recall my suburban hometown's impromptu candlelight vigil for local victims, as well as how moved I was watching then-president George W. Bush's "bullhorn speech" atop the World Trade Center rubble on September 14, 2001. At the tender age of twelve and having just been awakened to the contentious world of American politics, I immediately gravitated toward the moralistic nation-building imperatives and neoconservative foreign policy agenda of the Bush administration, which was best encapsulated by the president's (in)famous Second Inaugural Address, in which he introduced the "Freedom Agenda": "The best hope for peace in our world is the expansion of freedom in all the world."[2]

In hindsight, the results of what would come to be known as the "Bush Doctrine" were nothing less than catastrophic: immense American blood and treasure squandered, entire regions of the Islamic world destabilized, enemy regimes and terrorist networks emboldened, and America's reputation tarnished on the world stage. In my own defense, I was young, credulous, naïve, and generally had no idea what I was talking about when I began advocating for "Freedom Agenda" ideals in middle school. But what excuse did the adults in the room in Washington, DC, at the time have?

A half-century ago, when the term "neoconservative" first entered the American political lexicon, it referred to a subset of liberals who, dispirited with an increasingly illiberal and leftist Democratic Party, began to shift rightward in their politics. These new conservatives, or "neo"-conservatives, included Jewish intellectuals such as Irving Kristol and Norman Podhoretz. During the denouement of the Cold War, neoconservatives sought to push American foreign policy in a more aggressive and bellicose direction, and away from the realpolitik and détente advocated by Secretary of State Henry Kissinger and his allies. Neoconservatives proved to be very influential during the Reagan administration, encapsulated by the Gipper's famous "Evil Empire" speech delivered in 1983.

Ironically, when running for president in 2000, then–Texas governor George W. Bush had actually come out swinging against Clinton-era liberal internationalism. Indeed, Bush went so far as to declare during one presidential debate against then–vice president Al Gore: "If we are an arrogant nation, they will resent us; but if we're a humble nation, but strong, they'll welcome us."[3]

Less than a year later, Osama bin Laden successfully orchestrated the all-time deadliest Islamic terrorist attack, and the world changed. As the old Yiddish expression goes, "Man plans and God laughs." Almost immediately after 9/11, then–vice president

Dick Cheney, then–secretary of state Donald Rumsfeld, and other prominent Bush administration officials such as Paul Wolfowitz and Doug Feith began moving American policy in a more aggressively neoconservative direction.

Perhaps the best distillation of Bush-era neoconservatism, other than the "Freedom Agenda" articulated by Bush himself in his Second Inaugural Address,[4] came many years later from congressman and 2012 Republican vice presidential candidate Paul Ryan. In an August 2012 *Wall Street Journal* column published after Republican presidential candidate Mitt Romney tapped Ryan to be his running mate, columnist Bret Stephens quoted Ryan at length:

> America's foundations are not our own—they belong equally to every person everywhere. If you believe these rights are universal human rights . . . it leads you to reject moral relativism. It causes you to recoil at the idea of persistent moral indifference toward any nation that stifles and denies liberty, no matter how friendly and accommodating its rulers are to American interests.[5]

There is so much misguided thinking in this pithy summary—"Paul Ryan's Neocon Manifesto," as Stephens dubbed his *Journal* column that week[6]—that one hardly knows where to begin in unpacking it. But two glaring fallacies stand out above the rest.

The first fallacy is the idea that America was founded as a purely creedal nation with a universalist mission—the notion, per Stephens, that America "was the first nation born of an idea, and from an idea that is true not only for Americans."[7] This is a common misconception among right- and left-liberals alike.

In fairness, it is not *entirely* incorrect. Thomas Jefferson's Declaration of Independence famously asserted that it held certain liberal "truths to be self-evident," a creedal proposition if there ever were one. Abraham Lincoln, decades later, would similarly speak of the Declaration as "the electric cord . . . that links the hearts of patriotic and liberty-loving men together."[8] This is notable, of course. And the Declaration of Independence, more broadly, absolutely *does* have a role to play in how we think of America. But it is not the whole picture.

America, like any other nation, was founded by specific men, at a specific time in history, and within a specific cultural context and milieu. As John Jay described the nascent American republic in *The Federalist No.* 2, America was also, at least at the time it was founded, "a people descended from the same ancestors, speaking the same language, professing the same religion, attached to the same principles of government, [and] very similar in their manners and customs."[9] America has always been partially inspired by a unique overarching creed, but it has generally been guided by the same careful considerations of law, custom, culture, and inherited tradition that apply to all nations.

The second and even more pernicious fallacy in Ryan's "manifesto" is the insistence that America's philosophical "foundations" apply "equally to every person everywhere" throughout the world. This is pure, unadulterated nonsense. There is, quite simply, no such thing as universal values; it is ludicrous to assume that disparate cultures all around the world, including Islamic cultures, aspire to the same European Enlightenment–based conceptions of individual liberty and human dignity to which Paul Ryan—or any other American—subscribes. It is entirely plausible—indeed, it is all but assuredly true—that many other cultures yearn for rigid hierarchy, economic or social central planning, and explicit enforcement of prevailing orthodoxy in a way that offends Western right- and left-liberals' delicate sensibilities. To assume otherwise is to reek of hubris and chauvinism, and to discount one of the most important traits any man can ever possess: epistemological humility.

But even assuming for the sake of argument that some of America's core founding values (whatever they may be) *are* "universal," that still does not require us to "recoil at the idea of . . . any nation that stifles and denies liberty," let alone counsel a pugnacious foreign policy that categorically rebuffs alliance-building with illiberal or authoritarian foreign regimes "no matter how friendly and accommodating [their] rulers are to American interests."[10] A far wiser and soberer approach to American values and American foreign policy was expressed by then–secretary of state John Quincy Adams in his July 4, 1821, speech to the House of Representatives: "[America] goes not abroad, in search of monsters to destroy. She is the well-wisher to the freedom and independence of all. She is the champion and vindicator only of her own."[11]

Adams's famous "monsters to destroy" speech embodies the great virtue of epistemological humility. It captures the essence of a foreign policy that is based in prudence, empiricism, and realism—not abstraction, ideology, and utopian universalism. The former, more measured and realistic, foreign policy, when put into practice by American leaders, has resulted in peace and stability. The latter, more arrogant and quixotic, foreign policy, by contrast, has always resulted in war and chaos. Even if one accepts (which one should not do) the underlying neoconservative philosophical argument, rooted in universal values and forcible exportation of those values unto the world stage, this foreign policy has been a demonstrable failure in practice.

Tragically, American support for the State of Israel, and for strong and durable US–Israel relations, has in recent decades often been subsumed into the latter US foreign policy paradigm (universalist neoconservatism) at the expense of the former paradigm (prudential realism). This is a grievous analytical mistake and conceptual error that has brought about disastrous tangible consequences for US–Israel relations. Those relations have suffered an indirect casualty—certainly on the Left, and even on small but growing swaths of the America Right—due to the empirical failures and abiding deep unpopularity of the liberal internationalist and neoconservative agenda.

But the enduring value of strong US–Israel relations, in truth, is not in any way predicated upon the philosophical validity or political popularity of swashbuckling neoconservatism, which I also view with disdain. It is thus imperative that the record be corrected.

Because the Bush-era neoconservative agenda and the prosecution of the War on Terror against Islamist foes transpired concurrently with Israel's Second Intifada–era counterterrorist operations against militant Palestinian-Arab factions, and also because some of the high-profile internal architects and outside supporters of Bush-era foreign policy were either Christian Zionists or Jewish Zionists (for instance, administration staffers such as the aforementioned Wolfowitz and Feith on the inside, and intellectuals such as Bill Kristol on the outside), a pernicious trope emerged: Jews and Zionists had pushed the US into wars simply to benefit Israel. This is not merely inflammatory and dangerous; it is also wildly mistaken based on the actual historical record.

As liberal Democrat and failed professional "peace process" activist Dennis Ross nonetheless accurately put it in 2017:

> Of course, most Jews are not neoconservatives, and most neoconservatives are not Jewish. In any case, it was two influential non-Jews, Vice President Dick Cheney and Secretary of Defense Donald Rumsfeld, who played the central role with President Bush in deciding to invade Iraq in 2003.[12]

And as for the post-9/11 war in Afghanistan to uproot and eradicate al-Qaeda and its Taliban hosts, the Authorization for Use of Military Force (AUMF) of 2001 that President Bush signed into law on September 18, 2001, had *one* dissenter in both houses of Congress combined: Congresswoman Barbara Lee of California. That the AUMF would be interpreted expansively in subsequent decades, and that the United States overstayed its time in Afghanistan and wholly botched its 2021 withdrawal, does not negate its obvious post-9/11 legitimacy or basic correctness.

Prominent members of the Israeli Right were divided in the early 2000s as to whether the Bush administration should invade Iraq and depose its infamous dictator, Saddam Hussein. It is true that Benjamin Netanyahu, who was a private citizen at the time, testified in Congress in 2002 in favor of a US invasion of Iraq.[13] But it is also true that then–Israeli prime minister Ariel Sharon—who was still a famed member of the hawkish Likud and had not yet devised his ill-fated plan for Israel to unilaterally withdraw from the Gaza Strip—conveyed, along with a "procession of Israeli officials," a deep sense of concern that a reckless invasion would destabilize the Middle East and distract the West from the region's true aspiring hegemon, Iran.[14] As a Jerusalem-based *Los Angeles Times* journalist reported at the time, some in Israel also "question[ed] whether the status quo of a weakened and contained Iraq isn't better than a war that could further inflame anti-Israel sentiments in the Arab world."[15]

This ought to make a great deal of sense. The State of Israel is a tiny nation, forged with a particularist identity, a unique sense of dignity and transcendental purpose, and a historical sense of rootedness going back at least as far as King David's unification of the Kingdom of Israel. As a bastion of Jewish particularism, Israel is also necessarily a "humble nation," along the lines of what Bush said during the 2000 debate against Gore. It has no expansionist extraterritorial ambitions, and it certainly has no deep-set creedal aspiration to spread a misbegotten universalist sense of liberty, along the lines of Bret Stephens's aforementioned *Journal* column on "Paul Ryan's Neocon Manifesto." The State of Israel has a far more prosaic goal: It simply wants to live in peace. Israelis don't have time for delusions of grandeur, such as liberalizing or democratizing the Arab world.

Furthermore, since it is situated in the volatile Middle East, Israel is well-habituated to the geopolitical reality that it is often better to deal with the devil you know, rather than to risk something even worse emerging. Indeed, modern Israeli thinking takes this logic so far that it has sometimes engendered a *false* sense of complacency, which leads to catastrophic results; top Israel military and security brass deluded itself into thinking that Hamas could be contained and even economically appeased—via routine payments from Qatar—in the fateful years leading up to the Simchat Torah Massacre of October 7, 2023, for instance. On the eve of the Hamas pogrom, it was estimated that the Islamism-promoting emirate of Qatar had, with the tacit (and at times not so tacit) approval of the Israeli government, sent over $2.1 billion in total aid to Gaza.[16] Almost all of that funding, naturally, was gobbled up by Hamas.

There are glaring flaws with this grand strategy. By now, it should be obvious that the century-plus-long delusion of engendering peaceful relations through economic appeasement and outright enrichment has blown up in Israelis' faces. Be that as it may, the key point, for present purposes, is how firmly ingrained this hardened "better to deal with the devil you know" line of thinking is in the State of Israel's collective national conscience. Israel's foreign policy, to this day, is not in any way oriented toward neoconservative ends of dictator-toppling or nation-building; it is oriented toward the far less lofty end of crisis management and containment, and it employs humble means such as strategic pinprick strikes in service of those ends. For example, when Israel had struck Iranian convoys in Syria that transported weapons across the mullahcracy's "Shiite

Crescent"[17] of influence to reach Tehran's Hezbollah proxy in Lebanon, it was not that the Jewish state ever harbored any ambition to depose Syrian dictator Bashar al-Assad; when Assad was finally toppled in December 2024, it was Islamist rebels backed by the fiercely anti-Israel Turkish government that did the deed. Instead, Israel takes care of the necessary business to secure its homeland in the most efficient manner possible and then gets the hell out.

Accordingly, the decades-long, post-9/11 conflation of US support for the Israel with the fanciful neoconservative agenda does not pass the laugh test. Indeed, such a conflation is outright dishonest. Just look at recent US history. The neoconservative Bush administration, far from being staunchly supportive of Jewish nationalism throughout the Land of Israel, was obsessed—perhaps more than any US president until Joe Biden—with micromanaging the State of Israel's affairs and pushing it to revive the moribund "peace process" with the recalcitrant Palestinian-Arabs. The Bush White House described "building support for the two-state solution" between Israel and the Palestinian-Arabs as one of the president's "highest priorities."[18] In 2008, President Bush himself said from Jerusalem that "the establishment of the state of Palestine is long overdue."[19] This is the neoconservative nation-building impulse at work.

No true friend to Jewish nationalism in the Land of Israel speaks like this. And it is particularly egregious that George W. Bush, whose presidency was almost singularly defined by the catastrophic Islamist terrorist attacks of September 11, 2001, spoke like this in favor of a Palestinian-Arab cause whose revanchist and genocidal raison d'être was summarized in 1974 by former Palestine Liberation Organization Chairman Yasser Arafat: "We shall never stop until we can go back home and Israel is destroyed. The goal of our struggle is the end of Israel, and there can be no compromise or mediations. We don't want peace, we want victory."[20]

But the fundamental neoconservative instinct is to vanquish, liberalize (by force, if necessary), and build anew. This impulse is profoundly hubristic, and it helps explain why moralistic neoconservative "supporters" of Israel—as opposed to hardheaded realist, or "Jacksonian"[21] supporters—often tend to support the establishment of an independent Palestinian-Arab state. And it is not merely a Bush-era political phenomenon; there are still plenty of prominent neoconservative thinkers and scholars who either believe in the genuine ideological desirability or have otherwise made peace with the alleged inevitability of an independent Palestinian-Arab state between the Jordan River and the Mediterranean Sea.[22]

The conflation of neoconservatism and Zionism, which I fear has already done damage to the State of Israel's standing with younger American conservatives, is simply farcical. Neoconservatives, considered as a whole, are not even particularly reliable friends of the State of Israel! Neoconservatives and liberal internationalists recklessly topple regimes not constructed in their idiosyncratic Western image, thus laying the seeds for instability and the possible metastasis of Islamism—such as what we saw during the Barack Obama–era "Arab Spring," which saw the rise of the Muslim Brotherhood in Egypt and the strategically reckless toppling of Libyan dictator Muammar Gaddafi on misguided humanitarian grounds. The liberal internationalists' and neoconservatives' hubris leads them to support efforts to reach a permanent "two-state" settlement with the bloodthirsty Palestinian-Arabs.[23] Even holding aside the crucial issue of how disastrous Bush-era neoconservatism empirically proved to be for the United States, Israelis themselves might be forgiven for asking: With friends like this, who needs enemies?

On the flip side, it was Donald Trump's presidential administration, with an instinctual conservative realism and the American national interest at the core of its worldview, that brooked no tolerance for the many decades of Palestinian-Arab jihadism and Islamist rejectionism.[24] President Trump, who is nothing if not a nationalist and populist, oversaw a "Jacksonian" foreign policy. Walter Russell Mead explained the essence of "Jacksonian realism"—and how it drastically differs from a moralistic or idealistic "Wilsonianism"—in his seminal 1995 essay for the *National Interest*, "The Jacksonian Tradition":

> Jacksonian realism is based on the very sharp distinction in popular feeling between the inside of the folk community and the dark world without. Jacksonian patriotism is not a doctrine but an emotion, like love of one's family. The nation is an extension of the family. Members of the American folk are bound together by history, culture, and a common morality. At a very basic level, a feeling of kinship exists among Americans: we have one set of rules for dealing with each other and a very different set for the outside world. Unlike Wilsonians, who hope ultimately to convert the Hobbesian world of international relations into a Lockean political community, Jacksonians believe that it is natural and inevitable that national politics and national life will work on different principles from international affairs. For Jacksonians, the world community Wilsonians want to build is not merely a moral impossibility but a monstrosity.[25]

In fact, "Jacksonianism" and conservative realism in the American political tradition goes even further back than the eponymous Andrew Jackson—it goes back at least as far as John Quincy Adams, who admonished that "[America] goes not abroad, in search of monsters to destroy."[26] Is there anything more quintessentially "Wilsonian" than the failed liberal humanitarian and neoconservative project of "go[ing] . . . abroad, in search of monsters to destroy"? "Jacksonianism," or national interest–centric conservative realism, stands against these two ruinous strands of foreign policy dogma.

Donald Trump was, in practice, the single most pro-Jewish US president of all time—or at least since George Washington.[27] His nationalist, pro-Israel instincts cashed out in an extraordinary way, securing the most dynamic and transformative new peace deals in the Middle East—an unambiguous US national interest for *any* volatile and strategically important region of the world, let alone one routinely beset by radical Islam—in an entire generation.[28] Trump's highly successful Middle East foreign policy approach, which was emblematic of conservative realism or "Jacksonianism," reveals a clear path forward when it comes to both US foreign policy in general, and US–Israel relations in particular. Trump's Middle East foreign policy, culminating with the miraculous Abraham Accords peace agreements of 2020, underscores the distinctly *realist*, national interest–centric case for tight-knit US–Israel relations and staunch US support for Israel.

I proposed to my now-wife at the Kotel (Western Wall) in Jerusalem on December 20, 2022. Following the celebration, we spent another week in Israel, in which we covered terrain from a vineyard in the far northern Golan Heights near the Syrian border all the way down to a resort in the heart of the Negev desert. After that, we went to the airport to do something neither of us had ever done before: fly to an Arab country. Specifically, we boarded an EL AL flight at Ben Gurion International Airport to take a flight that had not existed just a few years prior: from Israel to Dubai, in the United Arab Emirates (UAE).

We spent a few days in the UAE, visiting three of the nation's seven emirates: Dubai, Abu Dhabi, and Sharjah. What we saw was remarkable. Jewish life, in recent years, has been thriving in the UAE.[29] By the time we got to our hotel room, we had a Shabbat "care package" already waiting for us, hand-delivered from a local Dubai-based rabbi who had messaged me after he saw me post online that I was coming to town. Dubai now has many fine kosher dining options, including an upscale meat restaurant in the iconic Burj Khalifa, the world's tallest building. There are multiple synagogues in the UAE, and Dubai even has a kosher supermarket.[30] Israelis now flock to the UAE to visit; when we were leaving the stunning Sheikh Zayed Grand Mosque in Abu Dhabi, my wife, who was born in Israel and speaks fluent Hebrew, overheard another couple speaking Hebrew to each other.

This is no small miracle; it was not that long ago that Israeli passport holders could not even travel to the oil-rich Gulf state.

All of this is due to the Abraham Accords, the extraordinary peace agreements between Israel and the UAE, Bahrain, Morocco, and Sudan achieved toward the end of Donald Trump's presidency. The Accords were a world-historic diplomatic triumph; if the US president at the time had been anyone other than the much-scorned Trump, the parties would have undoubtedly won Nobel Peace Prizes for their efforts. The Accords ushered in the first peace deals—*four* of them—between Israel and an Arab state in a generation. And unlike Israel's preexisting peace deals with Egypt and Jordan, which are cold and in constant jeopardy of being annulled due to the restive nature of the two nations' Islamism-sympathetic domestic populaces, the Abraham Accords peace deals have proven themselves to be personally warm and structurally durable—as evidenced by the fact that none of the signing Arab nations withdrew from them in those trying months following the Simchat Torah Massacre.

As counterintuitive as it may seem to America's bipartisan foreign policy establishment, realism and a hardheaded emphasis on pursuing and securing the national interest produced the fruits of regional peace the likes of which the modern State of Israel had never previously had since its founding in 1948.

It is important to understand just how the Abraham Accords, under the guidance of President Trump and Prime Minister

Netanyahu, came to be. The truth is that the Accords evince the folly of decades of trite "peace process," "land for peace," and "two-state solution" blather from the Washington establishment. Instead, the Accords point toward the burgeoning Israeli–Arab peace, prophylactic regional alliance formation, and concomitant containment of the baleful Iranian regime that can transpire when Western leaders ignore the decades-long so-called "Palestinian veto" and simply focus on emboldening Israel instead of forcing it to capitulate to its Islamist oppressors. Peace, it turns out, happens not by seeking to appease or mollycoddle foes. Rather, it comes from a hardened realist approach to foreign affairs that properly rewards America's allies as allies and punishes its enemies as enemies. Peace happens not from elaborate and starry-eyed wishcasting, but from simple and intuitive pragmatism.

Donald Trump was, as evidenced by his administration's track record, by far the most pro-Israel US president since the establishment of the modern State of Israel in 1948.[31] He withdrew the United States from President Obama's harrowing 2015 Iran nuclear deal, moved the US embassy in Israel from Tel Aviv to Jerusalem (as Congress had statutorily mandated since 1995, but which no prior president had fulfilled), recognized Israeli sovereignty over the Golan Heights, declared Israeli presence and Jewish settlement in Judea and Samaria to be *not* per se illegal, defunded the Palestinian Authority over its scandalous "pay for slay" program, brought the Iranian regime to the brink of bankruptcy via crippling sanctions, cut funding or outright withdrew the US from three notable anti-Israel United Nations bodies (UN Human Rights Council, UNWRA, and UNESCO), and more.

Crucially, Trump and his team also understood the Arab world—and, in particular, the intense rivalry throughout the region between Islamism and moderate non-Islamist Muslim rule. And Trump took a side in that battle—the correct side. His very first international trip was a May 2017 summit—which included his holding a mysterious and memorable orb[32]—in Riyadh, which over the past decade or more has dramatically cracked down on domestic Islamism and the problem of radical clerics. Trump's son-in-law, Jared Kushner, was known to have warm relations with the reform-minded Saudi crown prince, Mohammed bin Salman. Trump lavishly praised Egyptian president Abdel Fattah el-Sisi, perhaps a strongman but nonetheless an adamant non-Islamist who had himself supplanted the Obama-supported Islamist/ Muslim Brotherhood government of Mohamed Morsi. Only a realist can do such things in the name of the American national interest; it is the precise opposite of Paul Ryan lamenting how he "recoil[s] . . . toward any nation that stifles and denies liberty, no matter how friendly and accommodating its rulers are to American interests."

It was this specific ingenious combination of strong-willed US support of Israel to the hilt and support of specifically non-Islamist Arab nations that yielded historic peace, and which left the Middle East the most tranquil it had been in a generation or two. Israel and the non-Islamist Arab states saw a mutual threat in the Islamic Republic of Iran—which had been emboldened by President Obama's tragic nuclear accord with the mullahs— and reached a mutually beneficial series of peace deals to better secure their respective national interests and thus help stabilize the region.

Crucially, it is only a diplomatically and militarily emboldened Israel—such as the Israel we saw in the second half of 2024, when the Jewish state assassinated in rapid succession a bevy of top-ranking Hamas and Hezbollah officials, including Simchat Torah Massacre architect Yahya Sinwar and decades-long Hezbollah head honcho Hassan Nasrallah—that can send an unmistakable message to Abu Dhabi, Manama, and Riyadh: We are good and worthy allies because we have the fortitude and tactical precision to protect you from our common enemies, such as the Iranian regime. It is this demonstration of defiance and mutual protection that serves as the most legitimate basis for a stable and enduring peace—especially in the volatile Middle East.

Such a pragmatic rapprochement between the State of Israel and the more moderate Sunni Arab states could only have emerged from a foreign policy rooted in hardheaded realism—not the universalist ideologies of liberal internationalism or neo-conservatism. Indeed, hardheaded realism *produced*, in many ways, the genuinely warmest peace deals Israel has ever secured with any Arab nations.

The Abraham Accords model of diplomacy and statecraft demonstrates the myriad benefits of an American realist foreign policy done well. And in the case of the specific American Accords themselves, tight-knit US–Israel relations were at the very core of the entire endeavor. It should thus be evident that a realist, non-neoconservative American foreign policy and staunch US support for the State of Israel are not at loggerheads with one another—they are mutually reinforcing, two sides of the same "America First" coin.[33]

America is, in many ways, a decadent and declining empire. It is increasingly uninterested in or incapable of investing the blood and treasure that is necessary to deter and ward off malicious actors, and to best secure its own national interest, throughout the globe. America is massively in debt, its citizens lack faith in its ruling institutions, its military is suffering a recruitment crisis, and its failed regime-change wars have depleted the popularity and political capital that is necessary to sustain a robust military posture overseas. And to the extent that a strong American military presence overseas *is* either popular among the citizenry or otherwise indispensable as a matter of basic national security, it is imperative that such a presence be primarily based in the Indo-Pacific due to

America's already-well-underway twenty-first-century great power competition with Communist China.

But America's enemies have not gone anywhere. On the contrary, from Moscow to Beijing to Pyongyang to Tehran to other far-flung corners of the globe, enemies of America and the West have doubled down on revanchism, militant expansionism, and other softer forms of power projection. Hence, a quandary: Given the many domestic headwinds it faces, the oft-repeated desire of the war-weary American people to reduce the nation's military footprint abroad, and the overriding strategic priority of the Far East, what can the United States do to best protect and secure its interests in other regions throughout the world?

The Abraham Accords provide a clear template for resolving this conundrum.

In the Abraham Accords, the United States sought the fundamentally realist goal of uniting disparate nations that may ostensibly share little ideological common ground around a common threat: deterrence of the terrorist Iranian regime. In so doing, the United States hoped to lay the seeds of peace, cooperation, and Iranian containment that might permit it to extricate itself more from the region, as realism might suggest and as the American people indicate they desire. It worked—or, more accurately, it would have worked had the Biden administration not spent an entire term in office undoing virtually everything the Trump administration accomplished in the Middle East (and elsewhere) due to a lethal combination of narcissism and fixation upon ruinous ideology.

The Abraham Accords revealed the realist formula for allowing the United States to reduce its physical footprint in a volatile part of the world while not abdicating its solemn responsibility to secure its national interest in that same region. The recipe is to first embolden America's powerful and strategically important allies in a region, no matter how different those allies are and how unbridgeable their divides may superficially appear to be, and to convince them of each other's permanence due to their own friendships with the American superpower. Once that is accomplished, the second step is to wield diplomatic clout to bring the nations together so that they can better deter a common threat. In the Middle East, for instance, that common threat for Israel and the Sunni Arab Gulf states of the UAE and Bahrain (and Saudi Arabia) is the terrorist regime in Tehran.

Crucially, there is no limiting factor that might prevent the exportation and adaptation of the Abraham Accords model of diplomacy and statesmanship to other troubled regions of the world. Consider, for example, the Indo-Pacific, where Communist China looms as America's preeminent twenty-first-century civilizational threat.[34]

In the Indo-Pacific, applying the Abraham Accords model would first entail the United States supporting (and likely arming) key regional powers whose national self-interests—namely, deterrence and containment of China—are aligned with America's own national interest in the region. These powers would include culturally and ethnically distinct countries with no intrinsic sense of mutual kinship, such as Japan, South Korea, India, and the Philippines. After these nations are all sufficiently emboldened such that they are convinced of the other nations' permanence, the United States would then wield its diplomatic clout to bring them all together in a new formal alliance that perhaps includes intelligence-sharing, supply chain integration, and joint military exercises. This new Indo-Pacific alliance would then be oriented, whether explicitly or implicitly, toward the deterrence and containment of Communist China. As with deterring and containing Iran in the Middle East, the United States directly benefits from such an arrangement—likely with a reduced military footprint, to boot.

Even if an Indo-Pacific version of the Abraham Accords proves not to be realistic or feasible, doubling down on the original Middle East–based Abraham Accords in the years ahead must be a pressing American foreign policy priority. By nurturing the Abraham Accords and further emboldening Israel, the UAE, and Bahrain—and other aligned, non-Islamist Sunni Gulf states, such as Mohammed bin Salman's Saudi Arabia—in the years to come, the United States will be able to wind down its myriad far-flung military bases in the Middle East (such as the now-infamous Tower 22 in Jordan) and strategically retrench more generally. As the incisive foreign policy analyst Elbridge Colby argued in 2024, such a prudent foreign policy realism recognizes "that some threats matter more than others, that power has limits, and that a proper foreign policy should focus our nation's scarce resources on protecting the things that are most important for Americans."[35]

Think of the Abraham Accords foreign policy as something of a baton handoff in a relay race: Here, the US hands the Iran-containment baton to Accords signees and sympathetic onlookers, such as Saudi Arabia, to take the lead role in safeguarding the region. For the US, such a Middle East military retrenchment will be necessary in the decades to come, in order to redeploy scarce assets to the Indo-Pacific to ward off the Communist Chinese hegemony that is America's foremost twenty-first-century civilizational threat. Aryeh Lightstone, who worked closely on the Accords while on the diplomatic staff of former US ambassador to Israel David Friedman, observed in 2024 that "the Abraham Accords between Israel and four Arab countries created the basis for a US-led Middle East defense architecture," and the hopeful "result" is "a regional security architecture that could not only help counter US adversaries and protect US bases in the Middle East, but that would facilitate a shift of US assets to other theaters such as the Asia-Pacific."[36]

The Abraham Accords foreign policy model only works if the American focus is intensely realist and national interest–centric—or, to borrow from the Trump vernacular, "America First." When it comes to the Middle East and the State of Israel,

statesmen and diplomats cannot be distracted by thorny unresolved questions involving the Palestinian-Arabs; it was precisely
the mollycoddling of Palestinian-Arab intransigence and the
long-standing "Palestinian veto" of Israeli normalization with
Arab nations that, for decades, successfully obstructed and prevented greater regional rapprochement. And when it comes to
the non-Islamist Sunni Gulf states—including, hopefully in the
not-so-distant future, the Kingdom of Saudi Arabia, which gave
its implicit imprimatur to the Abraham Accords—it is crucial
that statesmen and diplomats not be distracted by recurring
concerns about the Arab regimes' human rights shortcomings
and their other perceived failures to abide by the various tenets
of Western liberalism. Only a ruthless, emotionally detached,
hardheaded realism that eschews any desire to remake the
Middle East in the image of Western liberalism can get the job
done.

It is also notable that, in the trying year that followed the
Hamas pogrom of October 7, 2023, none of the Arab Abraham
Accords signees severed or even curtailed their diplomatic relations with the State of Israel. Some of these nations, such as the
UAE, occasionally put out public-facing statements that were less
than fully supportive of all the Netanyahu-led Israeli government's articulated war aims in Gaza. They likely did so to try to
mollify certain segments of their domestic populaces that may
be more Islamist / pro–Muslim Brotherhood in their worldview
than are the regimes themselves. Such symbolic actions may be
irksome, but they are also irrelevant.

What is much more relevant is the fact that the first Arab
countries to make peace with Israel in two and a half decades
stayed the course, rejecting demands from domestic extremists
to sever ties with the Jewish state and openly side with Hamas
and other totalitarian Palestinian-Arab forces. These moderate,
non-Islamist Arab nations saw clearly and soberly that maintaining and even strengthening ties with Israel was in their direct,

unambiguous national interest. The Abraham Accords thus survived their first real stress test unscathed, proving the diplomatic resilience that comes with a tangible focus on military, national security, trade, and economic concerns, as well as the overarching need to ward off Iranian regional hegemony. The fact that the Abraham Accords survived the Simchat Torah Massacre and its tumultuous aftermath only accentuates the immense and lasting power of realist, national-interest considerations in foreign policymaking.

The neoconservative Bush administration accepted the premise of the "Palestinian veto" and pursued the white whale of Palestinian-Arab statehood; its Middle East diplomatic efforts were, accordingly, highly unsuccessful. The realist Trump administration, by contrast, rejected the "Palestinian veto" and emboldened Israel and key non-Islamist Arab nations; its Middle East diplomatic efforts were, accordingly, transformative and historic. Unfortunately, the Biden administration quickly reestablished the preeminence of abstract liberal ideology, and diminished the relevance of "national interest"–centric realism when it comes to American foreign policy in the Middle East. But the blueprint for American success in the Middle East is there, available to all who wish to seek it out and learn from its example.

Part of that blueprint entails robust, unapologetic American support for the State of Israel. The remarkable Abraham Accords peace agreements single-handedly exposed the long-standing analytical errors of University of Chicago political scientist John Mearsheimer and other older "realist" skeptics of Israel, to say nothing of long-standing ideological Israel-haters such as paleoconservative firebrand Pat Buchanan. In the aftermath of the Abraham Accords, one can make no mistake: Steadfast US support for the State of Israel helps yield the fruitful dividends of regional peace, permitting a reduced direct American military footprint while simultaneously helping to secure the American national interest throughout the Middle East.

■ ■ ■

As a concrete means of professing US support for the State of Israel, most of the American pro-Israel establishment has long supported large-scale annual US military aid to the State of Israel. This recurring aid package is the single most important Capitol Hill lobbying item of the well-known advocacy group the American Israel Public Affairs Committee (AIPAC)—and, in some ways, its very raison d'être. The consensus of the American pro-Israel establishment seems to be that the best way for the United States to support Israel is for Congress to pass, and for the president to sign into law, a military aid package that amounts to $3.8 billion annually under the terms of the current memorandum of understanding (MOU) between the two nations.[37]

I strongly dissent from this consensus.[38] It should be clear by now that such a large-scale annual appropriation from the United States to Israel—especially structured along the lines of the current MOU, reached toward the tail end of the Obama administration in 2016[39]—does far more harm than good for both countries.

The extant MOU severely curtails Israel's ability to spend the appropriated sums to procure arms and materiel from Israeli defense companies, instead requiring that the overwhelming majority of the funding be reinvested back into the United States. In practice, from an American taxpayer's perspective, this amounts to an indirect subsidization of Boeing, Raytheon, Northrop Grumman, and other titans of the modern military-industrial complex. This backdoor gift card to American defense contractors, who are among the biggest campaign donors to many elected officials in Washington from both major political parties, may help explain the aid deal's popularity. And while $3.8 billion in aid is a mere drop in the bucket of America's ever-mounting annual budget deficits, to say nothing of its debilitating accumulated national debt, foreign aid routinely ranks very high on the list of congressional budget items Americans say they are most willing to cut. At a bare minimum, it is shortsighted to risk making American support for the strategically vital US–Israel relationship subject to blunt fiscal policy considerations.

Even more troubling is the anti-Semitism that large-scale annual American military aid to Israel inadvertently risks exacerbating for some on both the fringe Left and (increasingly) the fringe Right. In the months following October 7, 2023, for instance, it became clear that loud online provocateurs on both the Left and the Right (both wrongly) viewed AIPAC as a nefarious foreign-directed entity that simply does the State of Israel's bidding in Washington, DC. Many even argued that AIPAC should be forced to formally register as a foreign agent under the Foreign Agents Registration Act.

Far be it from me to defend AIPAC, but the notion that AIPAC is foreign-directed is wildly misguided. AIPAC and similar mainstream/establishment pro-Israel groups, such as the American Jewish Committee, are all comprised exclusively of American citizens who lobby for federal policies that they themselves favor in their own capacities as politically attuned American citizens. But the fact that AIPAC and aligned organizations make a large-scale annual military aid appropriation such a pressing annual priority plays right into the hands of anti-Semites who are always eager to find a new conspiracy theory about alleged Jewish or Israeli control over American foreign policy. This isn't necessarily AIPAC's fault, but cultural perception can still be important in guiding policymaking. Perhaps most important, AIPAC is wrong on the substantive policy merits—namely, they are wrong in concluding that the bear-hug, bilateral relationship between the US and Israel fostered by massive annual military aid is somehow beneficial.

Whatever damage large-scale annual US aid to Israel entails for the United States, in terms of misaligned public spending, crony capitalism for defense contractors, and the inadvertent flaming of the fans of malicious conspiracy-mongering, that damage pales in comparison to the tremendous harm the current arrangement does to the State of Israel itself. The aid arrangement hinders Israel's pursuit of military self-sufficiency, disincentivizing its world-renowned technology and defense firms from putting in the work to innovate and produce the necessary arms and materiel at industrial scale. It fosters an excessive and deeply unhealthy reliance upon the United States—a nation in which support for Israel is rapidly dwindling in one of the two major political parties, and which has a dysfunctional political system. The annual aid package forcing the State of Israel to depend upon the whims of the famously capricious US Congress, in particular, is unwise and myopic.

In practical terms, moreover, the aid package permits hostile American administrations to wield an enormous amount of influence over Israeli domestic and foreign policy. Indeed, that seems to be one of the very *purposes* of the current (and "record-breaking") MOU—it was the rabidly anti-Israel Obama administration, after all, which secured it in the first place. The status quo of mass US aid to Israel amounts to a baleful sword of Damocles that empowers hardened anti-Israel US administrators, diplomats, and lawmakers to weaponize aid as a cudgel toward achieving capitulatory, Israeli sovereignty-sapping, Palestinian-Arab-empowering, and Iran-emboldening policy goals in the Middle East.

The all-too-predictable result is that US presidential administrations belittle Israel as little more than an American vassal state that must act according to the dictates of that foreign superpower.[40] Israel's own national interest and sovereignty are thus markedly impaired; its freedom of action to settle more Jews in Judea and Samaria, neutralize menacing Iranian weapons convoys traversing Syria and Lebanon, and even reform its own overweening judiciary are curtailed.[41] After all, who knows what the sugar daddy superpower in Washington might say?

The entire cause of Zionism—Jewish nationalism and Jewish self-dependency in the Land of Israel—is undermined by large-scale annual military aid to Israel. No one who values Jewish self-sufficiency and self-determination in the Land of Israel—indeed, no one who takes seriously the post-Holocaust vow of "Never Again"—should support the present financial arrangement.

That does not mean that the aid spigot can, or should, be recklessly turned off overnight. Nor, crucially, does it mean that one-off *emergency* aid to an ally in the midst of an existential defensive war—such as the multifront conflict Israel was forced into after the Simchat Torah Massacre—is inappropriate. Such *ad hoc* emergency aid *is* appropriate. But even that necessary emergency aid becomes a politically tougher sell in Congress than it ought to be, due to the fact that the United States *already* sends so much money every year to Israel. Perhaps counterintuitively, then, if Israel were to better attain military self-sufficiency and wean itself off annual US aid, the American public would likely more easily rally to Israel's side when jihadists make war and the Jewish state finds itself in dire need of materiel.

Nor, of course, does any of this mean that the United States does not tangibly benefit, in myriad ways, from having exceedingly close trade, economic, military-training, and intelligence-sharing ties with Israel. The United States' interests are absolutely advanced from maintaining such close ties with Israel.

The American and Israeli militaries effectively developed Israel's groundbreaking Iron Dome missile defense system—as well as its far more sophisticated David's Sling and Arrow 3 missile defense systems—in tandem with one another. Here, the United States directly benefits from Israel—as the West's proverbial and literal "man on the spot"—testing out previously untested systems in live-fire situations. Israel has been instrumental in allowing the United States to achieve missile defense parity—no small deal. More generally, the United States military and the American people themselves also directly benefit from Mossad's famed intelligence-gathering capabilities and tactical prowess, as well as the countless Tel Aviv–area tech startups that have given Israel its well-deserved "startup nation" moniker. The key point, however, is that there is no compelling reason why mass annual US aid to Israel is somehow necessary to secure these mutually desired bilateral benefits.

Winding down annual US military aid to Israel cannot happen overnight, of course. It will be a slow and perhaps painful process, and Israel will have to work hard to bolster its own arms and defense production, and to begin producing certain types of munitions that it currently only gets from America. But it is imperative, in the mid- to long-term, that both countries extricate themselves from this well-intentioned, but ultimately pernicious, poison pill arrangement. Authentic Jewish nationalism in the Holy Land demands nothing less.[42]

8

ANTI-ZIONISM, A MOST FASHIONABLE ANTI-SEMITISM

"And it shall come to pass on that day, that I will seek to destroy all the nations that come upon Jerusalem."

—ZECHARIAH 12:9[1]

THROUGHOUT MY ADULT LIFETIME, WESTERN ELECTED OFFICIALS claiming to be "pro-Israel" trot out in front of cameras to recite the same canned line: "I support Israel's right to exist." Usually, the follow-up statement is: "I support Israel's right to defend itself." In the United States, many Republican and Democratic officeholders alike are guilty of indulging in this well-worn ritual.

These banalities are outright insulting. The fact that so many politicians feel an instinctual need to blithely assert a wholly sovereign modern nation-state's "right to exist" and "right to defend itself" is belittling in the extreme and bespeaks an obvious (if unspoken) double standard. To wit: Is there any other nation in the world, other than the State of Israel, for which it is somehow considered an unwavering demonstration of support merely to take the side of the nation's right to exist and defend its territorial sovereignty against infringers and invaders?

Does it somehow make a politician "pro-Canada" to look sternly into a camera and assert that Canada has a right to exist and defend its Arctic air space against possible aerial intrusions from Russian warplanes? Does it somehow make a politician "pro-Zimbabwe" to defiantly declaim that Zimbabwe has a right to exist and defend its side of the Zambezi from menacing Zambian aggression upriver?

To pose such patently silly questions is to demonstrate the futility of this exercise. Normally, in order to demonstrate that one is a committed ally of a foreign nation, an official would advocate for much more salient and substantive measures than to regurgitate platitudes about that nation's "right to exist" or "right to defend itself." Truly, there is not a politician in the entire world who feels a need to speak in this condescending manner about any other modern nation-state. There is not a single other country on the contemporary global map for whom merely espousing their legitimacy in the post-1648 Westphalian nation-state order is somehow equated with a rousing expression of support. For every other contemporary nation-state not named Israel, the state's legitimacy, right to exist, and right to defend itself are simply assumed and are therefore undisputed.

Yet for the State of Israel, it is different. And this time-honored political rite of passage has bothered me to no end. The relevant question is thus: Why is the State of Israel, and the State of Israel alone, singled out for such patently infantilizing treatment?

The answer lies in the reality that the State of Israel is the literal and proverbial "Jew of the nations"—and just as the Jewish people throughout history have repeatedly been forced to prove their tenacity and existential worth in the eyes of their oppressors and tormentors, so, too, is the modern Jewish state repeatedly forced to defend and justify its existence on the world stage. Just as the nation of Israel has had to explain its continued existence to those who seek its eradication ever since God Himself first chose the ancient Israelites as His means for transmitting His truth to the pagan world, so, too, must the State of Israel continually explain its own existence to hostile powers as wide-ranging as Islamic supremacists, global neoliberals, and radical woke academics.

It is this logical analogy between the millennia-old nation of Israel and the post-1948 modern State of Israel that explains the essence—and the root—of the anti-Jewish, anti-Semitic double standard that many now tragically take for granted in the course of otherwise-polite political conversation. There is no other minority people—not the Kurds, not the Yazidis, not the Zoroastrians, nor anyone else in between—whose right to exist as a concrete nation and to defend itself as a concrete people have been as incessantly challenged as they have been for the Jews. And there is no other modern nation-state—not Japan, not Paraguay, not Ghana, or anyone in between—whose right to exist and to defend itself are as continually challenged and doubted as they are for the world's lone Jewish state. Anti-Semitism is a bigotry known around the world in a way that "Kurdophobia" or "anti-Zoroastrianism" simply are not; similarly, "anti-Zionism" is a bigotry known around the world in a way that "Japanophobia" or "anti-Argentinaism" simply are not.

There are many today who claim that anti-Zionism—that is, opposition to the State of Israel's existence as a Jewish state and a concomitant desire to see that Jewish state disbanded, either diplomatically or by force—is somehow not equivalent to anti-Semitism. This is a lie. They are two sides of the exact same coin.

The current leading internationally accepted definition of anti-Semitism was that put forward on May 26, 2016, by the thirty-one member states (including the United States) of the International Holocaust Remembrance Alliance (IHRA)—the so-called "IHRA definition" of anti-Semitism. The IHRA definition was invoked by the Trump administration in December 2019 as part of its Executive Order on Combating Anti-Semitism, and it remains the leading definition of anti-Semitism highlighted and invoked by the US Department of State today.[2]

The IHRA definition of anti-Semitism is, at first blush, somewhat unhelpful. It states: "Anti-Semitism is a certain perception of Jews, which may be expressed as hatred toward Jews. Rhetorical and physical manifestations of anti-Semitism are directed toward Jewish or non-Jewish individuals and/or their property, toward Jewish community institutions and religious facilities."[3] But as it pertains specifically to anti-Zionism, the definition becomes more helpful when one considers some of the enumerated examples: "denying the Jewish people their right to self-determination, e.g., by claiming that the existence of a State of Israel is a racist endeavor"; and "applying double standards by requiring of [the State of Israel] a behavior not expected or demanded of any other democratic nation."[4]

Under the IHRA definition, anti-Zionism as it is routinely peddled today by left-wing pseudo-academics and Islamic extremists is plainly and categorically anti-Semitic. That is not, of course, to stipulate that modern Israeli economic, social, legal, and military policies cannot be criticized; indeed, there are often no more vociferous critics of such policies than Israelis themselves! But to deny the Jewish people, the world's oldest and longest-surviving people, their right to self-determination in their ancestral and divinely promised homeland is necessarily anti-Semitic, under IHRA. Similarly, to imply that the State of Israel does not possess an inalienable right to defend its borders, protect its people, and militarily respond against aggressors when threatened is also necessarily anti-Semitic, under IHRA. So, it is nowhere near "pro-Israel" for a politician to reaffirm his or her support for Israel's right to exist and to defend itself. In fact, it is outright anti-Semitic to indulge the fantasy that its existence and right to defend itself should even be subject to debate!

In addition to the IHRA definition, another popular definition of anti-Semitism is the so-called "three Ds" test formulated in 2003 by prominent Soviet Jewish *refusenik*-turned-Israeli statesman Natan Sharansky.[5] Under this test, legitimate criticism of the policies and conduct of the State of Israel crosses the line into anti-Zionist anti-Semitism if the State of Israel as a whole is "demonized," "delegitimized," or held to "double standards."

Under the "three Ds" test, "demonization" refers to "having its actions blown out of all sensible proportion," such as by comparing the Israel Defense Forces to Nazis and Palestinian-Arabs to Jews held in World War II concentration camps; "delegitimization" refers to denying the Jewish people's right to self-determination in their ancestral homeland or otherwise declaring the modern Jewish state to be somehow racist or illegitimate under international law; and "double standards" can be seen, for instance, in the United Nations' obsession with condemning democratic Israel to the exclusion of actual serial human rights abusers such as Syria and Iran, or in the anti-Israel "Boycott, Divestment, and Sanctions" (BDS) movement's monolithic focus on ostracizing Israel while ignoring other situations around the world that are orders of magnitude worse.[6]

Under Sharansky's test, the majority of anti-Zionist demonstrations on Western university campuses and in city streets following the Simchat Torah Massacre—which have almost always "demonized" or "delegitimized" the Jewish state or held it to impossible "double standards"—crossed the line into outright anti-Semitism. And as it pertains to the United States in particular, universities ought to lose federal funding under Title VI of the 1964 Civil Rights Act—as the December 2019 Trump administration executive order held—when they fail to protect students from anti-Zionist anti-Semitism (or any other type of anti-Semitism), just as they would lose such funding if they fail to protect students from any other form of race- or sex-based discrimination.

From this perspective, efforts to enforce an IHRA-inspired definition of Title VI on campus, just as with the many "anti-BDS" state-level laws that prevent taxpayer money from enriching BDS proponents via government contracts, amount not to limitations on speech but to extensions of America's corpus of civil rights law. Such efforts to protect Jews from the world's oldest bigotry are also necessary, of course, in establishing the minimum baseline of decent moral behavior that ought to be acceptable in polite and well-functioning society.[7]

Judaism is not a universalist faith like Christianity. Rather, Judaism is, at its core, a particularist nationhood and peoplehood with an abiding and eternal attachment to a very specific plot of land—promised to that nation and people long ago by God Himself, and which overwhelming archaeological evidence corroborates has been continuously inhabited by that same nation going back millennia. As such, the people of Israel's attachment to the Land of Israel is not merely nonnegotiable; it is a core tenet of Judaism itself. To seek to sever the connection between the nation and people of Israel and the Land of Israel is, by definition, anti-Jewish and anti-Semitic. Holding aside the various Orthodox Jewish movements' differing theological approaches to the specific post-1948 Jewish state, one might reasonably argue that God Himself was the first proto-"Zionist" insofar as God Himself promised the Land of Israel to the Jewish people.

It is true that religious, Torah-observant Jews sometimes disagree among themselves over whether to embrace the mantle of Zionism and to self-identify as Zionist. Modern Orthodox Judaism, frequently associated in the United States with Rabbi Joseph B. Soloveitchik and Yeshiva University in New York City, is a Zionist movement; so was Rabbi Abraham Isaac Kook and his intellectual offspring in the modern *Dati Leumi* ("National Religious," or Religious Zionism) movement in Israel, including their allies in the *Haredi Leumi* ("Nationalist Haredi," or "Hardal") movement. Theologically, these Torah-observant Jews believe that the modern State of Israel represents the onset of what Jewish thought calls *Atchalta De'Geulah*—the beginning of the redemption prior to the arrival of the Jewish Messiah.

By contrast, with the exception of Hardal and some other subgroups, most self-identifying Haredi Jews—Torah-observant Jews defined by a generally strict interpretation of Jewish law and a more reclusive approach toward interacting with the modern secular world, and often pejoratively labeled "ultra-Orthodox"— reject the modern State of Israel as a theologically significant entity, including any relevance as *Atchalta De'Geulah*. Virtually all well-known Hasidic Jewish sects, such as Satmar, Breslov, and Chabad-Lubavitch, identity as either "non-Zionist" or "anti-Zionist." The Israeli Zionist intellectual Israel Eldad, for instance, once reported that Rabbi Menachem Mendel Schneerson, the last worldwide leader of Chabad-Lubavitch and to this day still referred to simply as "The Rebbe" in Chabad circles, took a dismissive approach toward Rabbi Kook when asked about the possibility of the modern State of Israel as *Atchalta De'Geulah* during a trip to Israel.

In reality, however, this is usually an intellectual and theological distinction—a difference in what Orthodox Jews call *Hashkafa*, or worldview—without much of a concrete or meaningful difference. Rabbi Schneerson, for instance, was in practice a staunch supporter of Jewish sovereignty throughout the entire Land of Israel, supporting the modern Jewish state's maximalist territorial ambitions and vehemently opposing the "peace process" with the recalcitrant Palestinian-Arabs via so-called "land for peace" appeasements.[8] As Rabbi Elisha Pearl, who published an authoritative book on the precise subject in 2024, noted in a contemporaneous interview with Chabad, the Rebbe "was skeptical of appeals to the international community," "dismissed the effectiveness of international peacekeeping forces," and "argued that ['land for peace'] concessions not only fail to bring about lasting peace, but also put Israel in a strategically vulnerable position."[9] Instead, he proffered a "three-pronged military strategy based on Torah principles," consisting of "credible deterrence," "proactive defense," and the need to "fully neutralize [enemy] threats."[10]

The local synagogue nearest my home, and which I most frequently attend, is a Chabad shul. Officially, our shul, like every other Chabad shul, is not theologically "Zionist." But I personally am, of course, an ardent Zionist—as are many, and in all likelihood, the vast majority of our congregants. Our shul is packed with many Israelis and veterans of the Israel Defense Forces, and our weekly Shabbat morning *minyan* (service) in the aftermath of the Simchat Torah Massacre has regularly featured one congregant, whose son is actively serving in Gaza, leading the entire synagogue in a heartfelt *Mi Sheberach* prayer (for healing) specifically for the brave soldiers of the IDF. I have been to many Chabad synagogues over the years, and I do not think I have ever met a Chabad rabbi or lay leader whose personally preferred approach to the Israeli–Palestinian conflict is meaningfully different than the hard-line stance of any prominent *Dati Leumi* / Religious Zionist Israeli politician, such as Itamar Ben-Gvir or Bezalel Smotrich.

Even Satmar, which is considered more "anti-Zionist" than "non-Zionist," clarified in December 2023 in response to a viciously anti-Semitic and anti-Israel social media user trying to misappropriate the Hasidic sect's theological anti-Zionism for his own malign purposes: "WRONG! Our anti-Zionist stance is deeply rooted in religious beliefs and is fundamentally distinct from political anti-Zionism. Our stance is a principled religious position and is clearly not a political tool to cover for anti-Semitic Jew-haters."[11] In general, there is simply no honest way that one can possibly compare the theological positions of various non-Zionist Haredi Jewish sects—which, in practice, still usually amount to unapologetic support for maximal Jewish sovereignty over the Land of Israel—with the genocidal and profoundly anti-Semitic anti-Zionism of woke leftism and Islamic supremacism. Some of these sects reject the *theological significance* of the modern *State* of Israel, but virtually none of them are confused as to the importance of Jews defending the *Land* of Israel—especially now that the modern state has, indeed, been established.

The *only* exception to this rule is Neturei Karta, a truly fringe group of Haredi extremists who were expelled from Satmar in 1967,[12] are miniscule in number, and actively campaign against the Jewish state and in support of the Jewish state's existential enemies in Ramallah, Tehran, and elsewhere. It cannot be emphasized enough how tiny and truly fringe this group is; to suggest that Neturei Karta somehow represents Torah-observant Judaism would be the functional equivalent of suggesting that the Westboro Baptist Church somehow represents biblical Christianity. To suggest as much would be an obviously ignorant argument that can only possibly be made by an ignorant individual, such as the disgraced former *Daily Wire* podcaster Candace Owens.[13]

In short, anti-Zionist anti-Semites are intellectually dishonest in the extreme when they glom onto abstruse Jewish theological debates over the Messianic era and prop up lunatics in groups like Neturei Karta to somehow justify their obvious hatred of the Jewish people. Those who traffic in such ignorance, such as Owens, are bigots in search of a fig leaf to invoke as a weak excuse. The straightforward, uncontested reality is that the nation of Israel has a timeless, irreparable connection to the Land of Israel. Scripture repeatedly speaks of this connection; simple common sense also bears it out. An eternal attachment to the Land of Israel is an unmistakable and indispensable characteristic of Judaism as a religion—and the Jewish nationhood as a distinct people. It has always been thus, and it will always be thus.

Religious Jews can—indeed, frequently do—disagree among themselves over the theological significance of the modern State of Israel, and whether it is the coming of the Jewish Messiah or the redemption of the Land of Israel that ought to first sequentially precede the other phenomenon in the course of human events. Religious Christians, for that matter, have their own, and not entirely dissimilar, theological disagreements. But with the truly fringe exception of Neturei Karta, *none* of these Jewish doctrinal disagreements and *none* of these differing theological stances can in any way support or justify modern Islamic- or leftist-rooted anti-Zionist anti-Semitism.

From at least the time Herzl published *Der Judenstaat* (*The Jewish State*) in 1896 through the modern State of Israel's founding in 1948, the Zionist debate over whether to establish a new Jewish nation-state in the Jewish people's ancestral and biblical homeland was a viable one. But since 1948, when a plurality—and now near-majority—of the world's Jews have come to reside in a Jewish state the approximate size of New Jersey, there simply cannot be any plausible anti-Zionist argument for the state's dissolution and eradication that would not result in catastrophic Jewish suffering, devastation, and death. This, by definition, makes any contemporary anti-Zionist stance anti-Jewish and anti-Semitic to its very core. As *Wall Street Journal* editor Elliot Kaufman wrote in 2024 about anti-Zionism and noxious contemporary attempts to wield anti-Zionism as a cudgel to break what Leo Strauss once referred to as the "moral spine of the Jews":

> Around half the world's Jews live in Israel, which has become the center of Jewish cultural creativity. The Jewish future, in every sphere, increasingly is built there. To seek to destroy or dissolve the state of Israel, as anti-Zionists do, and leave those seven million Jews and that Jewish future in the hands of an Arab majority that cheers the October 7 massacre, is beyond reckless.

For Jews, it betrays a cruel indifference to or contempt for one's fellows. To demand that Jews take such a position, or else be vilified and shut out, is extortionate.[14]

In reality, moreover, the debate over whether modern anti-Zionism constitutes anti-Semitism need not be overly intellectualized. Some very basic questions, and some simple common sense, will often suffice. To wit:

Do so-called "anti-Zionists" who advocate the eradication of the distinct Jewish state also care about eliminating any other modern nation-states, such as the world's many dozens of Arab and Muslim-majority states? Do so-called "anti-Zionists," when they bemoan the civilians—and only the Arab and not the Jewish civilian victims, it all-too-often seems—tragically killed during the Israel–Palestinian conflict, ever pause to think at all about the considerably greater number of civilians intentionally slaughtered in other recent raging Middle Eastern conflicts, such as the Syrian civil war and the Yemeni civil war? Do so-called "ant-Zionists," when they decry the State of Israel's continued military presence in Judea and Samaria (regarding which the Jewish state has the far superior claim under international law) and the State of Israel's (nonexistent) alleged continued presence in the Gaza Strip as a sort of "occupation," actually intend to only stop there—or, as is almost always the case, do they instead view even Israel's major Mediterranean cities such as Tel Aviv and Haifa as somehow "occupied"?

There are countless other possible questions that one could—and should—ask to expose the blatant dishonesty, glaring hypocrisy, and barely veiled Jew-hatred of those who don their keffiyehs, paint watermelons on their faces, and casually clamor for tossing the Jews of Israel into the Mediterranean Sea. Yet at the end of the day, it is actually even simpler than *that*. To borrow from US Supreme Court justice Potter Stewart's well-known First Amendment threshold test for recognizing obscenity from his concurring opinion in the 1964 case of *Jacobellis v. Ohio*: "I know it when I see it."[15]

When I saw the raging eyes of the many University of Michigan Hamas-supporting students who shouted me down—and one who tried to rush toward me before my bodyguard thankfully intervened—in Ann Arbor for thirty-five minutes in November 2023 while I was attempting to give a lecture on the war in Gaza, I saw the face of raw anti-Semitism.[16] When I was physically present to see law professor and international law expert Eugene Kontorovich get shouted down by radical BDS supporters at our mutual alma mater, the University of Chicago Law School, in April 2019, I saw the raw, hideous, unmistakable face of anti-Semitism.[17]

When I see on TV the unfurling of the Hezbollah flag on the Princeton University campus lawn, the trapping of "Zionist" (i.e., visibly Jewish) Cooper Union students in the school library such that they have to be evacuated by the NYPD via underground tunnel, the human blockade at the University of California, Los Angeles, that instantaneously sprouted up to prevent "Zionist" (i.e., visibly Jewish) students from entering the campus lawn, an anarchic pogrom and savage beating of Jews in the heavily Jewish Los Angeles neighborhood of Pico-Robertson in response to a synagogue hosting a speaker who simply presented to congregants about real estate opportunities in Israel, and the cretins who protested an Agudath Israel–hosted event on the sidelines of the 2024 Democratic National Convention that had nothing whatsoever to do with Israel, I do not merely see "anti-Zionism." These episodes are not ambiguous—not at all. The mask has slipped. I see—and everyone else can see—the raw, twisted, millennia-old face of anti-Semitism.

Justice Potter Stewart was right: I know the face of anti-Zionist anti-Semitism when I see it. So do you. And so does everyone else who has any common sense.

■ ■ ■

Jewish nationalism, sovereignty, and self-determination in the Jewish people's ancestral and biblical homeland is a truly beautiful thing. It is tragic beyond words that anti-Semitic moral ignoramuses have been as successful as they have been in besmirching "Zionism"—which simply refers to that self-determination and national liberation movement—and relegating its use in most fashionable Western quarters to that of a smear or pejorative. If Zionism is ever to make a rhetorical and theoretical comeback, and to regain moral legitimacy in the mainstream English lexicon and Western political conscience, then things in Israel must change quickly. The now-decades-long status quo, in which Zionism dies a slow and painful death by a thousand cuts at the hands of radical Islamists, woke leftists, and pseudo-academic theorists, is a surefire loser. It is a death knell for Jewish nationalism and Jewish self-determination in the Jewish people's ancestral and eternal homeland.

It is time for Zionists—all supporters of Jewish nationalism in the Land of Israel—to unequivocally renounce the fool's errand of appeasing the Jewish state's unappeasable Palestinian-Arab foes and finally do that which every successful national movement has done since time immemorial: actually *defeat* any rival national movement that stands in its way and whose enduring existence is incompatible with that movement's own thriving.

The Palestinian-Arabs' zero-sum civilizational jihad against the Jews of the Land of Israel predates the founding of the modern Jewish state. In 1929, Hajj Amin al-Husseini—the grand mufti of Jerusalem, a major Nazi ally during World War II, and an infamous guest of Hitler in Berlin in 1941—fabricated false rumors of alleged Jewish attacks in order to instigate a murderous pogrom in Hebron, Judaism's second-holiest city. Nearly seventy Jews were slaughtered in the 1929 Hebron massacre. Days later, twenty Jews were murdered by rioting Arabs in Judaism's third-holiest city, Safed. Similar anti-Jewish pogroms in the Holy Land raged throughout the 1930s, around the same time that the Third Reich laid the groundwork for what would become the systemic genocide of the Jews of Europe.[18]

The notion that the so-called "Palestinian-Arab" cause—which achieved its final crystallized and mass-propagandized form in the 1960s as a deliberate Soviet disinformation operation to sow discord in the West and destabilize Western geopolitical interests in the Middle East—is fundamentally about anything other than the utter eradication of any Jewish presence in the Holy Land is a bald-faced lie. As I noted earlier in this book, former Palestine Liberation Organization Chairman Yasser Arafat let the cat out of the bag in 1974: "The goal of our struggle is the end of Israel, and there can be no compromise or mediations. We don't want peace, we want victory."[19] Arafat's PLO purported to recognize the State of Israel's right to exist in the lead-up to the 1990s-era Oslo Accords, but that didn't stop him from leading the mass-murderous First and Second Intifadas. Hamas, of course, is even more explicit in its genocidal aims.[20] If there is any single sine qua non of the Palestinian-Arab cause, it is *existential rejectionism*.[21]

Indeed, what might seem straightforward to Western neoliberals has proven, in practice, to be anything but.[22] There are a number of tangible unresolved issues, without which the Oslo Accords framework remains a fanciful reverie of the professoriate and professional political class. There is the particularly thorny issue of Jerusalem. There is the issue of Israel's security requirement to maintain a robust military presence, under any eventual political settlement, in the Jordan Valley; even the dovish former Israeli prime minister Yitzhak Rabin, prior to his 1995 assassination, warned that the Palestinian-Arab entity formed under the Oslo Accords framework would be something "less than a state," though professional "peace process-ers" quickly memory-holed that. There is also the issue of the Palestinian-Arabs' so-called "right of return," under which subsequent generations of the original 1948 "refugees"—using a unique definition of "refugee" applied by the United Nations to *no other population in the world*— can claim a right to "return" to the territory of pre-1948 Israel.[23] The purpose of this "right of return" scheme is quite obviously to set a ticking demographic time bomb aimed at destroying Jewish nationalism and the Zionist project from within.[24]

The upshot is that these two national movements—Zionism and Jewish nationalism on the one hand, and Palestinian-Arab nationalism on the other hand—have their own competing, entirely distinct historical and moral narratives. Zionism / Jewish nationalism and so-called Palestinian-Arab nationalism as it has been conceived since the 1960s-era rise of Arafat and the PLO, in short, are mutually exclusive political and geographical phenomena. One of these two nationalist movements simply cannot endure for long while the other remains intact. The abiding hubris of the decades-long "two-state solution" cartel in Foggy Bottom (DC's US State Department neighborhood), Turtle Bay (the United Nations' New York City neighborhood), and Brussels (NATO headquarters) has blinded the cartel's professional "peace process-ers" from seeing with clear eyes the *sui generis* theological-civilizational nature of this particular epic struggle. As Middle East Forum President Daniel Pipes has explained:

> [W]ould-be peacemakers [thus] attempt to resolve the Palestinian-Israeli conflict through conventional diplomatic means, which predictably fail. The [1990s-era] Oslo Accords, for example, came between such breakthroughs as the ending of South Africa's apartheid regime between 1990 and 1994, the Soviet Union's dissolution in 1991, and Ireland's Good Friday Agreement of 1998; surely compromise would work here, too. In this spirit, US Presidents [Bill] Clinton and [Barack] Obama each separately dispatched George Mitchell to

build on his diplomatic success in Ireland; of course, his Palestinian-Israeli efforts ended in total failure.[25]

Consider something as simple as one of the Palestinian-Arab movement's most well-known and ubiquitous rallying cries: "From the river to the sea, Palestine shall be free." The exterminationists choose their words carefully. The infamous chant does not begin, "from the river to the 1948 armistice line," or "from the river to the 1967 borders." It begins, instead, "*from the river to the sea.*" To this day, the official logo of the PLO includes a map of the entire Land of Israel. That is not a coincidence; conquering the entire Land of Israel and expelling the land's Jewish inhabitants—by means of violent jihad, if necessary— always has been, still is today, and always will be the PLO's ultimate goal. And the PLO, lest we forget, is the supposed "moderate" Palestinian-Arab faction compared with the overtly militant Islamists of Hamas—the perpetrators of the Simchat Torah Massacre of 2023.

All of this, moreover, is based on a demonstrably historical lie. Recall from chapter 5 top PLO official Zuhair Muhsin's candid confession in a 1977 interview:

> There are no differences between Jordanians, Palestinians, Syrians, and Lebanese. We are all part of one nation. It is only for political reasons that we carefully underline our Palestinian identity. . . . Yes, the existence of a separate Palestinian identity serves only tactical purposes. The founding of a Palestinian state is a new tool in the continuing battle against Israel.[26]

The term "Palestine" has its origins in the invidious Roman-era attempt to de-Judaize the Land of Israel following the destruction of the Second Temple and the failed Bar Kokhba revolt about a half-century later. The Land of Israel was thus colloquially known as "Palestine" for roughly two millennia before the modern State of Israel's founding in 1948.

During that lengthy time period, to speak of a "Palestinian" would have simply been to refer to a Jew living in the Land of Israel. For instance, my wife's paternal grandmother—may her memory be a blessing—was a Jew born in the Land of Israel prior to David Ben-Gurion's declaration of Israeli independence in 1948. Accordingly, her birth certificate and passport would have indicated that she was a "Palestinian." By contrast, the actual original "Palestinian-*Arab*" state under the European powers' post–World War I carving up of the Middle East was the Emirate of Transjordan—today, the Hashemite Kingdom of Jordan.

All of this history has been conveniently—and intentionally—forgotten by Western elites today.

President Ronald Reagan, in formulating his Cold War foreign policy doctrine, once quipped that his "idea of American policy toward the Soviet Union is simple, and some would say simplistic. It is this: We win and they lose." Reagan's ruthless binary was not, and must not be misunderstood as, a universally applicable dictum—as some sort of one-size-fits-all bit of wisdom for every foreign policy conflict the world over. Some conflicts *do* have overarching moral gray areas, and some conflicts *do* have specific territorial gray areas wherein there is room for professional "peace process-ers" to jet in from Washington and Brussels and attempt to do their thing. The current conflict in eastern Ukraine and Crimea is a good example.

But some conflicts really do fit the binary Reagan Cold War paradigm. The modern Israeli–Palestinian conflict as it has existed since the 1920s-era rise of Hajj Amin al-Husseini and the 1929 Hebron massacre, and certainly since it has existed since the 1960s-era rise of Arafat and the PLO, *is* one such conflict.

Accordingly, the only way to end the conflict is with Israeli victory and Palestinian-Arab defeat: "Israel wins and the Palestinian-Arabs lose." This is the way that wars have historically been waged and won since time immemorial, and it is the only way that the war for Zionism and the Jewish state's soul can be won.

The only way to end the conflict and to vindicate Jewish nationalism in the Holy Land once and for all, in short, is to so systematically crush the Palestinian-Arabs' morale and hopes of realizing their misbegotten nationalist ambitions that they come to the negotiating table as humiliated losers, pleading for Western and Israeli mercy and begging for any scraps they can find. This is obviously *not* to suggest that the Israel Defense Forces should begin indiscriminately bombing Palestinian-Arab population centers such as Nablus and Jenin—although prudent counterterrorist operations in such terrorist-dense urban strongholds must, of course, continue. But it *is* to suggest that a comprehensive, whole-of-society effort must be launched and executed, from both Jerusalem and any other Western citadels that have not yet so succumbed to global neoliberalism or wokeism so as to be unable to defend basic Western civilizational imperatives, to convince the Palestinian-Arabs that they have *lost* their century-long war to eradicate the Jews of Israel.

Above all, this requires the United States—the most powerful Western nation and one of the last remaining Western nations that has not (yet) entirely capitulated to civilizational self-hatred due to reasons of metastasizing leftism and failed mass migration—to put a decisive thumb on the scale and say: *No. We will not support a new Palestinian-Arab terror state anywhere between the Jordan River and the Mediterranean Sea for the simple reason that such a state is manifestly not in the American national interest. On the contrary, moreover, an empowered Israel has quite obviously led to more peace, not less: more regional normalization agreements, better containment of Iran, more security for American interests, and more geopolitical stability. Only a stronger Israel "from the river to the sea," as it is said, can ever yield the fruits of a durable and lasting peace with the obstreperous Palestinian-Arabs.*[27]

Such a concerted American effort would take the form of more "outside-in"-style diplomatic initiatives to circumvent the "Palestinian veto" of old and seek further Middle East rapprochement, in the mold of the Abraham Accords. Such an effort would take the form of a muscular policy at the United Nations—presumably including no shortage of American vetoes at the UN Security Council—and throughout similar anti-Israel, anti-Western transnational bodies. It would build on then–US secretary of state Mike Pompeo's 2019 declaration that Israeli Jewish "settlements" in Judea and Samaria are *not* per se illegal under international law by going even further and forthrightly declaring that the State of Israel has the best claim to all of Judea and Samaria under well-established and incontrovertible principles of international law, such as *uti possidetis juris*.[28]

Such a concerted American effort would also dangle appropriate diplomatic and foreign aid sticks and carrots to strong-arm moderate Arab states into abandoning the Palestinian-Arab nationalist cause and accepting the newfound American position on the conflict—for instance, by threatening to sever Egypt's massive annual foreign aid package. Ideally, such an effort might even belittle the Palestinian-Arabs—ridiculing their failed century-long exterminationist jihad, for example, in a way that would resonate in the old-fashioned "might makes right" logic of the proverbial Arab street.

The goal is simple: to convince the Palestinian-Arabs that they are, in fact, *losers*—that they have lost the century-long war to eradicate the Jewish presence in the Levant. The State of Israel lives. And the *nation* of Israel lives—*Am Yisrael Chai*.

Other proud and self-respecting Western nations can, and should, join the United States in this effort. But there is no viable alternative to the United States as the singular country capable of earnestly taking the international lead and advancing the underlying diplomatic and geopolitical goals of forwarding Western interests by simultaneously vindicating Zionism and crushing Palestinian-Arab nationalism.

The specific final political resolution to the Israeli–Palestinian conflict itself is, perhaps counterintuitively, somewhat beside the point. One simple, elegant, and largely self-explanatory possibility is the one-state solution advanced by thinkers like Israeli commentator Caroline Glick and former US ambassador to Israel David Friedman.[29] Another intriguing idea is Bar Ilan University professor Mordechai Kedar's proposed "emirates plan," modeled after the eponymous Gulf nation-state.[30] Just as the United Arab Emirates was formed as a loose confederation of disparate Arab tribes, each overseeing its own tribal land, so, too, could the deeply fractious Palestinian-Arab tribes of Judea and Samaria confederate into a series of noncontiguous, Palestinian "emirates" based around the tribes' home cities. That kind of plan is "based on the sociology of the Middle East, which has the tribe [and not the Westphalian nation-state entity] as the major cornerstone of society," as Kedar has explained.[31] In other words, it is a plan based on how the Middle East actually *is*—not how blinkered Western elites and hubristic "peace process-ers" so desperately want to believe it *could* or *should* be.[32]

Far more important, in the near- to mid-term, is that Western diplomacy and foreign policy radically shift toward an emphasis on crushing the Palestinian-Arabs' national ambitions. Such a result would not merely redound to the American national interest insofar as another Iran-backed terror state in the Middle East will have been thwarted; it will also deal a fatal blow to the modern anti-Zionist cause as that cause exists today in the halls of Western left-wing political power and throughout the proverbial Arab street. The reality is that there is no daylight—*zero*—between modern anti-Zionism and modern anti-Semitism. Just as the Jew was historically a scapegoat for all of society's ills, so, too, is the Jewish State of Israel often vilified today as the scapegoat for all of the world's ills. And in order for anti-Zionism to be defeated as a political force throughout both the West and the Islamic world, the underlying Palestinian-Arab nationalist cause itself must be dealt a decisive and irrevocable defeat.

Indeed, such a physical, psychological, and philosophical defeat is ultimately the only way to ensure the survival of Zionism itself. Jewish nationalism in the Holy Land requires the utter and complete crushing of Palestinian-Arabs' own nationalist dream. This is the only way true peace in the Levant will ever be possible. The only way out, in short, is through.[33] Human history tells us this—as does basic common sense. That such a stark conclusion may fly in the face of decades of failed "two-state solution" cartel and professional "peace process-er" dogma is, if anything, a feature and not a bug.

9

THE **TWIN THREATS** OF THE **NIETZSCHEAN RIGHT** AND THE **DEI LEFT**

"The Lord your God you shall fear, and He will deliver you from the hand of all your enemies."

—II KINGS 17:39[1]

ANTI-ZIONISM, WHILE UNDENIABLY POTENT AND DISTURBINGLY trendy among young people and societal elites alike, is hardly the only major threat faced today by the Jewish people and the Jewish State of Israel. In fact, given the general relegation of the anti-Semitic "Boycott, Divestment, and Sanctions" campaign to a university-wide phenomenon and its decisive failure to make any kind of tangible impact in hamstringing the Israeli people or Israeli economy on the world stage, leftist and Islamist anti-Zionism has, in some respects, been fairly limited in its real-world impact. Harvard University or University of Michigan campus radicals might symbolically vote to divest endowment funds from Israel, or New York University's Gender and Sexuality Studies program might categorically refuse an academic exchange program with Israeli universities, but neither Wall Street nor Silicon Valley has any interest in ostracizing or punishing the dynamic, innovative, and productive Jewish state. And therein lies the rub.

But in our new post–October 7, 2023, reality, it has never been clearer that the Jewish people are under greater sustained threat than they have been ever since World War II. And leftist and Islamist anti-Zionism, as wrongheaded and wretched as it is, is not the pathology singularly responsible for the terrible predicament now facing the Jewish people and the Jewish state. There is much more than those "keffiyeh-clad activists who construct their entire politics on opposition to Zionism; who obsessively catalogue the sins of one, and only that one, nation; and who call for boycotts targeting the world's sole Jewish state, even as they ignore or play down rights violations elsewhere."[2] Indeed, there are *numerous* other menacing threats that the Jewish people and the Jewish state face today beyond leftist and Islamist anti-Zionism. Some of these distinctive anti-Semitic threats to the Jewish people and the Jewish state have strong thematic overlap with a specifically anti-Zionist strand of anti-Semitism; some of them do not.

Above all, the two most pressing threats to the global Jewish population and the Jewish State of Israel besides rote anti-Zionist anti-Semitism are the twin threats posed by the Nietzschean Right and the DEI Left.

Historically, Anglo-American conservatism has been linked to the broader tenets of the Judeo-Christian religious, moral, political, and legal tradition.[3] One would certainly be hard-pressed to find an American conservative luminary in the latter decades of the twentieth century or the early decades of the twenty-first century who did not publicly profess that Christianity and the Bible had an enormous influence on political conservatism's self-conception, purpose, and sense of duty. As Russell Kirk, one of the leading architects of the modern postwar American conservative movement, famously put it in his 1953 *magnum opus, The Conservative Mind: From Burke to Eliot,* the very first of the "six canons of conservative thought" is "belief in a transcendent order, or body of natural law, which rules society as well as conscience."[4] Such a foundational role is appropriate because, as Kirk put it, "political problems, at bottom, are religious and moral problems."[5]

Kirk's sentiment would have been readily recognized by those patriotic intellectuals and statesmen who preceded him. President George Washington, in his 1796 Farewell Address, captured this idea perhaps better than anyone:

> Of all the dispositions and habits which lead to political prosperity, religion and morality are indispensable supports. . . . And let us with caution indulge the supposition that morality can be maintained without religion. Whatever may be conceded to the influence of refined education on minds of peculiar structure, reason and experience both forbid us to expect that national morality can prevail in exclusion of religious principle.[6]

In recent decades, religious Americans—and those Americans, more generally, who believe in the indispensable nature of revealed religion and biblical morality to the nation's flourishing—have largely gravitated toward partisan support for the Republican Party, the more self-consciously (if highly imperfectly) conservative of America's two major parties. That trend largely continues unabated today: Religious Christians still remain the electoral heart and soul of the American Right more generally, and the Republican Party specifically.

Yet there have always been dissidents within the American conservative movement—those who do not arrive at their political rightism through a religious or biblical prism. There are now some reactionaries on the Right, for example, who are so ardently opposed to ever-evolving conceptions of "egalitarianism"—as that term has indeed been horribly corrupted and bastardized, for example, in the service of faddish left-wing ideologies such as transgenderism and critical race theory—that they go significantly further and question divinely ordained human *equality* as that equality is established by the *b'Tzelem Elohim principle established* toward the beginning of the Book of Genesis: "And God created man in His image; in the image of God He created him."[7] This seemingly growing strand of right-of-center thought is typically unchurched and irreligious, and finds itself opposed to such rudimentary Judeo-Christian sentiments as that additional paean to equal human dignity found in Proverbs 22:2: "A rich man and a poor man were visited upon; the Lord is the Maker of them all."[8]

For many years now, there has been a roiling current of (mostly online) right-of-center thought, centered chiefly around the pseudonymous right-Nietzschean writer "Bronze Age Pervert" (or "BAP"). This misbegotten sect of the contemporary Right broadly rejects the God of the Bible for pagan infatuations such as aggressive masculine bodybuilding and, as journalist Sohrab Ahmari has phrased it, even "the restoration of 'natural hierarchies' among large human groups, as supposedly revealed by IQ bell curves."[9] Whatever morality and guidance BAP—who has been revealed to be Costin Alamariu, a mid-forties man of Romanian and Jewish descent—preaches and seeks to impart to his sizable cultlike audience, it is surely not coming from the Bible or the broader Judeo-Christian tradition.

The Jewish people, despite Ashkenazi Jews' famously high collective verbal and mathematical intelligence, are hardly left unscathed in the toxic neo-Nietzschean world of BAP and his fellow travelers. As Ahmari has written elsewhere, in the disturbing right-Nietzschean online world of BAP and other influential "anons" such as "Raw Egg Nationalist" (a mid-late-thirties loser who flexes his muscles for an adoring and perhaps homoerotic audience while living at home with his mother in Britain[10]) and (the seemingly self-hating Jewish writer/editor) "Dr. Ben Braddock," "the heroic white subject is assailed by dysgenic black and brown hordes, a project of dispossession engineered by Jews seeking their own racial triumph."[11]

There is nothing good down this fetid rabbit hole, as both history and common sense suggest. Much as with the woke Left, the Nietzschean Right sees revealed religion and biblical morality not as the foundation of the West and our foremost civilizational inheritance, but as a nettlesome hindrance to the realization of social Darwinism or John C. Calhoun–esque racial/ethnic superiority yearnings. That such pining for these atrocious racialist ideologies of yesteryear stands no chance of real-life vindication and success—it is all a big "LARP" (live action role-play), to stick with online nomenclature—does not necessarily limit the perniciousness of such profoundly ugly sentiments seeping into America's national political and intellectual bloodstream.

For instance, BAP is a deeply anti-Semitic pseudonymous figure, despite allegedly being Jewish himself. A self-described "fascist," BAP repeatedly decries, to quote from his book *Bronze Age Mindset*, "the Judaizing tendency that promotes facility with words and numbers, but approaches mental deficiency and even retardation when it comes to anything visual."[12] Suffice it to say that BAP does not hold Judaism and the Jewish people's collective influence on modern Western society in particularly high esteem. And unsurprisingly, BAP hardly thinks better of Christianity itself. Insofar as Anglo-American conservatism is inextricably from the Bible, the new Nietzschean Right is decidedly non-conservative.

It is no coincidence that the rise of the Nietzschean Right has coincided with the contemporaneous rise of a new breed of prominent anti-Semitic and anti-Israel commentators on the Right, such as podcaster Candace Owens. The recent demotion of the Judeo-Christian tradition within American conservatism to something less than a universal touchstone and rallying cry on the Right, as well as the concomitant rise of the petulant rightist nihilism closely affiliated with BAP and other online "anons," has laid the seeds for such noxious views gaining traction in certain nominally right-of-center quarters.

A previous generation of American conservatives with troubling views on the Jewish people and the Jewish state, such as longtime commentator (and former presidential candidate) Patrick J. Buchanan, viewed the State of Israel as a diplomatic and national security liability for the United States. In past decades, paleoconservative proponents of this view typically argued that, even if solely for energy sufficiency purposes, the United States erred in allying so closely with the oil-deprived Jewish state while alienating major petroleum-producing Arab states across the Middle East.[13] This argument, whatever its merits may (or may not) have been, was thoroughly repudiated in real time by the Abraham Accords and the still-emerging Israeli–Sunni regional rapprochement and Iranian containment alliance. The Abraham Accords have demonstrated that, far from being a diplomatic and national security liability, America's close alliance with Israel is actually a tremendous strategic asset. It is only with an Abraham Accords–style Iranian containment alliance in place that America can strategically and militarily refocus on the Indo-Pacific, in order to counter the civilizational threat posed by Communist China.

But in that failed old paleoconservative argument's place, something far darker and more insidious has emerged.

As with so much else that addles contemporary American and Western life, one of the root problems of rising rightist disaffection with the Jewish people and the Jewish state is declining church attendance, increasing godlessness, and a rejection of the very Bible that first gave concrete form to, and which still ought to shape and undergird, our nation and our civilization. For young conservatives who may think they exist in a more secular "Barstool conservative"[14] or "post-Religious Right"[15] milieu, wherein conservative Christianity takes a back seat to other analytical prisms and substantive emphases, there is a temptation to downplay or ignore the centrality of the Jewish people and the Jewish state to Western conservatism at large. I see this play out on social media on an almost daily basis—often in ugly ways, and usually egged on by pseudonymous "anons," anti-Semitic mega-platform commentators such as the cartoonish Candace Owens and the more insidious Tucker Carlson, and occasional outright neo-Nazis such as the Holocaust denier and "Groyper" leader, Nick Fuentes.

But as tempting as it may be to mingle with an "edgy" online crowd and prove one's iconoclastic bona fides, the fundamental reality is that younger American conservatives are the heirs to a much richer tradition than "Bronze Age Pervert" and "Pepe the Frog": the Judeo-Christian tradition, hearkening back to Sinai and Jerusalem and pulsating throughout American history. If being a "conservative" means anything whatsoever, then surely it means "conserving" the very Bible and the two great religions— Judaism and Christianity—which birthed, developed, and nourished that which we today call "the West." As Yoram Hazony has written, it ought to be axiomatic that "conservatives hold that the only stable basis for national independence, justice, and public morals is a strong biblical tradition in government and public life."[16] This was once common sense on the American Right, if nowhere else. Younger conservatives risk downplaying and discarding this truth not just at their own peril—but at our entire civilization's peril. They are playing with a very serious fire.

Nor can the Right abide any tolerance for Jew-hatred within its ranks—period. Even holding the right-Nietzscheans aside, the past few years, both before and after the Simchat Torah Massacre of 2023, have seen an unambiguous increase in anti-Semitism coming from certain pockets of the broader American Right. This is truly despicable. The scourge of anti-Semitism—the shape-shifting chameleon of all historic bigotries, which molds to fit any given society's scapegoats and pathologies—must be unequivocally rejected, combated, and repelled wherever and whenever it raises its ugly head. It makes no difference at all whence the anti-Jewish bigotry comes.

Podcasters such as Candace Owens and Tucker Carlson, as well as lesser-known decrepit public-facing social media "influencers" who are vaguely affiliated with portions of the BAP-centric "Frog Twitter" social media universe or with other portions of the so-called "dissident Right," such as the repulsive human trafficker Andrew Tate and the oleaginous womanizer Dan Bilzerian, have in recent years been increasingly comfortable trafficking in and promoting some of the most loathsome, unvarnished, barely disguised raw hatred of the Jewish people that can be seen anywhere in the Western world. Sometimes this newly reascendant form of rightist anti-Semitism is pushed by those disingenuously embracing a false mantle of Christianity—although those who traffic in Jew-hatred for these ostensible reasons, such as Owens, are often wholly unpersuasive in cosplaying as purported zealous converts for their brain-dead audiences. The American Right has a complicated history with gatekeeping both real and perceived cranks, but if there is to be any exclusionary line drawn whatsoever, *this must surely be it.*

This distinctly right-wing anti-Semitism has often reached outright farcical depths of insanity over the past couple of years, such as Owens's peddling of the infamous medieval blood libel—the monstrous pogrom-inducing lie that Jews utilized the blood of Christian children for ritual purposes—and Carlson letting a crackpot pseudo-historian podcast guest (Darryl Cooper) speak uninterrupted about how Adolf Hitler was a man of peace and the *real* villain of World War II was actually Winston Churchill. Whether it is Owens's unhinged diatribes, Carlson's occasional deeply disturbing guests, or any number of more obscure online content creators and social media "influencers," Jew-skeptical or anti-Jewish provocateurs on the nominal "Right" often claim they just want an "honest debate" on Zionism or on the United States' long-standing support for the State of Israel. Sometimes, the mask slips a bit more and a commentator may assert a desire to debate "Jewish power" or "Jewish influence." ("Power" or "influence" over what, exactly, is typically left unspecified.)

Unfortunately, having an "honest debate" on the anti-Semites' own terms is a bit difficult when Jews are asked to somehow "prove," just as so many medieval Europeans egregiously did all those centuries ago, that they are not poisoning wells and baking Passover matzos from the blood of slain Gentile children. This is patently insane. It is abhorrent in the extreme. Any decent human being with an iota of integrity must unequivocally reject and denounce such Nazi-like propaganda, no matter its source. At this point, these rightist Jew-haters, such as Candace Owens, Andrew Tate, Dan Bilzerian, and Darryl Cooper, would make Joseph Goebbels proud.

From a specifically conservative, rightist, or Western civilizational preservationist perspective, moreover, it ought to be clear that targeting the Jews is simply a convenient stepping-stone for those who wish to target and ultimately destroy Western civilization itself. There is no shortage of malign actors in right-Nietzschean and white nationalist circles who act as if the Jewish people are somehow interlopers in the broader arc of Western civilization—that the Jews are somehow *extrinsic*, and not *intrinsic*, to the entire Western corpus and edifice. This is utter mendacity—nothing could possibly be further from the truth. If one accepts the unrivaled centrality of Christianity and Christendom to the millennia-long development and contemporary self-conception of the West, then one cannot possibly view Judaism—the progenitor and older Abrahamic sibling of Christianity—as anything other than foundational to the West, as well. The West, as we have seen, really did begin at Mount Sinai.

Attacks on the Jewish people—and the Jewish State of Israel—are thus not merely about the Jews themselves. The ultimate target is so much bigger than a small national and religious minority such as the Jews. Every so often, these contemptible low-lifes let the mask slip and say the quiet part out loud. In August 2024, for instance, the Columbia University student chapter of the (egregiously misnamed) pro-jihadist outfit "Students for Justice in Palestine" posted to social media: "We are Westerners fighting for the total eradication of Western civilization."[17] Such candor is terrifying in its explicitly countenanced ramifications, but it is nonetheless welcome insofar as it helps clarify the stakes for anyone who may still struggle to see them clearly.

Christians and Western civilization–sympathetic secularists alike who might have a fleeting inclination to ditch the broader nation of Israel—and the specific State of Israel—in the rear-view mirror would be wise to remember that the stakes of our civilizational clash are considerably higher than the mere future of the Jews. There are real people out there who really do seek nothing less than the destruction of Western civilization itself. And it is incumbent upon good men and good women to rise up, stand their ground, and tell the would-be conquerors of the West: "*No.*" More often than not, those courageous individuals must, by definition, be *conservatives*—those who seek to "conserve" the Judeo-Christian heritage of the West from the preying talons of those who seek to eradicate and build anew in the West's vanquished stead. No self-respecting member of the *Right* can possibly make common cause with such petty totalitarians, including Jew-haters—and Christian-haters—of all nominal political stripes.

Self-identified conservatives and those on the contemporary Western Right, by very definition of being *conservatives*, must also be students of history. And, accordingly, they should be aware of all the various nations and empires throughout human history—from the Babylonians to the Romans to the Nazis to the modern Islamists, with so many others in between—who died off and met history's ash heap after attacking, assaulting, pillaging, and exterminating the original People of the Book. There has *never been a single nation in the entire history of the human race* that has thrived and prospered *after* persecuting its Jewish population.

Truly, there is not a single example. The rise of virulent anti-Semitism is here, there, and everywhere a symptom that something has gone deeply wrong in a given society. American conservatives and Western right-wingers, perhaps above all, would be misguided in the extreme to ignore history's most glaring warning signs. To desire to "conserve" one's own tradition, heritage, and customs necessarily also means to know what one does *not* seek to "conserve": the traditions, heritages, and customs of history's greatest monsters and most profound losers.

At a family wedding in 2024, a relative asked me whether I was optimistic or pessimistic about the future of Jewish life in America. I replied that I was optimistic, and I quoted the Book of Genesis: "And I will bless those who bless you, and the one who curses you I will curse, and all the families of the earth shall be blessed in you."[18] President George Washington, a man of faith himself, certainly understood and channeled this, as when he famously wrote to the Hebrew Congregation of Newport, Rhode Island, in 1790: "The Children of the Stock of Abraham who dwell in this land . . . shall sit in safety under his own vine and fig tree, and there shall be none to make him afraid."[19] So must those now on the Right intuit and comprehend this, as well. *So goes the Jews, so goes America. And, so goes the Jews, so goes the West.* It has always been thus, and it will always be thus.

Accordingly, conservatives and all those on the Right must ditch seducing nihilist, neo-Nietzschean nonsense such as BAP and "Raw Egg Nationalist," ditch the neo-Nazi so-called "Groypers" and their "Pepe the Frog" anonymous online army, toss unhinged and patently moronic anti-Semitic propagandists such as Candace Owens to the curb, and rediscover the necessity and the unrivaled preeminence of God and Scripture in Western civilization and the Western conception of what constitutes the good life. Our present moment requires nothing less than that.

But as dangerous as right-Nietzschean and other newly reascendant strands of right-wing anti-Semitism are—and I do not in any way whatsoever diminish their corrosive influence or potency—they still pale in comparison (for now, at least) to the threat posed by the cancerous left-wing woke ideology to both the Jewish people and the Jewish State of Israel. Indeed, the single most pernicious threat facing the viability and flourishing of the Jewish people—and, by logical extension, the flourishing also of Christians, Christendom, the United States, and all of Western civilization as a whole—is the spread of the woke ideology.

Most troubling for the Jews has been the incubation, promulgation, and dissemination of so-called "Diversity, Equity, and Inclusion" (DEI) initiatives—the most visible public-facing tip of the spear of wokeism—throughout American higher education, corporate America, and American life more generally. Through DEI, an entire generation of impressionable minds has been indoctrinated into believing that the Jews, the most frequently oppressed group of people in all of human history, actually constitute an "oppressor" class. And Christians, it ought to go without saying, are if anything even "lower" than Jews on the intersectional hierarchy of perceived victimhood—meaning that they are viewed as "oppressors" par excellence.

As an "oppressor" class under this harrowing paradigm, Jews and Zionists deserve the unmitigated scorn and vitriol of various subgroups deemed "oppressed" according to the subjective dictates of prevailing intersectional taxonomy. So, too, for that matter, do Christians—and above all white Christian men, the paradigmatic "privileged" group in the vengeful eyes of wokeism. American universities have been cesspools of anti-Western thought for decades, and the metastasis of the noxious—if perhaps superficially anodyne-sounding—DEI catechism is blameworthy for much of the unhinged anti-Western sentiment and loathsome Jew-hatred we have seen on higher education campuses since the Simchat Torah Massacre of October 7, 2023.

What exactly *is* wokeism? "There is nothing new under the sun,"[20] we know from the Book of Ecclesiastes, and so it is true here as well. The modern woke ideology, a vogue form of leftist illiberalism that in many ways reduces to an oversimplified clashing dichotomy of "oppressors" and "oppressed," is, argues Yoram Hazony, simply "an updated version of Marxism."[21] And under this new Marxism, instead of the prescribed proletariat overthrow of the patrician and capitalist class as in the economic-based Marxism of old, wokeism's rough hierarchical pecking order is, as journalist Jamie Kirchick once put it, "Muslim > gay, black > female, and everybody > the Jews."[22] Hazony elaborated on this new Marxism in a 2020 essay for *Quillette*:

> The new Marxists do not use the technical jargon that was devised by nineteenth-century Communists. They don't talk about the *bourgeoisie, proletariat, class struggle, alienation of labor, commodity fetishism,* and the rest, and in fact they have developed their own jargon tailored to present circumstances in America, Britain, and elsewhere. Nevertheless, their politics are based on [Karl] Marx's framework for critiquing liberalism . . . and overthrowing it.[23]

The dire threat posed by this neo-Marxism—the woke ideology—is not in any way limited to the Jewish people or the Jewish state. It is the single most dire comprehensive threat facing all of us in the Judeo-Christian West. Wokeism is appallingly totalitarian, insofar as the woke wield the levers of power to suppress all dissident speech, root out all wrong-think, and attempt to secure by brute force a stifling intellectual homogeneity—often by means of deliberately blurring the lines between the state and the purportedly "corporate,"[24] which once upon a time would have been readily recognized as a hallmark of the very fascism the woke unpersuasively claim to abhor. Wokeism is outright racist, insofar as intersectionality and "identity politics," to say nothing of vogue concepts such as "critical race theory" and "racial equity," overtly discriminate on the basis of race and thus directly undermine the preeminent biblical and American ethos of Divine Image–rooted equal moral worth and equal protection under the law.[25]

Wokeism purports to supplant and fill the void of traditional religion—and, in particular, seeks to fill the vacuum of a Western civilization increasingly unmoored from its Judeo-Christian roots and sensibilities. Like traditional monotheistic religions, wokeism is replete with sacraments, rituals, rites of passage, sins, excommunications, and enticing promises of group solidarity and personal salvation. It is a form of neo-Marxism, but it is also a form of neo-paganism—a return to the worship of the false gods of past millennia.

Making matters considerably worse, wokeism also has the power of the state behind it. As journalist Matthew Schmitz put it in a 2020 *Tablet* essay, "Governmental authorities and corporations now coordinate in enforcing the dictates of th[is] new secular progressive faith."[26] Wokeism is the singular unifying creed of America's decadent ruling class, extending its impressive tentacles from public-sector bureaucracies to Fortune 500 boardrooms to the heights of corporate media to leading Hollywood studios to countless other institutions in between. As journalist Bari Weiss noted in a post-Simchat Torah Massacre essay, "[t]he [woke] takeover is so comprehensive that it's now almost hard to notice it—because it is everywhere."[27]

But as dangerous as DEI and wokeism are to America—and the West—as a whole, these faddish ideologies pose a *uniquely* dangerous threat to the already highly vulnerable Jewish people.

(Christians are of course threatened, too, as they constitute the preeminent "privileged" and "oppressed" class according to wokeism's neo-Marxist taxonomy.)

One of the leading tenets of wokeism is that equality of opportunity is an unattainable illusion that must be discarded in favor of equality of outcome—no matter the totalitarian means that might be necessary to "immanentize the eschaton" and realize such a quixotic result. Thus, during the ur-woke days of the Barack Obama presidency in particular, we saw the forty-fourth president's administration fixate upon so-called "disparate impact"—social and economic practices in which some groups of people are disproportionately affected more than others, even though the relevant promulgated rules are officially neutral—as a key legal concept in civil rights litigation and enforcement.

In practice, "disparate impact" is a convenient shorthand for wokesters who wish to impute nefarious racial and otherwise discriminatory intent whenever an economic or societal result manifests that is somehow disproportionate to the underlying groups' percentage-based apportionment across a broader sample size or populace. For example, if blacks in America constitute 12–13 percent of the US population but over 50 percent of all arrests for homicide, woke-addled statistical or economic analysis would deem this to be a "disparate impact"—and therefore evidence of "systemic" racism afflicting the entirety of the US justice system.

Once one accepts that "disparate impact" is necessarily evidence of racism, the next logical conclusion is that infamously reached by the "critical race theory" pseudo-intellectual Ibram X. Kendi in his book *How to Be an Antiracist*: "The only remedy to racist discrimination is antiracist discrimination. The only remedy to past discrimination is present discrimination. The only remedy to present discrimination is future discrimination."[28] Wokesters thus arrive at a harrowing, and quite self-serving, conclusion: Not only is discrimination against "oppressors" by those in "oppressed" groups justified—it is *compelled*. Indeed, such discrimination is actually the quintessence of virtue and justice!

In the not-so-distant past—for example, in the 1960s-era America of Martin Luther King Jr., who famously exhorted others to judge their fellow Americans not by the "color of their skin," but by the "content of their character"—such an overtly hateful sentiment as Kendi's would have been instantly recognized not as so-called "anti-racism," but as racism *tout court*. Sadly, such basic intuition and common sense seem today to be increasingly rare. Once we reapply Kendi's shocking "insight" to the woke neo-Marxist dichotomy of "oppressor" and "oppressed" classes, we immediately see the problem for the Jews. To again quote Weiss:

> If underrepresentation is the inevitable outcome of systemic bias, then overrepresentation—and Jews are 2 percent of the American population—suggests not talent or hard work, but unearned privilege. This conspiratorial conclusion is not that far removed from the hateful portrait of a small group of Jews divvying up the ill-gotten spoils of an exploited world.[29]

This is *Protocols of the Elders of Zion*–style anti-Semitism—dressed up and refashioned for new, uneducated, and impressionable twenty-first-century progressive audiences. (Wokeism's more "conspiratorial" elements also share a great deal in common with BAP-esque right-Nietzschean anti-Semitism.)

Neo-Marxist wokeism is explicitly racist. Classes of human beings subjectively deemed "oppressed" are typically more "brown," while classes of human beings subjectively deemed "oppressors" are typically more "white." For many contemporary proponents of "critical theory" or "intersectionality," in the Levant this translates to standing in solidarity with the purportedly "brown" Palestinian-Arabs—and perhaps Arabs as a

whole—over the purportedly "white" Israelis, who are errone-
ously viewed as European colonizers and interlopers. Taken to
its logical conclusion, woke neo-Marxism also view the Jews as
benefiting from "white privilege"—and perhaps as even being
"white supremacist"–adjacent themselves.

All of this is ludicrous on its face. The assertion that the Jews—
the most systematically oppressed and discriminated against
group of people in human history, and the vastly disproportionate victims of history's most notorious race/ethnicity-based genocide less than a century ago—are somehow beneficiaries of "white
privilege" would have been quite a shock to the Aryan racial
supremacists of Nazi Germany. Furthermore, as I have already
addressed, the notion that the Jews today are somehow "colonizers" in their ancestral, millennia-old homeland is an ahistorical,
archaeologically disproven, and empirically debunked myth.
There has been a continuous, uninterrupted Jewish presence
in the Land of Israel ever since Joshua led the ancient Israelites
across the Jordan River to conquer it following the death of Moses
at Mount Nebo.

When it comes to race and ethnicity, the Israeli government
does not officially keep tabs of such demographic data for its
Jewish population—but according to a 2019 study, Mizrahi and
Sephardic Jews (those generally swarthier Jews who descend from
the Iberian Peninsula, North Africa, and across the Middle East)
in Israel far outnumbered all Jews of combined Ashkenazi (those
generally lighter-skinned Jews of Central European, Eastern
European, and Russian) descent.[30] The notion that Israeli Jews
all look like prototypical "white" American Ashkenazi Jews, such
as Jerry Seinfeld or Larry David, is an absurd—and typically
disingenuous—misconception.

For anyone who has actually visited the State of Israel and witnessed the rich tapestry of Jewish life that now thrives there, furthermore, such a sentiment would be immediately recognized as a
bald-faced lie. For example, in Israel today there are an estimated

169,000 black Ethiopian Jews. Personally, I also live this lie every day of my life. I am a fairer-skinned Ashkenazi Jew of mixed Eastern European descent, but my wife—who is a considerably darker-skinned Israeli-born Jew of mixed Sephardic/Mizrahi lineage—is not. When we were traveling together in Mexico a couple of years ago, a hotel attendant tried speaking to my wife in Spanish since he thought she was a local Mexican. Similarly, when we visited Egypt together, some Arabs tried speaking to my wife in Arabic. As the case may be, the Egyptians were not terribly far off the mark: My mother-in-law, whose parents were born in Morocco and Tunisia, is herself perfectly fluent in Moroccan Arabic.

More to the point, of course, even deigning to play this racial identitarian game—this "sordid business, this divvying us up by race," to quote the current chief justice of the United States Supreme Court—is a fool's errand.[31] It represents the antithesis of everything Western civilization, and the United States of America, was founded upon—going as far back as the Divine Image imperative in the Book of Genesis. It represents a return, whether consciously or not, to the toxic race-centric pathologies of yesteryear. Ironically, it would have made such avowed antebellum racists as former vice president and US senator John C. Calhoun—he of the slavery is a "positive good" school of thought—blush.

Indeed, the centrality of race to the worldviews of hard-line modern wokesters and antebellum southern slaveholders is nearly identical; it is merely the relative position and perceived favorability of the underlying races themselves that have changed. This is extraordinarily wrong—racism must be rejected *everywhere* and in *every context*. But wokeism also amounts to a perpetual "scarlet letter" for those individuals deemed to belong to an "oppressed" social group. In practice, therefore, the woke ideology is belittling and dehumanizing in the extreme. As Justice Clarence Thomas explained in his blistering concurring opinion in the landmark 2023 US Supreme Court case of *Students for Fair Admissions, Inc. v. Presidents and Fellows of Harvard College*, which overturned race-conscious "affirmative action" admissions programs in higher education:

> Individuals are the sum of their unique experiences, challenges, and accomplishments. What matters is not the barriers they face, but how they choose to confront them. And their race is not to blame for everything— good or bad—that happens in their lives. A contrary, myopic world view based on individuals' skin color to the total exclusion of their personal choices is nothing short of racial determinism.[32]

The Judeo-Christian West's justice system is premised upon individualized guilt and innocence—on sons being held harmless for the misdeeds of their forefathers. (At maximum, under the Mosaic Law, God does not visit the sins of the fathers past the third or fourth generation of sons.[33]) To speak of collectivized, hierarchical class- or group-based rewards and punishments may tickle the fancy of Marxist academics and impressionable young leftist students. But such talk is utterly anathema to our tradition, our creed, and our most basic and cherished values.[34]

Wokeism represents the singular totalizing rejection of the West's Judeo-Christian inheritance, which has always emphasized inherent individual human dignity insofar as Scripture tells us that "God created man in His image."[35] Wokeism is an affront to the biblical values system—cherished by Jews and Christians alike—that has defined the West ever since Divine Revelation at Mount Sinai. And as is so often the case, where revealed monotheistic religion and biblical values in general are targeted, it is the original People of the Book who are singled out for a uniquely harsh condemnation.

Crucially, that Jews are singled out for such opprobrium and outright hatred by wokeism must be understood not merely on an intrinsic level, but also on an instrumental level. It is of course true that, as the original recipients and transmitters of God's will, the Jewish people are uniquely scorned by those wokesters who ultimately seek nothing less than the full-on supplanting of the biblical, Judeo-Christian worldview with an obsessive, one-size-fits-all, enforced neo-Marxist dichotomy of dueling "oppressor" and "oppressed" classes. But it is also true that wokesters, just like countless anti-Semites throughout history, view the Jews as a convenient stepping stone to be utilized as a beachhead in a far broader and more systemic civilizational assault.

Just as Karl Marx singled out the Jews in his noxious 1840s writings even though his real goal was to undermine and overthrow all of Western capitalism and Christendom, so, too, do contemporary wokesters often single out the Jews even though they share Marx's goal of eradicating the entirety of the Judeo-Christian West. In the eyes of the wokesters—and, incidentally, also the Islamists—Judaism and Christianity are forever intertwined. They are the two biblical religions. So, if the issue is the Bible itself, as it is for the wokesters who seek to supplant it with their own neo-paganism, then both Jews and Christians must be targeted. It is imperative that Christians understand what the stakes of our civilizational struggle really are.

It is only in this broader context that one can begin to fully make sense of the paroxysms of pro-Hamas, pro-Islamist, anti-Semitic, anti-American, and anti-Western rage that have so engulfed higher education and left-wing street thug activism alike since the October 7, 2023, pogrom. Yes, the civilizational arsonists soiling our campuses and rioting in our streets harbor a special disdain for, and abhorrence of, the original People of the Book—those who have passed down God's will in an uninterrupted, millennia-long intergenerational chain, going all the way back to Moses ascending Mount Sinai to receive the stone tablets. But the wokesters also detest Christians—and, above all, according to the often race-obsessed intersectional taxonomy, white male Christians. Without Christianity, after all, there would certainly be no entity that we can identify today as Western civilization. It often begins with the Jews but, we know from history, it rarely ends with the Jews. And in this case, as in so many others, the explosive anti-Semitism we have seen since the Simchat Torah Massacre is only partially *about* the Jews in the first instance.

The terrifying woke mask has been lifted for all to see. There is no more hiding. Jews, Christians, and their Western civilization–sympathetic secular allies must now all join forces to repel this terrifying social conflagration before it devours all of us.

Where societies have been generally—and authentically— meritocratic in nature, Jews have historically thrived. My great-grandfather Bernard Berkley, of blessed memory, grew up extremely poor in a Lower East Side tenement in New York City. As he would later recount to my grandmother, he was a lifelong dreamer who lived according to this maxim: "If you can conceive it, and you can believe it, then you can achieve it." He ultimately had an extraordinarily successful and prosperous business career in real estate, although he sadly gambled away most of his life savings before succumbing to cancer. To the extent the American Dream exists—and tragically, that is an increasingly debatable proposition today—my great-grandfather lived it with every fiber of his being.

But perhaps the most interesting part of my great-grandfather's story is actually how *unextraordinary* it is. There were countless Ashkenazi Jewish immigrants to the United States from around the same late-nineteenth to early-twentieth century time period who grew up mired in poverty but built for themselves impressive careers. America was a fundamentally different place, in those days—worse in many material ways, of course, but also better in some crucial ways. Immigrants were expected to learn English and seamlessly assimilate into the dominant culture. And with some obvious and terrible exceptions, such as the infamous early-twentieth-century Ivy League Jewish matriculation quotas, Jews were given ample opportunities to succeed and rise up the economic ladder based on their own skills, talents, and merits.

Throughout history, Jews have thrived when they have been given the opportunity to thrive. By contrast, it is when they are discriminated against and otherized that Jews have historically suffered. As such older ideals as divinely ordained equal moral worth and constitutionally required equal protection under the law are rejected as "quaint" or "antiquated," only to be replaced by a neo-Marxist worldview that proposes overt, naked discrimination against economic or social "oppressors," it is naturally the Jews—history's perennial scapegoats—who disproportionately suffer. So, too, on the international stage and in the diplomatic arena does the State of Israel, the proverbial and literal "Jew of the nations," suffer.

Wokeism represents nothing less than an existential threat to all that the United States and Western civilization stand for. And while it is also fiercely anti-Christian, the woke mind virus is acutely dangerous—perhaps more than anyone else—for the Jewish people and the Jewish State of Israel. All defenders of our Judeo-Christian heritage must work together to reject, discredit, and defeat wokeism by any means necessary. The future of Jewish thriving in the Diaspora depends on it. But so, too, does the fate of these United States—and the West.

10

THE **MACCABEAN** **IMPERATIVE**

"I am the Lord; I called you with righteousness and I will strengthen your hand; and I formed you, and I made you for a people's covenant, for a light unto the nations."

—ISAIAH 42:6[1]

I THINK I WAS BORN WITH A FEAR OF GOD INSTILLED IN ME; NOT necessarily in the proper Jewish sense of a righteous fear of God—*yir'at shamayim*, or "fear of heaven," stemming from the belief that God is one, God is eternal, God is our King, and God's will must at all times be obeyed. Rather, I think I was born with a fear of relationship, of acknowledging God's all-encompassing sovereignty and trying to understand Him and what He wants of us, His creation. I think I was scared, in short, to seek Him out and develop a bond with Him.

One of my lifelong projects—one I used to struggle mightily with—has been to jettison that inexplicable, primordial "fear" of God in favor of a righteous and robust embrace of the foundational Jewish concept of *yir'at shamayim*, properly understood. I have made a great deal of progress on this front in recent years, although the personal work to improve one's sanctification of God and best live out His Will will always continue.

I was raised in a home full of love. In so, so many ways I had a peaceful, supportive, and generally happy and wonderful upbringing. For that, and for my loving parents, I am eternally grateful. President Abraham Lincoln, on whose birthday I am most fortunate to have been born and whose insights I have often echoed in my lay commentary and legal scholarship,[2] famously said: "All that I am, or hope to be, I owe to my angel mother." I find that sentiment entirely relatable.

But my childhood home, as I only came to truly appreciate as I matured, was also lacking in structured religion. Like most secularized American Jews, we acknowledged some of the holidays and kind of, sort of celebrated them. We lit the Chanukah menorah, spun the dreidel, exchanged presents, and listened to Adam Sandler's "Chanukah Song." My father would drive me and my brother to a local Reform synagogue on Yom Kippur, the holy Day of Atonement on which Jews famously fast and "afflict ourselves"[3]—and then we would discuss what we were having for lunch afterward. On Passover, the Festival of Matzot where *chametz* (foods made from wheat, rye, barley, oats, and so forth) is strictly verboten, we would drive to my uncle's house for an abridged and unserious Seder—and then probably eat pizza the very next day.

This experience is all too common among non-Orthodox American Jews. In the suburban town where I grew up and in which Jewish infrastructure—kosher restaurants, a ritual *eruv* that surrounds a Jewish community and is important for Shabbat purposes, and so on—was generally lacking, I doubt many of my Jewish childhood friends observed the religion of our forefathers much more stringently. Our family's secularized, assimilated American Jewish lifestyle was similar for all the other Jews I knew. I simply did not know any better. With the exception of the rare trip into Brooklyn or another town or city with an observant Jewish community, I never saw an Orthodox Jew and I was never in any way exposed to authentic, Torah-observant Judaism. I don't think I even knew what a Shabbat dinner was until I was well into my teenage years. There was no *chinuch*—instruction on Torah observance—in our home.

Our household growing up was, as it is often said, "spiritual but not religious." My father's mother laudably kept kosher and tried to instill some *Yiddishkeit* (Jewish customs and folkways) in us whenever we saw her, but my mother's mother—a Halachic Jew who nonetheless dabbled decades ago in other religions as far-flung as Buddhism—talked about "spirituality" in the abstract and often referenced a vague belief in a "higher power." Because my mother's mother's mother (herself also a Halachic Jew whose parents, in turn, immigrated to America to escape repression in Eastern Europe and find a reliable *minyan*) had dabbled in "messianic" thought, my maternal grandmother adopted the custom of setting up a well-decorated Christmas tree and stockings every year. My grandmother (like my mother) is a beautiful human being and I of course loved the presents at the time. But I nonetheless cringe when I think back to how, well into my late teenage years, I had greater exposure to Christmas trees and Easter eggs than Shabbat candles and *tefillin* (phylacteries).

Besides the obvious risk of fomenting an identity crisis in children exposed to conflicting cultures and differing household practices, there is also a much more glaring problem with the entire notion of "spiritual but not religious": It is a total fraud on both an intellectual and a practical level. To be "spiritual but not religious" is to declare oneself free of all religious constraints while, simultaneously, somehow believing in . . . well, *something.* To be "spiritual but not religious" is to declare war, no matter how implicitly, against the customs, folkways, rituals, values, and principles of one's forefathers. It is to pronounce oneself as somehow better than one's own inherited tradition.

"How benighted the ways and rituals of my forebears are," such an individual might intone. "I am too rational—or perhaps just too lazy—to transmit my atavistic tradition for the next generation, which will surely be more enlightened!" Such thinking evinces the soft tyranny of a heightened conceit. Appeals to "reason" may be seductive, but they are also very dangerous, as discussed in chapter 2.

Appealing to "reason" might make an individual feel better or somehow more justified in abandoning the faith and way of life of his forefathers. It might make an individual Jew sleep better at night in spite of his fundamental failure to uphold his duty to help transmit the Jewish tradition to the next generation, as the Jews have done since the Divine Revelation at Mount Sinai. Indeed, *Pirkei Avot* ("Ethics of the Fathers"), one of the most famous tractates of the Talmud, opens by emphasizing the intergenerational transmission of the Jewish tradition: "Moses received the Torah from Sinai and gave it over to Joshua. Joshua gave it over to the Elders, the Elders to the Prophets, and the Prophets gave it over to the Men of the Great Assembly."[4]

To do one's own part in transmitting the tradition of our forefathers, and therefore pass on the tradition to one's own children, is to lead a life enriched by meaning and purpose—a life that recognizes its significance in the broader story of God, His creation man, and the teleology and destiny of mankind. To subscribe to the vacuous ideology of "spiritual but not religious," by contrast, is to fall prey to narcissism and solipsism. True human flourishing is not available for a "reason"-addled, "spiritual but not religious"–abiding narcissist or solipsist, no matter how "liberated" he might feel in breaking free from the "restrictive" shackles of his own inherited tradition. To be "liberated" from unchosen obligations is a fundamentally false conception of human freedom, as discussed in chapter 3. And such a "reason"-centric worldview does not offer true contentment, as recent decades of declining membership and attendance numbers for "reason"-based Reform synagogues—and concomitant gains in membership and attendance for tradition-centric Orthodox congregations—demonstrate.

Only by living within a specific framework of law, order, family, and community—most obviously, the framework of the forefathers—can one truly be free. In Judaism, that framework is, of course, the Torah and *Halacha* (Jewish law).

I never would have reached such a conclusion about the importance of living a meaningfully Jewish life when I was younger, of course. When I was in elementary school, my parents, to their great credit, enrolled me on two separate occasions in after-school classes and Sunday school at the local Reform synagogue. I had no previous meaningful introduction to the religion, and my childhood friends—most of whom had been taking such classes for far longer—seemed more knowledgeable and advanced. I felt out of place; the whole experience seemed foreign to me, and I grew frustrated. What's more, I was still hamstrung by that fear of God that had nagged me ever since childhood—a fear drastically exacerbated by my total lack of familiarity with the subject matter. It was a vicious cycle. So, I dropped out of Reform Jewish after-school and Sunday school classes not once, but twice.

My parents and my grandfather, again to their great credit, encouraged me to work with a private rabbinical tutor to become a bar mitzvah. We found a rabbi who I connected with: Reuben Modek, a native Israeli who was living in New York at the time, but who has since moved back to Israel.[5] Even then, after months of tutoring, I almost dropped out before the big day. Rabbi Modek and I took a stroll around the neighborhood, and we sat on a lawn a few houses down. We were both entirely silent. I didn't realize it at the time, but in retrospect it seems clear that the *yetzer hara* ("evil inclination") tied my tongue, and the *yetzer tov* ("good inclination") led Rabbi Modek to pray on my behalf. The *yetzer tov* conquered the *yetzer hara*, because I emerged with full conviction that I needed to become a bar mitzvah. My bar mitzvah ceremony, held in the backyard of my childhood home, was highly untraditional, to say the least. It bore no resemblance to the Orthodox services I now attend. But it was beautiful, meaningful, and special in its own way.

I joined the Jewish fraternity Alpha Epsilon Pi, at Duke University, and I had a thoroughly memorable first-ever visit to Israel on my Taglit-Birthright trip between my junior and senior years. As I mentioned a few chapters ago, I became a political conservative on September 11, 2001, when, as a seventh-grader in suburban New York, I saw the billowing smoke emanating from the destroyed World Trade Center in downtown Manhattan. When one intuits that there is real good and real evil in this world, and that utopian idealism is entirely impractical, he is already a conservative—whether he realizes it or not. As I discussed in chapter 6, I vividly recall having the exact same emotional experience that I had on 9/11 when, as a twenty-one-year-old college student visiting Israel for the first time on my Birthright trip, I stood at an outlook point in Sderot and looked out into Hamas-controlled Gaza.

Many Americans derive their political beliefs from their inherited religious tradition, but for me it was actually the exact opposite: I became more meaningfully attuned to my religious tradition, and embarked upon the journey toward greater embrace of Jewish tradition that I am very much still on, due to my already-strong political convictions.

I have never been on the political Left in my entire life. I developed my first real political thoughts and opinions as a middle school student when the 9/11 jihadists struck, and I became a young but reliable defender of the Bush administration's policies. (My foreign policy views have since changed quite a bit, as I have also discussed.) I distinctly remember arguing on my own against two dozen liberal classmates in my AP US Government and Politics class senior year, when I defended President George W. Bush's controversial use of the Guantanamo Bay Naval Base during the War on Terror. During my sophomore year at Duke, I was one of the only people in my fraternity not celebrating when Barack Obama won the historic 2008 presidential election; I had voted for John McCain.

But I studied economics, not politics, in college. And it wasn't until around the time I was graduating college and getting ready to move to Washington, DC, for my first post-college job that I really started to dig deep on what it means to be a *conservative*: meaning, someone who does not merely identify with a specific American political party, but a genuine philosophical conservative. As I became more acquainted with Anglo-American conservatism, personified by men such as the great eighteenth-century British statesman Edmund Burke, one theme emerged above all: tradition. Burke famously conceived that "the nature of a people" is "a partnership of generations dead, living, and yet unborn."[6] Conservative societies, in other words, are distinguished by their safeguarding and transmitting of the culture's dominant customs, rituals, principles, and folklores from one generation unto the next.

At some point, it finally hit me: If I find these ideals so intellectually appealing, then shouldn't I actually try it out for myself—by looking into *my own inherited tradition*, Judaism? The Burkean idea of intergenerational transmission, after all, bears a striking resemblance to the aforementioned opening Mishnah of *Pirkei Avot*: "Moses received the Torah from Sinai and gave it over to Joshua. Joshua gave it over to the Elders, the Elders to the Prophets, and the Prophets gave it over to the Men of the Great Assembly."[7] That resemblance makes a great deal of sense, naturally. Western civilization, which Anglo-American conservatism self-consciously seeks to preserve and protect, began long ago at Mount Sinai.

■ ■ ■

It is incumbent upon every Jew—just as it is incumbent upon every other person—to realize that he is not merely an individual who exists in the philosophical abstract. Nor, furthermore, is that Jew merely a member of a family or a community—or a certain town, city, or state. Rather, each and every Jew is a member of the Jewish nationhood, *Am Yisrael*—the oldest continually existing and distinct people on the face of the earth. Any Jew bogged down (heaven forbid) in a crisis of meaning or who is otherwise tempted to succumb to solipsism or hyper-individualism could do worse than to ask the question Mark Twain famously asked in an 1899 essay: "All things are mortal but the Jew; all other forces pass, but he remains. What is the secret of his immortality?"[8]

The answer is that no matter how far His chosen people stray from His word, and no matter what humiliations and harms they suffer while in exile, God never forgets His covenant with the nation of Israel. As it says in Scripture: "For the Lord your God is a merciful God; He will not let you loose or destroy you; neither will He forget the covenant of your fathers, which He swore to them."[9] God may punish the nation of Israel and even banish them from the Land of Israel when they stray from His word—as is prophesied in the Book of Deuteronomy—but He still never completely abandons His chosen people.

As Jews recite every year during the reading of the Haggadah at Passover: "This is what has stood by our fathers and us! For not just one alone has risen against us to destroy us, but in every generation they rise against us to destroy us; and the Holy One, blessed be He, saves us from their hand!"[10] It was the *nation* of Israel that entered into the covenant with God, and it is the *nation* of Israel that keeps the covenant. The Jewish experience and the teleology of the Jews as it relates to their Creator, in other words, is fundamentally *communitarian* and *nationalist* in nature. The entire biblical concept of a chosen people is inextricably inter-twined with the idea of *collective* holiness.[11]

Jews who were raised in a strong Jewish household—whose parents did their best to observe *Halacha* and to fulfill their obligation of *chinuch* (instruction of Torah observance to one's children)—likely already understand this. But as someone who grew up in a very secular, Reform Judaism–adjacent home, I know that not all Diaspora Jews are able to intuitively grasp this. (For Jews living in the modern State of Israel, the cultural milieu and knowledge gleaned by sheer osmosis is perhaps a bit different.) It is thus imperative that more Jews who did not grow up in authen-tically Jewish households, such as me, come to think of themselves as indispensable cogs in the broader intergenerational transmis-sion and preservation of the Jewish nationhood and way of life, stretching all the way back to Mount Sinai.

The prevalence of nontraditional and non-Orthodox Judaism in America—and especially Reform Judaism—makes this task difficult. Reform Judaism and its now-barely distinct offshoot, Conservative Judaism, are theologically problematic for the very simple reason that they reject the strict binding authority of *Halacha* and the centrality of Jewish tradition more generally in favor of a solipsistic obsession with "reason." (The minuscule progressive denominational offshoot known as Reconstructionist Judaism is, if anything, even more radical.)

That a plurality of American Jews now identify as Reform is nothing short of tragic.[12] The first-ever graduating class of Hebrew Union College, which has served as the major Reform Jewish seminary in the United States since its late-nineteenth-century founding, quite literally celebrated its launch with a lavish ban-quet that featured clams, crabs, shrimp, frogs' legs, and both (non-kosher) meat and dairy dishes—all in overt violation of the laws of kashrut, and thus *Halacha*. Attendees proudly dubbed it the "Trefa Banquet" due to the fact that it primarily served *treif*—non-kosher food.[13]

Then, just as now, the callous offensiveness and flippant rejection of one's own tradition is the whole point. In lieu of any affirmative claim to grounded substantive religious commitments, duties, or obligations, Reform Judaism instead places a tremendous—almost singular—emphasis on the somewhat arcane Jewish ideal of *tikkun olam*, or "repairing of the world." Throughout the Talmud, *tikkun olam* is used to refer to enacting and utilizing law to preserve social order. Unfortunately, Reform Judaism since the eighteenth–nineteenth century *Haskalah* ("Jewish Enlightenment") has tendentiously reinterpreted and reintroduced *tikkun olam* as a sweeping "social justice" call to arms—whether that entails radical environmentalism, an open-borders immigration policy, sexual liberation, or whatever a modern *tikkun olam*–ist might otherwise subjectively believe. In practice in the United States, therefore, *tikkun olam*–ist Reform Judaism simply exists—via its political Religious Action Center, or "RAC"—as an appendage of the Democratic Party.

This is an utter tragedy. Reform Judaism is inauthentic and, based on my own personal experience, also spiritually unfulfilling: It fails to provide any meaning or sense of purpose for those who sit in its pews. As I told the liberal Jewish magazine *Jewish Currents* in a 2023 interview: "When you're so vehemently anti-tradition that driving to synagogue on Shabbat is fine, that eating a cheeseburger at a synagogue event is fine, you're not going to have any attachment to conserving tradition."[14] When something as abstract and amorphous as anything-goes-style *tikkun olam* becomes the nominal center of a Jewish congregation instead of Halachic observance itself, the community loses its interdependent and reciprocal bonds of loyalty, as well as the intergenerational collective holiness that has sustained the broader nation of Israel since God's Divine Revelation at Mount Sinai all those millennia ago.[15] And without either traditional Halachic observance or a sense of collective holiness, it is difficult to see how the Jewish people can long endure. Reform Judaism is thus anathematic to Jewish survival and self-preservation. Sadly, it has already done tremendous damage.

The strong plurality of Reform Jews within the broader community of American Jewry helps explain why the United States is the only major anglophone country in the world with a Jewish population that largely votes for the party of the Left. There is a nice silver lining for us Jewish conservatives and traditionalists, however: The demographics are unambiguously on our side. The percentage of American Jews under the age of thirty-five who identify as Orthodox is roughly twice that of their parents' generation, and the next generation of American Jews will therefore be more religious and observant (and thereby politically conservative). This shift is due not merely to higher birth rates among traditional and Orthodox Jews, but also the fact that progressive Jewish communities have shockingly high intermarriage rates and thus often fail to raise Jewish children.

Assimilated American Jews will naturally not think of it as such, but every Jewish intermarriage—and *especially* a Jewish man marrying a non-Jewish woman, since Judaism is matrilineal in its descent—is a tragedy. As former Israeli minister of education Rafi Peretz was reported to opine during a 2019 meeting of the Israeli Cabinet, the intermarriage rate among American Jews—estimated to be 61 percent of all American Jews, including an astounding 72 percent of non-Orthodox American Jews, according to a 2021 Pew Research Center study[16]—is "like a second Holocaust."[17] That is a blunt—and some might say harsh—assessment. But intermarriage does pose an existential crisis for Diaspora Jewry, and for American Jewry—given the metastasis of theologically liberal Judaism in the United States—in particular.

But however awful progressive Judaism is at a structural and theological level, this awfulness pales in comparison to how terrible a job nontraditional/non-Orthodox American Jewish communities typically do in instilling a sense of Jewish identity, belonging, and (above all) meaning and purpose in the younger generations. When a Jew is raised thinking that noshing on bagels and cream cheese and watching old reruns of *Seinfeld* encapsulates what it means to be Jewish, then he will be hopelessly confused and lost. Everyone loves a good bagel, and Jerry Seinfeld and Larry David are indeed talented comedians, but to reduce the world's oldest monotheistic religion and longest-surviving extant nation to such trifles is truly pathetic.

Arguably even worse is a definition and self-conception of Judaism that emphasizes above all the singular horrors of the Holocaust. That is, of course, not to deny that the Holocaust was the single most systematically executed mass genocide against a specific people in recorded human history. As I mentioned at the beginning of the book, I have a rock from the Auschwitz crematorium that a rabbi once gave me in Jerusalem, which I keep on my desk at all times next to a smaller rock that I took myself from Treblinka. There is rarely a day of my life that goes by where I *do not* think about the Holocaust at some point—especially in a post–October 7, 2023, world.

Rather, what I mean is this: If what it *means to be Jewish* is to personally remember the worst tragedy to befall a particular people and particular nation in all of recorded human history, and maybe to meet a Holocaust survivor or two and go pay one's respects at a concentration camp, then the Jew hearing such a message will be depressed and immediately repelled. No one in his right mind would gravitate toward such a nationhood and way of life that places at the center of its worldview and actions an intense and always-simmering fixation with six million murdered coreligionists.

Holocaust education and awareness is vitally important, especially at a time of skyrocketing global anti-Semitism. And the percentage of younger Americans who think the Holocaust was exaggerated or fabricated is outright harrowing.[18] But Holocaust education and awareness must not be the center of contemporary Jewish education and identity formation. Instead, the center of

Jewish education and identity formation must be a deep-seated love and appreciation for the *mitzvot* (commandments) that constitute the inherited Law of Moses from Mount Sinai—and a concomitant love for the Jewish people's special and unique role in the broader story of God, His creation, and the teleology and destiny of mankind.

In short, modern Jewish education and identity formation must be predicated upon the three authentic pillars of Judaism: Torah, *Am Yisrael* (the nation, or people, of Israel), and *Eretz Yisrael* (the Land of Israel, which now entails the modern State of Israel). Reorienting the American Jewish experience toward these authentic ends, and away from meaningless culinary or pop cultural totems, would go a very long way in sparking a fire in the belly of nontraditional/non-Orthodox Jews and persuading them to rise to the challenge of being selfless transmitters of their own inherited tradition. This is easier said than done, but *kiruv*—traditional or Orthodox Jewish outreach—from movements such as Chabad can certainly help. Prominent Torah-observant Jews with a deep and abiding love for *Am Yisrael* and *Eretz Yisrael*, such as my former *Daily Wire* colleague Ben Shapiro and my present Edmund Burke Foundation colleague Yoram Hazony, can also help by setting good examples of how Torah-observant Jews can lead in the public square.

And if you are a Jew who already has an innate love of your own people, the easiest and most impactful thing you can do to demonstrate your commitment is to simply lead by example. Thoughts and words can be nice, but Judaism, by and large, is a religion of *action* and *deed*.

My full English name is Joshua Benjamin Hammer. Since I grew up in a secular home, I did not grow up aware of any other Hebrew name. So Rabbi Modek gave me one while we were finalizing preparations for my bar mitzvah. (In 2024, I found the original certificate for my *brit milah* [circumcision], where the officiating rabbi apparently did provide me with a Hebrew name. I was not previously aware of it.)

My paternal grandfather, may his memory be a blessing, was Polish—so Hammer is a Polish Jewish surname. And the actual word "hammer"—i.e., the hardware tool—translates in modern Hebrew to "*pateesh*." But I was instead given the powerful Hebrew surname *Maccabee* because, in ancient times, Judah Maccabee himself was nicknamed "Judah the Hammer." This is likely because "Maccabee" itself derives from the Aramaic word "*maqqaba*," which means "hammer," although scholars are not sure.

My Hebrew name is therefore Yehoshua Binyamin Maccabee. On my *tallit* (ritual prayer shawl) bag, which I use for daily prayer, this full name is stitched in Hebrew. (On my accompanying *tefillin* bag, which is smaller, it is simply "Yehoshua" that is stitched in Hebrew.) My daily *siddur* (prayerbook), which I customized, also has "Yehoshua Binyamin Maccabee" in Hebrew engraved on its cover.

I am proud to be a Maccabee. But even if a Jew is not *named* Maccabee, it is imperative that he take to heart the Maccabees' warrior spirit and anti-assimilationist defiance. Years ago, my friend Elliott Hamilton explained the real meaning of the Jewish holiday of Chanukah, which is a story of the Maccabean triumph of Torah Judaism over the assimilationist and Hellenized forces within the broader Jewish fold:

> What most American Jews do not realize about the story of Chanukah is that it was . . . also a story of a civil war between two camps of Jews: One who believed that the Jewish people should maintain their Halachic traditions and the other who wished to assimilate with their [Seleucid Empire] oppressors. . . . [The lighting of the menorah] should also serve as a reminder that

it never helps the Jewish people to side with those who openly seek to destroy us.[19]

This is indeed the true lesson of Chanukah. Americans, and most other Diaspora Jews, typically associate Chanukah with spinning the dreidel, exchanging presents, eating oily foods, and, yes, lighting the menorah. With the exception of the menorah, though, this mostly misses the point of the holiday. Chanukah, and the underlying Maccabean impulse and imperative that it commemorates, is a recurring annual witness to Jewish particularism, Jewish nationalism, and the Jewish people's unique eternal role as God's chosen toehold in His creation. Chanukah, and the victory of the Maccabees over the Hellenizers and the Seleucid Empire, memorializes the rejection of Jewish assimilation. It reaffirms the nation of Israel's true purpose in this world: sanctifying God's name in all that we do on earth.[20]

The reality is that an assimilationist mentality has characterized weak-kneed Jewry ever since the original sin of the golden calf at Mount Sinai. That same mentality reared its ugly head again during Second Temple–era Judaism, in the form of the Hellenizers who yearned so strongly for assimilation and secular "acceptance" that they fought a bloody civil war against the Jewish Maccabees over it. In medieval times in Europe, this mentality surfaced countless times during murderous pogroms and the other tragically recurring episodes of anti-Semitic repression. And in the direst crucible of twentieth-century totalitarianism, this same mentality rose yet again in the form of Jewish collaborationists and *kapos* who actively abetted unspeakable Nazi crimes against their fellow Jews. We see a similar instinct on display today when left-wing Diaspora Jews abandon their brethren in *Eretz Yisrael* and advocate for the Palestinian-Arab cause.

American Jews, much like their forebears and ancestors throughout Jewish history, therefore have two basic options: (1)

Be a Maccabee and defiantly tell the world that, against all the odds, we are still here and that our nationhood will never be extinguished; or (2) be a Hellenized Jew and forsake the uniqueness of Jewish particularism at the sacrificial altar of assimilationism or secularism.[21] There is an obviously correct choice here: *Always be a Maccabee, and always be proud and authentic representatives of the broader nation of Israel.* Every Jew must do his part to ensure the nation of Israel always remains a "light unto the nations."[22] That is only possible by remaining a proud Jew who leads an authentic Jewish life, with a deep love for the Torah and the Law of Moses, *Am Yisrael* (the people of Israel), and *Eretz Yisrael* (the Land of Israel).

I have always been inspired by the message and story of Chanukah. I deliberately proposed to my now-wife on the third night of Chanukah in December 2022, in the Old City of Jerusalem. I did it from a scenic balcony at the Aish HaTorah World Center yeshiva overlooking the Kotel (Western Wall) and the Temple Mount, the holiest site in Judaism. I wrote out a short speech, which I read before dropping to one knee on the Aish yeshiva balcony with diamond ring in hand. As part of the speech, I referenced the fact that it was Chanukah and that I am a Maccabee:

> My Hebrew family name, as you know, is Maccabee, and I have always taken a special interest in the victory of the Maccabean Revolt. During this very time, which we now call Chanukah, we recall that revolt, which happened over two thousand years ago. The Maccabean revolt, against the forces of Hellenistic assimilation, helped confirm that the Jewish people's true home remains Jerusalem. It has always been, and it will always be, such.

For female readers in particular: Don't fret, there were plenty of other more personal and touching parts to the speech! Most important, of course, she said yes. God is good.

Another vital component of being a modern-day Jewish Maccabee, especially in today's fraught times, is to arm yourself, train with your firearms, and take your security—and your family's and congregation's security—into your own hands as much as possible. For American Jews in particular, who—unlike most other Diaspora Jews—have the extraordinary constitutional guarantee under the Second Amendment to keep and bear arms, it is malpractice to not purchase firearms and train with them.

I attended law school in the very anti-gun city of Chicago, so I waited until after I moved to Texas after graduation to purchase my first firearms. My first purchase was a compact handgun, intended for daily concealed carry. I trained with it and obtained my carry license. I have been carrying that same weapon on a near-daily basis for over eight years now. I own other firearms, as well, including my modern sporting rifle (a gun that tendentious leftists and corporate media ignoramuses inaccurately describe as an "assault weapon"), which I have decked out with numerous add-on features such as iron sights and a red-dot sight.

My concealed carry handgun, as it is for every American who regularly carries, is the weapon I take out most frequently. But my passion for gun rights is deeply informed by my reading of Jewish history, and for that reason I am most passionate about my rifle. I call that rifle my "Warsaw Ghetto gun," since it is the gun the oppressed Jews of the Warsaw Ghetto would have (literally) killed to have during their extraordinarily courageous, albeit ultimately unsuccessful, 1943 uprising against the occupying Nazi forces. As a lawyer by background, one of my all-time favorite judicial opinions was an extraordinarily powerful dissent from denial of *en banc* (i.e., full court) rehearing written by then-judge Alex

Kozinski of the US Court of Appeals for the Ninth Circuit in the 2003 case of *Silveira v. Lockyer*:

> All too many of the other great tragedies of history—Stalin's atrocities, the killing fields of Cambodia, the Holocaust, to name but a few—were perpetrated by armed troops against unarmed populations. . . . If a few hundred Jewish fighters in the Warsaw Ghetto could hold off the Wehrmacht for almost a month with only a handful of weapons, six million Jews armed with rifles could not so easily have been herded into cattle cars. . . .
>
> The prospect of tyranny may not grab the headlines the way vivid stories of gun crime routinely do. But few saw the Third Reich coming until it was too late. The Second Amendment is a doomsday provision, one designed for those exceptionally rare circumstances where all other rights have failed.[23]

Unfortunately, the most recent available public polling on the topic indicates that American Jews barely even support the Second Amendment, let alone take seriously and put into practice its afforded protections. It is true that many American Jews rushed to purchase firearms in the months immediately following the Simchat Torah Massacre, which is laudable.[24] Hopefully that was not a flash in the pan, but the beginning of a deeper and more profound American Jewish commitment to responsible gun ownership. Because as recently as 2018, an American Jewish Committee survey found that 70 percent of American Jews believe that pursuing gun control and anti-gun regulation is more important than protecting and securing the rights of gun owners—compared to 25 percent of American Jews who disagree.[25] The historical collective lack of American Jewish interest in responsible firearm ownership is simply tragic.

In a post–October 7 world, it has never been more important for Jews to buy guns, buy ammunition, and to train extensively. American Jews constitute an unfathomably high percentage of all religiously based hate crime victims in America: 68 percent of the total according to the FBI's most recent annual Uniform Crime Reporting statistics, despite constituting roughly 2 percent of the US population.[26] The American Jewish security situation has gotten markedly worse since October 7—especially in the urban cores with large Jewish populations, such as New York City and Los Angeles. A July 2024 poll found that nearly half (44 percent) of Jews living in New York City, which has the largest single-city Jewish population in the world, feel unsafe.[27] Indeed, that poll found an even higher two-thirds majority of Orthodox Jews agreed with the same sentiment.[28]

Despite these deeply worrisome trends and statistics, many Jewish institutions in America remain soft targets. True, many shuls and Jewish Community Centers have added armed security in recent years—but many also have not. And as a pure statistical matter, American Jews are far less likely to own guns—and to be carrying them while attending religious services—than are American Christians.[29]

Truly, this is unconscionable. I carry my loaded handgun on me—in addition to a backup gun magazine and a knife—most times I leave home, but I *always* do so whenever I attend shul, eat at a kosher restaurant, go to a communal Jewish event, or anything of the sort. Other than certain special events that have a mandatory metal detector, I cannot even remember the last time I attended any kind of Jewish gathering without my firearm at my side.

The reality is that Jews, who are the most systemically and consistently persecuted group of human beings in the history of the human race, have more reasons to want to train with firearms, become proficient with firearms, own firearms, and carry firearms than do *any other group of Americans.* Jews, who for millennia have been demographic minorities in every land except for the modern State of Israel itself, ought to be uniquely willing and eager to take advantage of the protections secured by the Second Amendment to the US Constitution.[30] Jews who were properly armed instead of forced to live at the behest of tyrannical oppressors could have better resisted any number of pogroms and atrocities committed throughout history—as Kozinski's powerful Ninth Circuit dissent and my beloved "Warsaw Ghetto gun" both attest.

The State of Israel's gun laws are a mixed bag. Israel's civilian gun ownership regime is much stricter than the Second Amendment would tolerate in the United States: Firearm ownership is considered a privilege, not a right, and firearm license applications are largely left to the discretion of regulators, who may or may not deem the applicant's interest to be compelling. At the same time, guns are far more prevalent in Israel than they are in most European nations; anyone who has ever visited the Jewish state has likely encountered dozens of uniformed IDF soldiers and civilian rapid response teams who are armed with so-called "assault weapons." This is considered entirely routine; there is no eyebrow-raising when a soldier or civilian responder brings his rifle out in the street or into a shop or restaurant, as there would be in the US.

After the Simchat Torah Massacre, Israel moved to liberalize some of its gun laws. Israel had historically rejected a large percentage of firearm carry permit applications, but that is starting to change. In January 2024, for instance, I met a friend for dinner in Jerusalem—it was a tony restaurant, but he came straight from the shooting range and openly carried his handgun in the restaurant. Between October 7 and December 25, 2023, more than 270,000 Israelis applied for new gun licenses; during the same time period, armed civilian rapid response teams expanded in number from 70 to 900.[31] This auspicious trend must continue: Israelis are surrounded by enemies who want to kill them on virtually all borders. Many Israelis (and most Jewish Israelis) served in the military, and thereby have a basic proficiency with firearms. Indeed, a better-armed Israeli civilian populace might have been able to substantially limit the mass casualties of October 7, 2023.

A modern Jewish Maccabee, whether in the Land of Israel or in the Diaspora, must be trained, armed, and proficient in the use of firearms. He is necessarily the Jew who the anti-Semites fear the most. He is a Jew who is ready, willing, and able, if need be, to heed the Talmudic principle that one must rise to take the life of someone who is trying to kill him. As the Gemara famously says in Tractate *Sanhedrin*: "The Torah stated a principle: If someone comes to kill you, rise and kill him first."[32]

A modern Jewish Maccabee is a Jew who understands and internalizes this. He is a Jew who, while praying in shul, is trained and prepared to act in his and his congregation's defense, if need be. He is a Jew who is physically capable and emotionally prepared to take down an active shooter, if need be.[33] He is the Jew who fought back against the SS shepherding Jews to their certain deaths via cattle car. He is a Jew who will protect himself, protect his family, protect his congregation, protect his tribe, and protect his nation against mortal threats and oppressors. He is the warrior Jew—the Jew who takes comfort in the opening line of King David's Psalm 144: "Blessed is the Lord, my Rock, Who trains my hands for battle, my fingers for war."[34]

I do not pretend that this comes easily for every American Jew. I grew up in an assimilated and very anti-gun home. As a child, I distinctly remember my mother initially rejecting my desired first purchase of a first-person shooter video game: *GoldenEye 007* for Nintendo 64. (She eventually relented.) But as I matured and learned more about both Jewish history and American history, I came to appreciate and cherish the constitutional right to keep and bear arms. A well-armed citizenry is not simply an outgrowth of any particular natural or legal right; rather, when exercised safely and responsibly, the right to keep and bear arms is fundamentally just, virtuous, and conduces to the common good of a well-functioning, harmonious society.[35]

That responsible gun ownership is usually no longer viewed as *just* or *virtuous* is due to the fact that manliness itself is increasingly viewed not as a noble virtue to be nourished and cherished, but as a "toxic" vestige of a bygone barbarism that must be tamed and ultimately excised.[36] To be sure, that is a broader sociological problem beyond the scope of this book. But for present purposes, if a weak, secular, assimilated Jew is to ever break out of his shell and become a modern, manly Jewish Maccabee—to be a "wolf" and not a "sheepdog," to borrow the phraseology of the 2014 blockbuster film *American Sniper*—then it is incumbent upon him to take up the cause of responsible gun ownership.

It is of course appropriate for us to demand concrete action, and not mere virtue-signaling and grandstanding, from those elected officials who have allowed this despicable years-long resurgence of the world's oldest bigotry to fester under their negligent watch. But ultimately, the imperative is on each individual Jew to be the guardian of his own security—and on each Jewish congregation to be the guardian of that congregation's own security. Why would Jews, the most systemically persecuted group of humans to have ever lived, ever delegate responsibility for their own lives to third-party actors?[37]

In the Land of Israel—for which the Israel Defense Forces have served, ever since the modern Jewish state's founding in 1948, as a living, breathing embodiment of "Never Again"— the elegant solution to Jewish control of the Jews' own security and destiny is Zionism and Jewish nationalism. And regulations on civilian firearm ownership in the State of Israel should certainly also be liberalized. But in the Diaspora—and particularly in America, due to our Constitution's glorious Second Amendment—the *only* acceptable approach is for each and every individual Jew to arm up and train extensively. There is simply no other game in town.

Arm and train yourselves, fellow Jews. *Now.*[38]

As I mentioned at the beginning of this chapter, I think I was born with a literal fear of God. I distinctly recall, as a child, shuddering as I walked by houses of worship. While I still have a long way to go on my religious journey, I have also come a long way already in ridding myself of that primordial fear and developing a more Jewishly proper *yir'at shamayim*. Such a righteous fear can only possibly come by accepting the truth of God's existence and the truth of the Torah, which He revealed to His chosen people at Mount Sinai. Indeed, Judaism teaches that such a fear is more than righteous—it is a necessary condition for a life well lived. As the psalmist says, "The beginning of wisdom is the fear of the Lord."[39]

Ultimately, it is this premise—the truth of God's existence and the Divine Revelation at Mount Sinai—that every would-be Maccabee should accept, and from which subsequent actions can logically build. Put more concretely: It is laudable and commendable to advocate on behalf of the Jewish people and the State of Israel, but it is even more laudable and commendable to do that after first investing in the proper intellectual and moral foundation and leading a correspondingly proper personal life—one that places at its center the three Jewish pillars of Torah, *Am Yisrael*, and *Eretz Yisrael*.

Today, the nation of Israel desperately needs more of its own people—in both the Land of Israel and the Diaspora—to reject the many vogue manifestations of Hellenization that plague our troubled times and to instead make a stand on the world stage as modern Maccabees who will proudly protect, defend, preserve, advocate on behalf of, and live according to the customs and laws of the nation of Israel. Practically, that means that Jews who have moved away from the religion of their forebears or who (like me) grew up with great ignorance of their own tradition, but who nonetheless retain an instinctive attachment to their people and their inherited way of life, must take concrete steps to learn about or refamiliarize themselves with Judaism and then commit to living an authentically Jewish life themselves.

In order to be a modern Maccabee, a Jew today must adamantly reject the false modern manifestations of our forefathers' ancient religion, such as Reform Judaism, which rejects the binding nature of *Halacha* in favor of an unwarranted heavy emphasis on *tikkun olam*—the obligation to "repair the world," a venerable (if abstruse) Talmudic concept twisted by the Reform movement into rote left-wing political activism. A modern Maccabee should not go to any synagogue service that is not at least highly traditional in its liturgy, rituals, and practices. As a religious Jewish friend told me years ago, it doesn't matter if you go to synagogue and cannot immediately follow all the Hebrew in the liturgy; you are still getting an authentic experience, and you will certainly learn a great deal (as I did, and still do) by sheer dint of observance, osmosis, and repetition. And for those Jews who harbor lingering doubts and may struggle to accept the authenticity of the faith and way of life of their forefathers, there is nothing better than sheer repetition—in liturgy, ritual, and practice.

Above all, every Jew must take upon himself the weight and gravity of the thousands of years of our people's history. If you are Jewish, then you can directly trace your history back to the Divine Revelation at Mount Sinai. (Indeed, you can trace it back even further, to the patriarch Abraham himself.) That is a beautiful and powerful thing to contemplate, but it also comes with a solemn responsibility. The Jewish people, the original People of the Book who first introduced the world to monotheism and whose legal and ethical code laid the foundation for what we today call Western civilization, have a unique role to play in the fate of mankind and in mankind's relationship with our Creator. If you are a

Jew alive today, don't you *want* to be a part of that history? Don't you *want* to be a part of the unfolding of that story in real time? You certainly *should* want to be a part of it.

Maybe you think that leading a Jewish lifestyle and abiding by Jewish law is too "restrictive"—and that leading a secular lifestyle and following secular teachings is "liberating." Perhaps you are worried that you might miss the taste of a juicy cheeseburger or a tangy shrimp cocktail. Or maybe you just think that some signature Jewish rituals, such as a man's donning of *tefillin* on his arm and head every morning during the *shacharit* prayer, are too "primitive" or otherwise unsuitable for today's enlightened age of "reason" and "rationality."

You might be forgiven for harboring such thoughts, especially if you grew up as secular as I did. I understand and can personally relate to that. But to wallow in such existential doubts is to entirely miss the point. The Jewish people exist not to chart out the "easiest" path in life, or to demonstrate a self-indulgent lifestyle free of unchosen burdens and restraints. Rather, the Jewish people exist to sanctify God's name in all that we do on earth. Only in doing that can we credibly claim to serve as a "light unto the nations" of Gentiles all throughout the world, as we are called to do. As Rabbi Pesach Wolicki has noted, "One of the primary purposes of [the nation of] Israel, if not *the* primary purpose, is to be a vehicle for the revelation of God in this world."[40] And as it says in Scripture: "The sum of the matter, when all is said and done: Revere God and observe His commandments!"[41]

If the Jewish people are to serve their divinely ordained purpose as God's toehold on earth and as the cornerstone of His creation, then it is imperative that we Jews not merely think, speak, or write nice thoughts; we must also affirmatively *act* and *do*. We Jews must all do our very best to lead by example—by demonstrating and acting in accordance with *yir'at shamayim*, a righteous fear of God. So buckle up, all Jews who may need to hear it: Get your head out of the secular gutter, grab a *siddur* and a set of *tefillin,* and let's roll.

The times are very tough these days for the Jewish people. They have been tougher in the past, certainly; I saw it for myself at Treblinka. But everywhere one now looks, we see enemies of the Jews: from the egregiously biased corporate media to the lofty corridors of political power to the censorious Big Tech oligarchs to the K–12 and higher education establishments to the corporate "Diversity, Equity, and Inclusion" ("DEI") bureaucracies, and so much else in between. The world's oldest bigotry is not just back; it is back with a vengeance, and it is now positively *fashionable.*

A young Abraham Lincoln had this to say about America during his prophetic Lyceum Address of 1838: "At what point then is the approach of danger to be expected? I answer, if it ever reach[es] us, it must spring up amongst us. It cannot come from abroad. If destruction be our lot, we must ourselves be its author and finisher."[42] With full confidence that God will never renege upon His covenant, the destruction of the Jewish people would similarly never come from "abroad," but only from within. And such a destruction could only transpire if the Maccabees relent to the tyranny of the Hellenizers—and their natural accomplices, the Hellenized.[43]

If you are Jewish, are you ready to answer your calling and become a modern Maccabee?

11

THE JEWISH–CHRISTIAN
ALLIANCE TO SAVE THE WEST

*"Trust in the Lord with all your heart and do not rely
upon your understanding."*

—PROVERBS 3:5[1]

THE BRITISH HISTORIAN ARNOLD TOYNBEE FAMOUSLY ARGUED THAT
civilizations die from "suicide," and not by "murder."[2] And a
young Abraham Lincoln said in Springfield, Illinois, in 1838: "If
destruction be our lot, we must ourselves be its author and finisher."[3] Lincoln's 1838 Lyceum Address sentiment is certainly apt
for the Jewish people's present predicament, as discussed in the
previous chapter. But Lincoln and Toynbee must be heeded not
only by the beleaguered Jewish people and the besieged Jewish
State of Israel, but also by the broader West itself—namely, its
Jews and Christians alike. Every way one looks, it is impossible to
escape the conclusion that self-hating elites across the Western
world now scorn our Judeo-Christian inheritance in a kamikaze
mission to commit civilizational suicide.

Western civilization now faces an existential crisis. The barbarians have breached the gate. The hegemonic threats of illiberal leftist wokeism and illiberal totalitarian Islamism have combined, with a dastardly "red-green" alliance, to put the West in a position of historic precarity.[4] Meanwhile, homogenizing global neoliberalism continues to stamp out and subjugate those dissenters who resist its tyranny of lifestyle and mind. What we are living through right now is easily Western civilization's most tenuous position since the height of the Cold War—perhaps even since the Battle of Vienna in 1683, when a coalition of European Christendom successfully repelled the invading Ottoman Empire and saved the European Continent from Muslim conquest.

Whether European leaders today care to preserve that legacy or to dilute their own civilization via unfettered third-world immigration and Islamization is another matter. And whether Western leaders as a whole now care to preserve their heritage from ideological ruin, cultural decadence, and demographic collapse is the foremost question of our time.

If the West is going to survive as a semi-concrete entity and not either be subsumed into an amorphous global neoliberal blob or be conquered by wokeism and Islamism—that is, if the West is not going to commit "suicide" and be the "author and finisher" of its own "destruction"—it is imperative that its core constituent parts all stand boldly together.[5] Specifically, Western Jews and Christians must stand shoulder-to-shoulder like never before. Immense theological and eschatological differences that will not be bridged any time soon must be put aside in favor of a focus on Jews' and Christians' overwhelming moral and civilizational-historical overlap as the two preservers of our biblical inheritance, on the one hand, and the urgent practical necessity of forging a united front.

The Judeo-Christian tradition, which began with God's world-transforming revelation to the incipient Israelite nation at Mount Sinai, birthed Western civilization and has nourished it over the course of thousands of years. The West's manifold gifts to the world all directly or indirectly flow from this great patrimony. If Western civilization is now going to prevail as a distinct entity and resist the existential challenges posed by stifling globalism, metastasizing wokeism, and subjugating Islamism, it is going to require the West to rededicate itself to that very inherited Judeo-Christian tradition.

Both Jews and Christians have distinct and indispensable roles to play.

For Christians, adherents of the West's dominant religion, it is imperative to internalize the basic truth that the civilization they were so instrumental in building and developing is largely predicated upon values and principles derived from the Hebrew Bible. And it is not just the Hebrew Bible—and the Talmud, as well—that has been so central to the formation of Western civilization as a unique strand of the human experience. Rather, it is also the *Jews themselves*—the original preservers of our biblical inheritance, who introduced monotheism to the world—who have always been foundational to the entire construct.

As Eric Hoffer, known as the "longshoreman philosopher," wrote in a 1968 essay, "I have a premonition that will not leave me; as it goes with Israel so will it go with all of us. Should Israel perish, the holocaust will be upon us."[6] Hoffer was referring to the State of Israel, writing in the aftermath of the Jewish state's miraculous victory in the Six Day War one year prior. But his sentiment holds true not only for the specific State of Israel, but also for the broader nation of Israel.

Through the centuries, those who have sought to physically or intellectually conquer the West have taken a peculiar interest in targeting the Jews. There are reasons for this focus. As argued in an earlier chapter, the Jew is an enduring testimony of God's existence, His Kingdom, and His Divine Will. The Jew is a living,

breathing testament to the fact that God has affirmative expectations of us, and expects us to think, act, and more generally live
our lives within certain moral parameters. Jewish life—including,
but hardly limited to, the perpetuation and thriving of the modern State of Israel—is thus an incessant nagging weight on the
World's collective moral conscience.

Thus, Jew-hatred is pervasive, diffuse, and supra-rational.
Jew-hatred affects Jews of all levels of observance (fully assimilated, fully Torah-observant, or somewhere in between)—
because the Jew represents more than himself as an individual
person. The fact that he is a Jew, no matter how secular or assimilated his station in life or how lowly his behavior, recalls that
there is such a thing as a "Jew"—and a distinct, particularist
Jewish *people*. That Jewish people, in turn, has a specific heritage
of God's covenant, His promising them the Land of Israel, His
liberating them from Egyptian bondage, His giving them His
Torah, His protecting them in the wilderness, and His settling
them in the Land of Israel wherein they established a kingdom
and built a permanent home for Him in that kingdom's united
capital, Jerusalem.

As I have previously discussed, the stifling centripetal forces of
globalism despise the defiant particularism of the Jewish nation
and the modern Jewish state. The globalists' impulse is to homogenize and stamp out all underlying differences, in line with the
insidious message of John Lennon's well-known song, "Imagine."[7]
For the intellectual and geopolitical homogenizer, there can be no
greater foe than the Jewish people, bound as they are by the particularist Mosaic Law and inextricably intertwined with the particular Land of Israel promised to them thousands of years ago.

To celebrate human variation and resist forced conformity
means supporting the eternal symbol of the particularist refusal
to assimilate into the masses: the Jew. Christians who want to
safeguard their own traditions from the globalist and neoliberal imperialists in the lions' dens of Turtle Bay, Brussels, and

so forth will find no better allies than the Jews. The Jews' entire existence, to say nothing of their flourishing, necessarily hinges on successfully thwarting the centripetal force of modern global neoliberalism.

But it is not merely the hegemonic globalists and intellectual conformists who have a rather large bone to pick with the Jews. It is also atheists, reprobates, and all those who seek to rupture and ultimately sever Western civilization from its underlying mono-theistic moral basis—and thus destroy the West itself as a con-crete entity.

Christianity, after all, derives from Judaism. The Second Vatican Council's official Declaration on the Relation of the Church with Non-Christian Religions ("*Nostra Aetate*"), promul-gated in 1965, officially affirmed the "common patrimony" and "spiritual bond" that unites Christians and Jews.[8] Quoting the New Testament, *Nostra Aetate* also referred to the Jewish people as the "good olive branch onto which has been grafted the wild shoot, the Gentiles."[9] Pope John Paul II elaborated further in 1986 during his visit to the Great Synagogue of Rome, where he famously declared: "The Jewish religion is not extrinsic to us, but in a certain way is intrinsic to our own religion. With Judaism we have a relationship we do not have with any other religion. You are our dearly beloved brothers, and in a certain way our elder brothers."[10] Decades earlier, as looming war gripped the European Continent in 1938, John Paul II's predecessor, Pius XI, declared that anti-Semitism is "incompatible" with Christianity and ought to be "inadmissible," since Christians "are all spiritu-ally Semites."[11]

It is not merely Christian philo-Semites, such as Pope John Paul II, who have advanced such claims. For better or for worse, the undeniable kinship of Jews and Christians—and the broader relationship between the two biblical religions—has also been appreciated by those who wish harm or destruction to Jews, Christians, and the West.

Perhaps no one made this connection more clearly than Karl Marx, who sought to overthrow the Western order—which he viewed as capitalist and thus economically "oppressive"—with an international communist workers' revolution. As Marx wrote in his deeply anti-Semitic 1843 essay, "On the Jewish Question," which he penned just a few years before *The Communist Manifesto* itself:

> The Jew has emancipated himself in a Jewish manner, not only because he has acquired financial power, but also because, through him and also apart from him, money has become a world power and the practical Jewish spirit has become the practical spirit of the Christian nations.

Therefore, Marx ultimately sought nothing less than the "emancipation" of humanity from Judaism itself.[12] It is not difficult to draw a straight line from such a vile sentiment to modern left-wing, DEI-based, and "anti-Zionist" manifestations of anti-Semitism.

A century later, the same Soviet hatred of the capitalist/ Christian West would similarly manifest itself in appalling Jewish repression at home, precipitating the rise of the refuseniks— oppressed Russian Jews denied emigration to Israel by the Soviet government. In the Jews, the Soviet Communists saw a useful proxy for the broader Western monotheistic and biblical order that they sought to upend and supplant. It is surely no coincidence that around the same time American social conservatism and Christian Zionism began to rise as a political force, such as with the "Moral Majority" of Jerry Falwell Sr., American Christians were simultaneously largely united in the goal of restraining and defeating the atheistic Soviet Union.

In general, when the ultimate target is Christendom, the Jews will always be the first ones in the crosshairs. It is incumbent upon Christians to recognize that stark reality. Islamists seek to conquer the entirety of the Middle East—indeed, the world, if they could—and they do not discriminate between Jews and Christians. Christians have been ethnically cleansed for decades in Lebanon and Palestinian Authority–controlled parts of Judea and Samaria, such as Bethlehem. Coptic Christians have similarly been targeted for decades by fanatical Islamists in Egypt. Islamists' top target in the Middle East is the Jewish State of Israel, but one should not be under the impression that the radicals do not similarly seek to exterminate the region's last remaining Christians.

It is also incumbent upon Western Christians of all stripes to appreciate, and not simply take for granted, just how much of the prevailing Western order they predominantly built owes a moral, legal, and cultural debt of gratitude to Judaism, Torah, and the Jewish people.

Thousands of years before John Locke and Thomas Jefferson popularized the Enlightenment-era natural rights theory that all men are created equal, the Hebrew Bible introduced to the world the same basic principle of equal moral worth and dignity: "And God created man in His image; in the image of God He created him; male and female He created them."[13] Millennia before the English common law popularized its own notion of blind justice and equality under the rule of law, the Hebrew Bible articulated it right in Leviticus: "You shall commit no injustice in judgment; you shall not favor a poor person or respect a great man; you shall judge your fellow with righteousness."[14]

Large swaths of the Anglo-American common law of property, including the law of squatters' rights, adverse possession, and easements as they are still taught in American law schools today, are derived from the well-known Talmudic Tractate of *Bava Batra*.[15] A similarly sizable corpus of modern Anglo-American tort law traces its origin to the related Talmudic Tractate of *Bava Metzia*. And millennia before Sir Edward Coke first drew a criminal law distinction between *actus reus* ("guilty act") and *mens rea* ("guilty mind"), the Mosaic Law provided precisely such a distinction in chapter 35 of the Book of Numbers.[16] So often in the Anglo-America legal tradition, we find that before there was an English- or Latin-language principle, there was that same ancestral principle appearing in the original *Lashon Hakodesh* ("holy tongue").

There are simply too many other examples to enumerate. As Steven Grosby has written: "We can praise our own Western accomplishments, or rather the source from which we have drawn the sacred truths that sustain us, only as long as we can give no less credit to the unmatched authority and wisdom of the ancient Hebrew nation."[17] Without the myriad contributions of Judaism, Torah, Talmud, and the Jewish people themselves, there simply would not be such a cognizable entity as "the West." And the notion that Western civilization can long survive without the eternal witness and flourishing of its founding "olive branch," to again quote *Nostra Aetate*, is foolish and shortsighted beyond measure.[18] History, Rabbi Pesach Wolicki has explained, is "filled with examples of nations that attacked the Jewish people, only to be destroyed while the Jewish people prevailed."[19]

Accordingly, Western Christians should support and promote policies that best ensure the survival and flourishing of the Jewish people. Such policies can take any number of possible forms: robust free exercise and freedom of conscience protections for religious minorities, securing the continued legality of *shechita* (ritual kosher slaughter) against anti-Semitic European-style efforts to outlaw it,[20] education and tax policies to better enable universal school choice and affordable access to Jewish day school, universal workplace accommodations for Jews who fully observe the Sabbath and the Jewish holidays, funding for adequate security at synagogues and Jewish civic and communal institutions, and so forth. Western Christians should recognize that when the Jews are safe, secure, and thriving, so, too, is the West safe, secure, and thriving. Accordingly, Western public policy—and certainly American public policy, given that America is home to the largest Diaspora Jewish community—should be as supportive of Jewish life as is possible.

Similarly, Western Christians should support policies that best ensure the survival and flourishing of the Jewish State of Israel. Such policies can take any number of possible forms: increased military or economic ties, expanded academic and diplomatic ties, improved intelligence-sharing, *ad hoc* aid in times of need, support and cover at hostile globalist institutions such as the United Nations, sober hostility toward existential mutual enemies such as the terrorist Iranian regime, appropriate scorn toward the obstinate Palestinian-Arabs, and so forth. Western Christians should recognize that when the State of Israel is safe, secure, and thriving, so, too, is the West safe, secure, and thriving. The West will not long endure without its man on the spot—a man on the spot, incidentally, that happens to be derived from the world's first-ever concrete nation, and which is specifically earmarked for the world's longest-surviving concrete people. Accordingly, Western public policy must be as supportive of the State of Israel as is possible.

Christianity is the West's predominant religion, but Christians cannot stand alone in the defense of the West against the three menacing ideologies of homogenizing global neoliberalism, wokeism, and Islamism. Only an alliance of the original People of the Book and the "grafted [Gentile] wild shoot" can rise to meet that challenge together.[21] There would necessarily be no Christianity today were it not for Judaism, and there will be no thriving Christian future if there is no thriving Jewish future as well.

Just as Christians should appreciate the value and utility of their Jewish allies in the broader struggle to ward off the subjugation of Western civilization at the hands of homogenizing global liberalism, cancerous wokeism, and imperial Islamism, so, too, should Jews reciprocate in kind to their Christian allies engaged in the same struggle.

Jewish liberals first need to finally get over any vestigial skepticism—let alone outright animus—they may still harbor about Christians. I have had to talk numerous (almost exclusively secular) Jewish friends and family members out of skeptical attitudes, which primarily emanate from one of two starting points: They either mistrust Christians' professed philo-Semitism or they cling to anachronistic bitterness from past decades, wherein America's regnant "WASP" culture would sometimes exclude Jews from membership in various elite country clubs, reject Jews from admission to elite universities, refuse to hire Jews at elite law firms and investment banks, and so forth.

Both of these "reasons" that many Jewish liberals tend to distrust Christians are patently silly. First, evangelical Protestant affinity for the Jewish people and the Jewish State of Israel is generally rooted in what must be the very last thing any Jew could possibly be offended by: God's promises made to Abraham and the other Jewish patriarchs in the Book of Genesis.[22] And Catholics who have a natural affinity for the Jews tend to follow Pope John Paul II, who spoke of the Jews as Catholics' "elder brothers" in faith.[23] But even more to the point: Why exactly should a Jew particularly care *why* a Christian supports the Jewish people and/or the Jewish state? For goodness' sake, accept the support—Jews right now are pretty short on allies, as it is!

Second, when it comes to the harm some American Jews may have endured in previous generations as a result of elite "WASP" culture: We are way past the year 1955. Sure, right-wing anti-Semitism exists on the peripheries of society and our fractious online discourse.[24] But it is still a tiny, and politically and intellectually disenfranchised, minority. Even more to the point, it is *very* rare that even contemporary right-wing anti-Semitism comes from a starting position of biblical Christianity, as opposed to (as I discussed in chapter 9) the nihilism and iconoclasm of neo-Nietzscheanism. Explicitly Christian anti-Semitism in the twenty-first century ought to be condemned, just as any other strand of anti-Semitism ought to be condemned, but such a specific type of anti-Semitism is (thankfully) such a rare modern phenomenon that it is simply not worthy of our time.

It is past time for Jewish liberals, including the leaders of the failing major American Jewish establishment institutions such as the Anti-Defamation League (ADL) and the American Jewish Committee (AJC), to ditch the suicidal progressive attachment to intersectionality, identity politics, and a concomitant racial/ethnic "coalition of the oppressed." In a TV appearance on MSNBC shortly after the Simchat Torah Massacre, ADL CEO and National Director Jonathan Greenblatt appeared apoplectic at how favorably his progressive friends running the network were portraying the butchers of Hamas. It is incumbent upon liberal Jews like Greenblatt to finally recognize that militant identitarian leftism and groups such as Black Lives Matter and "Queers for Palestine" are *not* the Jews' friends—and that religious Christians, whether or not secular Jews fully agree with them on all hot-button "social" or "cultural" issues, *are* the Jews' natural friends.

But merely standing with Christians and defending them from left-wing smears is insufficient. It is also crucial that Jews encourage their Christian allies to be their authentic religious selves and to express their religiosity without fear of rebuke or negative repercussions. Jew-hatred may be the world's last remaining socially acceptable—indeed, in some quarters even "commendable"—form of bigotry, but Christophobia is not terribly far behind.

Throughout most of the West today, religious Christians are often derided simply due to the biblical nature of their beliefs—and how countercultural those beliefs may be viewed in light of today's prevailing orthodoxies, which are profoundly non-biblical (indeed, often *anti*-biblical). If the West's Christian majority is to be emboldened to help protect and preserve our civilization from the menacing tyrannies of global neoliberalism, wokeism, and Islamism, then Jews—Christians' "elder brothers" in faith, with whom they share a "spiritual bond"—should fulfill their role as supportive allies.[25]

In the United States, this will require a Jewish–Christian anti-"separation-ism" alliance. The anti-"separation-ism" goal must be nothing short of legal, political, and cultural in nature. Allow me to elaborate on this crucial point at some length.

In the 1947 case of *Everson v. Board of Education*, the US Supreme Court for the very first time interpreted the Establishment Clause of the First Amendment, which states that "Congress shall make no law respecting an establishment of religion,"[26] as effectuating a "wall of separation between church and state." Justice Hugo Black's majority opinion in *Everson* resuscitated a hitherto obscure 233-word letter sent by then–president Thomas Jefferson to the Baptists of Danbury, Connecticut, in which the nation's third president deployed that precise phrase.[27]

Never mind that Jefferson's pithy and unremarkable letter was penned in a distinctly political context: a desire to make inroads among the New England clergy, which at that time was more partial to the rival Federalist Party. Never mind that the Jeffersonian conception of a "wall of separation between church and state" has no textual, contextual, or historical basis in the actual words of the First Amendment. Never mind that Jefferson himself was not even present at the time the Bill of Rights amendments were passed by Congress and ratified by the states—he was gallivanting off in revolutionary France.

The liberal misnomer of "separation of church and state" soon ossified into a core tenet of America's postwar civic experience, and a touchstone of the Supreme Court's First Amendment jurisprudence. And it was all based on a lie. As Justice William Rehnquist explained in his dissent in the 1985 case of *Wallace v. Jaffree*:

> [Jefferson's] letter to the Danbury Baptist Association was a short note of courtesy, written fourteen years after the Amendments were passed by Congress. He would seem to any detached observer as a less than ideal source of contemporary history as to the meaning of the Religion Clauses of the First Amendment.[28]

But "separation-ism" is not merely wrong as a constitutional matter. It has led to results that are both ludicrous and tragic.

The Supreme Court courtroom itself features a frieze of Moses holding the stone tablets on which the Ten Commandments are inscribed, but similar displays outside the marble palace are deemed suspect. The theologically heterodox Jefferson asserted in the Declaration of Independence that our rights and duties come from our Creator, but to posit as much today is to risk denunciation as a "Christian nationalist."[29] To outwardly display either general religiosity or one's personal piety in contemporary America is to invite secularist scorn, dismissal as a retrograde troglodyte, and probably a lawsuit.

The result is that religious Americans are made to feel like second-class citizens. This is true in private life, and it is certainly true in the public square. But religious men *built* the United States; they should never feel like second-class citizens in their own country. And don't just take it from me. As Barack Obama noted in a 2006 speech:

> Secularists are wrong when they ask believers to leave their religion at the door before entering into the public square. . . . [T]o say that men and women should not inject their "personal morality" into public policy

debates is a practical absurdity. Our law is by definition
a codification of morality, much of it grounded in the
Judeo-Christian tradition.[30]

It is not often that I say this, but Barack Obama was precisely
right.

In recent years, the Roberts Court has led a long-overdue
course-correction in Establishment Clause jurisprudence. In
2019, the court upheld the constitutionality of the Bladensburg,
Maryland, "Peace Cross," a World War I memorial erected in
1925. In 2022, the court vindicated Coach Joseph Kennedy's right
to lead a voluntary on-field prayer following high school football
games, overturning the infamous 1971 case *Lemon v. Kurtzman* in
the process. The highly dubious practice of permitting so-called
"offended observers" to bring Establishment Clause challenges in
court has not quite been fully eradicated, but it is on its last legs.
The overall trend line is positive.

Yet "separation-ism" still broadly remains. It is not merely the
fact that *Everson* remains on the books at the Supreme Court.
Rather, at a deeper and more profound level, "separation of
church and state" remains a key civic framework inculcated in
today's impressionable young Americans. If one were to poll a random sample of American adults to ask what the First Amendment
says about religion, I predict most respondents would answer,
"separation of church and state."

Unfortunately, most of the liberal American Jewish establishment defaults toward a position of ardent "separation-ism." But
the American Jewish establishment's embrace of "separation-ism"
is not only misguided; it is myopic and outright counterproduc-
tive. A legal and civic culture of "separation-ism" harms not only
America's Christian majority and the American republic as a
whole, but it also harms Jewish–Christian relations and ultimately
endangers American Jews themselves.

The ADL, an iconic liberal Jewish establishment institution, boasts on its website that it "safeguards religious freedom for all Americans by protecting the separation of church and state mandated by the First Amendment."[31] Two of the Supreme Court's then-three Jewish justices joined the court majority upholding the Bladensburg "Peace Cross," but ADL head Jonathan Greenblatt nonetheless expressed "alarm" at how "separation of church and state" was purportedly undermined.[32] Similarly, AJC General Counsel Mark Stern criticized the "Peace Cross" ruling as "regrettable," and decried the Coach Kennedy ruling as a "serious blow" to "separation of church and state."[33]

In June 2024, Louisiana governor Jeff Landry signed a law making his state the first to mandate display of the Ten Commandments in all public school classrooms from kindergarten through university. As Landry, himself a Catholic, said before signing the bill, "If you want to respect the rule of law, you gotta start from the original law given, which was Moses. . . . He got his commandments from God."[34]

Unfortunately, the governor's lavish praise of Moses—whom religious Jews consider "the father of all the prophets that were before him and that arose after him," per Maimonides's well-known Thirteen Principles of Faith[35]—was not appreciated by secular Jewish families in Louisiana, three of whom immediately filed suit in federal court. The families cited concern that their children might feel suppressed in expressing their "own Jewish background and beliefs."[36] One cannot help but wonder whether these families realize it was the Jews themselves whom God chose as His intermediary for introducing the Ten Commandments to the world.

Truly, there is so much wrong with this picture that it is difficult to know where to begin.

America, which was founded in 1776 with an appeal to our "Creator," has long been a Godlier nation than its peers. This

Godliness is one reason why John Winthrop first described America as a "shining city upon a hill," and why Ronald Reagan reiterated the sentiment centuries later. In a somewhat similar vein, the Jewish people are famously called in the Book of Isaiah to be a "light unto the nations."[37]

In a great and Godly country such as America, it is incumbent upon the original People of the Book to be that "light" and to lead by example. As Rabbi Tuly Weisz wrote in 2024 following Louisiana's Ten Commandments controversy, "a return to basic principles is in order, and the Jewish community should promote biblical teachings."[38] To oppose the introduction of biblical principles in the public square is to necessarily also undermine Jews' unique mission on earth—to be a "light unto the nations" by sanctifying God's name in all that we do.[39] To oppose the teaching of the Ten Commandments in schools is to fail to be a "kingdom of princes and a holy nation" in the eyes of the Lord.[40]

As a practical matter, the end of "separation-ism" and the return of Christianity to the public square would, perhaps counterintuitively to some, also do a great deal to safeguard the Jewish future in America

One does not need a microscope to examine the origins of the recently ascendant anti-Semitism in America and throughout the Western world: It is almost entirely coming from woke leftist radicals who have replaced the one true God with the false gods of intersectionality, and who suffer from a debilitating case of Western civilizational self-hatred. What is needed to withstand and roll back totalizing woke revanchism is to cut through the liberal illusion of public "values-neutrality" and promote an alternative affirmative conception of the good life—which in America means Judeo-Christian ecumenism at minimum, and in many instances a Christian majority promoting Christianity *tout court*.[41]

John Adams, one of the most devoutly Christian of the Founding Fathers, famously wrote that the Jews "are the most glorious nation that ever inhabited this Earth."[42] Adams added: "They have given religion to three quarters of the Globe and have influenced the affairs of Mankind more, and more happily, than any other Nation ancient or modern."[43] Adams's sentiment is hardly aberrant; rather, he is representative of American Christianity, which has often tended toward philo-Semitism ever since the founding of the republic.

It is no coincidence that, as regular church attendance has declined and secular wokeism has ascended in America and throughout the West in general, anti-Semitism has skyrocketed. In the year 2024, any Jewish American who throws in his lot with wokeism and not the one entity pragmatically capable of subduing wokeism, the American church, is foolish beyond measure.

The more biblically oriented and the more authentically Christian America is, the better off both America and American Jews will be. The alternative paradigm—the doctrinaire "separation-ism" of liberal groups such as the ADL and the AJC, which rejects Christianity in the public square—diminishes the very Bible that is the Jewish people's greatest inheritance, embitters the very Christians who are the greatest natural friends of both the Jewish people and the State of Israel, sours Jewish–Christian relations, and vitiates the only affirmative force capable of vanquishing the hegemonic wokeism that poses an existential threat to the American Jewish experience.

American Jews should therefore advocate for an American public square that is more explicitly oriented toward God and Scripture—even if that is not strictly limited to the *shared* Judeo-Christian inheritance, such as the Ten Commandments, and will at times take the inevitable form of sectarian Christianity. The Judeo-Christian tradition, more generally, is the only affirmative positive force capable of withstanding and possibly rolling back the three hegemonic forces that today threaten ruin for the West: wokeism, Islamism, and global neoliberalism.

At times, it will also be necessary for American Christians to move beyond more abstract appeals to the Judeo-Christian tradition at large, and to simply promote *Christianity qua Christianity*. Even if one does not believe in the truth of the Christian faith—and any God-fearing Jew, by definition, does not—there is a compelling tactical reason to promote a biblically oriented public square that will, in America, sometimes take sectarian Christian form. Christianity is America's predominant religion, and it is the only concrete force in existence that is truly capable of providing a totalizing worldview alternative to wokeism, Islamism, and global neoliberalism. Thus, the Jewish–Christian anti-"separation-ism" alliance must be comfortable with a public square that, while often ecumenical and oriented toward promotion of foundational moral components of the Hebrew Bible such as the Ten Commandments or the Seven Noahide Laws, will nonetheless sometimes veer into promotion of Christianity *tout court*. There is a strong tactical basis for even non-Christians, such as myself, to make peace with such an arrangement.

Liberal "separation-ists"—Jewish and Christian alike—assuredly blanch at that. It is worth addressing their concerns.

First, religious free exercise in America has probably never been more robustly enforced in the federal courts than it is right now. The Roberts Court has repeatedly strengthened religious liberty jurisprudence in the areas of the Religious Freedom Restoration Act (RFRA) and the First Amendment's Free Exercise Clause. It is also notable that the Supreme Court rendered a *unanimous* ruling in the 2023 Title VII case of *Groff v. DeJoy*, an opinion rightly celebrated by Orthodox Jewish organizations because it mandated greater workplace accommodation for Sabbath observers. Free exercise for religious minorities is very secure in America, and it is often not even a divisive issue in the courts. Not only is Christian dominance of American Jewry not a viable or even remotely plausible threat, but our jurisprudence is more than capable of withstanding such a threat even if it were to somehow materialize.

Second, over the longer run, American Jews need a stronger American church so that, in George Washington's famous words, the "Children of the Stock of Abraham who dwell in this land . . . shall sit in safety under his own vine and fig tree, and there shall be none to make him afraid."[44] The present threat to American Jewry comes not from Christians, but from leftist intersectionalists, keffiyeh-clad Hamasniks in progressive enclaves, and imperial globalists in places like Brussels and Davos who seek to homogenize the world in their image and eradicate all particularist distinctions that might stand in the way. It is only a differing affirmative, all-encompassing force that can possibly withstand this onslaught and preserve Western civilization's biblical and national inheritance. At this time, the only affirmative force now capable of saving America from the woke mind virus, from totalitarian Islamism, and from the softer tyranny of homogenizing global neoliberalism, is the church. That is the simple truth.

Ergo, if one believes that wokeism, Islamism, and global neoliberalism must be decisively rejected—as every God-fearing Jew, Zionist, and American patriot should—then one must support measures to fortify the American church. But church attendance has been declining, and Christians are repeatedly told they suffer from excessive "privilege." Ending a legal and cultural paradigm of "separation-ism" can help tame anti-Christian hostility, embolden individual Christians, and fortify the church. For tactical purposes and also for reasons of basic survival and preservation, American Jews must enthusiastically support all of this.

It is imperative that Jews and Christians unite to defeat our common civilizational foes. That necessitates, among other things, a public square that is hospitable once again for expressions of authentic biblical religiosity. And that, in turn, requires a Jewish–Christian anti-"separation-ism" alliance between the original People of the Book and the "grafted [Gentile] wild shoot."[45]

Western civilization now finds itself at a crossroads. The Jewish people and Jewish civilization are under sustained and comprehensive assault as they have not been since the defeat of Nazi Germany in 1945. The Jewish State of Israel is under military assault the likes of which it has not endured since the Yom Kippur War in 1973, and under its worst assault in the amorphous court of international "legitimacy" in decades—perhaps since its founding in 1948. Meanwhile, Christianity, which has done more than any other force in history to develop and build the contemporary West, is treated by sneering societal elites as a regressive influence and a relic of a benighted past. Christians in Western countries are not necessarily physically endangered in the same way Jews increasingly are, but they are certainly mocked, disparaged, scorned, and sometimes even legally discriminated against.

This predicament is exacerbated by the harrowing nature of the forces that now rise in the Judeo-Christian tradition's stead, hoping and intending to supplant it. Wokeism, the cancerous species of "progressive" leftism that follows the well-worn path of its noxious Marxist forebear by arbitrarily dividing society into "oppressor" and "oppressed" classes, places Jews and Christians alike squarely in its crosshairs. Totalitarian Islamism, whose barbarism the United States experienced on September 11, 2001, and which the world vividly saw in the Simchat Torah Massacre of 2023, threatens to conquer and replace Western nations through a combination of bloody conquest and mass migration—with the latter all too frequently encouraged and abetted by subversive elites eager to tailor immigration policy to corporate or "politically incorrect" interests rather than their actual national interests.

Meanwhile, the ever-ascendant tide of global neoliberalism continues to snuff out all the various patchworks of laws, principles, beliefs, customs, religious traditions, and folkways that constitute modern Westphalian nation-states. Homogenizing neoliberalism continues to spread like a conflagration, engulfing and extinguishing all the particular nations, subnational entities, and inherited ways of life that long predominated before its ascent. This neoliberalism, promulgated by leading transnational institutions such as the United Nations and the World Trade Organization and predicated as it is upon free and open movement of labor, goods, and capital, is fundamentally anti-border, anti-sovereignty, and anti-tradition—and therefore anti-Jewish and anti-Christian. It is emblematic of perhaps a "softer" tyranny, but a tyranny that threatens to eliminate cherished national and particular traditions nonetheless.

It is ultimately inconsequential that the three great existential threats to the biblical, Judeo-Christian, nationalist heritage that has long defined the West—wokeism, Islamism, and global neoliberalism—are in deep intellectual tension with each other at best, and are fundamentally incompatible with each other at worst. It matters not to the rainbow flag-flying wokester that Islamists consider homosexual conduct to be a capital offense; and it matters not to the globalist sitting in Turtle Bay or Brussels that the Islamists seek to conquer in the name of Islam, not neoliberalism. What wokeism, Islamism, and global neoliberalism have in common with each other is something that has served as perhaps the oldest basis for an alliance in the entire history of human affairs: a mutual enemy. For wokester, Islamist, and global neoliberal alike, that mutual enemy is Western civilization itself: the Bible, Christianity, Judaism, the Anglo-American legal inheritance (which is itself broadly downstream of Scripture), and the post-1648 modern Westphalian nation-state. The enemy of my enemy, as it is said, is my friend.

If traditional Jews and Christians—and the biblical Western order, more generally—are to survive this harrowing multifaceted onslaught and endure with their own unique customs, values, and ways of life intact, they must emulate the humility and restraint of biblical Israel and the ancient Israelites. Thousands of years ago, the United Kingdom of King David rejected any temptation to forcibly export its values elsewhere, or to invade or conquer lands beyond the borders that God Himself had decreed to the Jewish patriarchs long before David came to Jerusalem from Hebron. In modern times, if Jews and Christians want to resist the eradication of their distinctive traditions and withstand both subsumption into the amorphous global neoliberal blob and conquest at the hands of wokeism or Islamism, they, too, must be prudent and exercise great humility.

It would be great to authoritatively roll back and defeat once and for all the Western order–destabilizing and Judeo-Christian tradition–threatening three-headed monster of wokeism, Islamism, and global neoliberalism. But given how firmly entrenched all three forces now are, the most promising realistic path forward for Jews and Christians is to repel their hegemonic advance in a few key nations, thereby establishing a beachhead for a larger sustained civilizational counterinsurgency at a later (and more propitious) time.

The most obvious location for a leading pro-Western beachhead, due to historical, cultural, sociological, and political institutional reasons, is the United States itself. It thus follows that if Western civilization is going to have any chance of surviving as a distinct entity, it is first necessary that pro-Western, Judeo-Christian forces begin to build new civic institutions in the United States and recapture many of the extant civic and governmental institutions that have been taken over in recent decades by wokesters, global neoliberals, and Islamists.

This is easier said than done. The development of successful new institutions requires tremendous courage, time, patience, intellectual and financial resources, and an entrepreneurial sense of risk tolerance. Furthermore, the sheer scale of Judeo-Christian recapture of existing woke-overrun institutions that is now required to establish a counterinsurgency beachhead in the United States is nothing less than daunting. It is no secret that, well over a half-century past the ascendance of 1960s-era cultural radicalism and Western civilizational self-hatred, menacing forces have made substantial inroads in their broader Gramscian "march through the institutions."[46] The task is made even more daunting when one considers the sheer stubbornness of America's current woke-addled ruling class. But the tall nature of the order does not lessen the gravity and necessity of the task.

If today's societal elites and elite institutions are dedicated to the metastasis of wokeism and global neoliberalism, then the solution is to replace those addled, unpatriotic elites with a fresh group of patriotic, Judeo-Christian elites. Jewish and Christian parents must instill in their children, and educators must instill in their pupils, a genuine patriotism, a love of their hearth and home, and a distinctly public spirit and sense of civic-mindedness. They must inculcate in those children and pupils sound republican habits of mind in the hopes that they might contribute, in their own small way, to the saving of America and the survival of the West.

Where opportunities exist for new institutions that might rival the impotent and failing institutions of the status quo, they must be seized. And where opportunities exist within extant elite institutions to make inroads and embed Western civilization–saving Judeo-Christian traditionalists into positions of power and influence, they must be taken advantage of as well. These two approaches—rival institution-building and institutional recapture—are entirely complementary. Let's consider some examples.

The laudable development of new Hillsdale College–like liberal arts colleges that reject federal money and are oriented toward the Scripture-rooted good life, for instance, do not militate against efforts to elevate traditional Jews or Christians to positions of administrative and pedagogical prominence within the Ivy League and states' flagship public universities. Nor, for that matter, do efforts at launching new private classical schools or "Great Books" curricula–based charter schools militate against other efforts to make existing K–12 public schools more hospitable to the traditionalist American way of life. Nor, furthermore, do efforts to build less hostile technology and social media platforms militate in any way against efforts to embed defenders of the grandeur of Western civilization into positions of prominence within Big Tech companies (however far-fetched that may seem).

In short, both the "build new institutions" and "recapture existing institutions" paths must be pursued whenever, and wherever, the proper conditions exist and the opportunity is ripe. These will necessarily be *ad hoc*, case-by-case situations. Only careful discernment, prudence, and sound judgment can dictate which path—or paths—to embark upon, in any specific context. But in general, a comprehensive "all-of-the-above" strategy is necessary to fend off our subjugation and to meaningfully push back with cultural, civic, and political counteroffensives.

In the American political and legal arena, the traditionalist Judeo-Christian imperative is to embrace a robust, muscular statecraft that decisively rejects the liberal illusion of "values-neutrality" and unapologetically advances the Judeo-Christian substantive conception of human flourishing and the common good. The aforementioned Jewish–Christian anti-"separation-ism" alliance is one particularly illustrative example of what this might look like in practice, but such statecraft must go even further, touching upon all areas of American public and communal life.

The hour of our decadent and seemingly declining republic is sufficiently late that in every area of public American life—from the tax code to immigration policy to constitutional interpretation, and everything in between—it is necessary to promote and incentivize Judeo-Christian values and the Judeo-Christian way of life and to degrade and disincentivize the values and way of life of our opposing forces. We cannot rest until every intermediary between citizen and state—from the market to the rule of law—is rightfully and justly oriented toward American and Western civilizational self-preservation.[47]

The rot is simply too deep, at this juncture, for fainthearted alternative political paradigms, such as appealing to a "values-neutral" middle ground that is content to merely let the proverbial chips fall where they may so long as traditionalists put up a good fight in the "marketplace of ideas." This is a loser's mentality—the very mentality, in fact, that has gotten us into this terrible mess in the first place. For the better part of a century, those politicians purporting to act on behalf of Judeo-Christian traditionalists have done exactly this—speak their piece against physically and intellectually hegemonic foes and then bask in the undeserved contentment that, no matter how things shape up at the end of the day, they gave it their all. These elites have been bringing knives to gunfights for longer than I have been alive.

If the West is going to be saved, then the United States must first be saved. And if the United States is going to be saved, then traditionalist Jews and Christians must work in tandem like never before. Such a Jewish–Christian alliance must embrace the superiority of our values, our inheritance, and our way of life, and commit to fighting like hell across all avenues of public, political, and civic life to ensure our dispensation prevails—and that our foes' dispensation is vanquished. The only way out is through.[48]

In the end, it is not possible for "both sides" to have their say when it comes to the fate of Western civilization. There was no "both sides"–ing the Simchat Torah Massacre of October 7, 2023. There can be no "both sides"–ing the United Nations' ceaseless assaults on traditional biblical values, on Jewish particularism, and on Christian morality. And there can be no "both sides"–ing pedagogy and education, where ineffectual resistance and failure to organize a traditionalist response has resulted in the near-complete brainwashing of multiple generations of impressionable young Americans. There can be no "both sides"–ing of those who understand that America was predicated upon the ethics and political theory of the Hebrew Bible and cannot possibly be understood without it, and those who do not.

There can be no "both sides"–ing any of this because one way of life, one vision, one order, and one dispensation must ultimately prevail. "Live and let live," the classical liberal's preferred escape hatch ever since the days of John Stuart Mill, is not just woefully insufficient against such a threat—it is outright suicidal.[49] Western civilization's cold civil war, roiling now for at least a century, necessarily ends up as a zero-sum game: One side must win, and the other side must lose.

For nearly a century, traditionalist Jews and Christians have been losing to the forces of progressive wokeism, totalitarian Islamism, and global neoliberalism—and losing badly. Any chance that the West has of stemming this poisonous tide begins with a concerted Jewish–Christian alliance to build, fortify, and sustain an American institutional foothold in defense of the biblical values and ideals upon which our entire civilizational edifice developed in the first instance. If the West is to have any chance, the turnaround must commence with the special people that Abraham Lincoln described so long ago as "almost chosen"—Americans.[50]

American Jewish and Christian defenders of the West: Are you up to the task? The hour is late. We are running out of time. And we have a civilization to save.

NOTES

CHAPTER 1

1. "Psalms Book 1, Chapter 23," Chabad.org https://www.chabad.org/library/article_cdo/aid/6323/jewish/Chapter-23.htm.

2. "Psalms Book 1, Chapter 23," Chabad.org https://www.chabad.org/library/article_cdo/aid/6323/jewish/Chapter-23.htm.

3. Josh Hammer, "The People of Israel Live," *Newsweek,* October 23, 2023, https://www.newsweek.com/people-israel-live-opinion-1834391.

4. "Hamas Covenant 1988," Yale Law School, Lillian Goldman Law Library, August 18, 1988, https://avalon.law.yale.edu/20th_century/hamas.asp.

5. Michael Oren, "Hamas Mortally Threatens Israel's Existence," *Wall Street Journal,* October 22, 2023, https://www.wsj.com/articles/hamas-mortally-threatens-israels-existence-1a805475.

6. J. Sellers Hill and Nia L. Orakwue, "Harvard Student Groups Face Intense Backlash for Statement Calling Israel 'Entirely Responsible' for Hamas Attack," *Harvard Crimson,* October 10, 2023, https://www.thecrimson.com/article/2023/10/10/psc-statement-backlash/.

7. Olivia Land, "'Reprehensible' Anti-Israel Protesters Chant 'Gas the Jews' Outside Sydney Opera House: Video," *New York Post,* October 10, 2023, https://nypost.com/2023/10/10/reprehensible-protestors-chant-gas-the-jews-outside-sydney-opera-house/.

8. Luke Tress, "Jewish Students Locked in NYC's Cooper Union as Protesters Chanted 'Free Palestine,'" *Times of Israel,* October 26, 2023, https://www.timesofisrael.com/jewish-students-barricade-in-nycs-cooper-union-as-protesters-chant-free-palestine/.

9. Phil Hilsel and Todd Miyazawa, "Jewish Man Killed in Altercation at Dueling Pro-Israel and Pro-Palestinian Rallies in California," *NBC News,* November 6, 2023 (updated April 5, 2024), https://www.nbcnews.com/news/us-news/man-dies-hitting-head-israel-palestinian-rallies-california-officials-rcna123942.

10. Jaryn Crouson, "Violent Protesters Disrupt Speech Condemning Hamas; University Police Sit Back & Do Nothing," Young America's Foundation, November 17, 2023, https://yaf.org/news/violent-protesters-disrupt-speech-condemning-hamas-university-police-sit-back-do-nothing/.

11. Josh Hammer, "The University of Michigan Failed to Protect My Right to Free Speech," *Newsweek,* November 24, 2023, https://www.newsweek.com/university-michigan-failed-protect-my-right-free-speech-opinion-1846259.

12. "Loyola ends Jewish speaker event early after pro-Palestinian disruption," The College Fix, November 4, 2024, https://www.thecollegefix.com/loyola-cancels-jewish-speaker-after-pro-palestinian-disruption/.

13. "3 Contentious Exchanges at the College Antisemitism Hearing," *New York Times*, December 26, 2023, https://www.nytimes.com/2023/12/06/us/harvard-mit-penn-presidents-antisemitism-hearing.html.

14. Phil Helsel, "Gaza War Protesters Shut Down Golden Gate Bridge, Block Traffic in Other Cities," *NBC News*, April 15, 2024, https://www.nbcnews.com/news/us-news/gaza-war-protesters-shut-golden-gate-bridge-block-traffic-rcna147945.

15. Jessica Blake, "New Study Highlights Campus Antisemitism 'Hot Spots,'" *Inside Higher Ed*, December 15, 2023, https://www.insidehighered.com/news/students/free-speech/2023/12/15/new-study-highlights-campus-antisemitism-hot-spots.

16. Sharon Otterman and Alan Blinder, "Over 100 Arrested at Columbia After Pro-Palestinian Protest," *New York Times*, April 18, 2024, https://www.nytimes.com/2024/04/18/nyregion/columbia-university-protests-antisemitism.html.

17. Caroline Downey, "Columbia Rabbi Urges Jewish Students to Go Home as Protesters Openly Cheer Hamas, Chant 'Burn Tel Aviv to the Ground,'" *National Review*, April 21, 2024, https://www.nationalreview.com/news/pro-palestinian-protesters-outside-columbia-urge-hamas-to-burn-tel-aviv-to-the-ground.

18. "The Ivy League's Anti-Israel Protest Meltdown," *Wall Street Journal*, April 22, 2024, https://www.wsj.com/articles/ivy-league-protests-palestine-israel-hamas-columbia-yale-1b66od95.

19. Matthew Impelli, "Hezbollah Flag at US College Protest Sparks Fury," *Newsweek*, April 26, 2024, https://www.newsweek.com/pro-palestinian-protest-princeton-hezbollah-1894654.

20. Greg Wehner, "Video Shows Anti-Israel Protesters Block Jewish Student from Getting to Class; UCLA Responds," *Fox News*, April 30, 2024, https://www.foxnews.com/us/video-shows-anti-israel-protesters-block-jewish-student-getting-class-ucla-responds; *Yitzchok Frankel v. Regents of the University of California*, United States District Court, C.D. California (August 13, 2024), available at https://caselaw.findlaw.com/court/us-dis-crt-cd-cal/116482817.html.

21. Josh Hammer, "How to Lock Up Those Nasty Pro-Hamas and Gaza Protestors," *New York Post*, June 15, 2024, https://nypost.com/2024/06/15/opinion/how-to-lock-up-those-nasty-pro-hamas-and-gaza-protestors.

22. See Josh Hammer, *"How to Lock Up Those Nasty Pro-Hamas and Gaza Protestors."*

23. "We're Protecting You: Full Text of Netanyahu's Address to Congress," *Times of Israel*, July 25, 2024, https://www.timesofisrael.com/were-protecting-you-full-text-of-netanyahus-address-to-congress (transcript of Netanyahu's speech to Congress on July 24, 2024).

24. See Steven Stalinsky "Who's Behind the Anti-Israel Protests," *The Wall Street Journal,* April 22, 2024, https://www.wsj.com/articles/whos-behind-the -anti-israel-protests-hamas-gaza-hezbollah-talking-points-d2f538ca.

25. Brie Stimson, "Anti-Israel Protesters Heard Shouting 'We Are Hamas,' 'Long Live Hamas' amid Columbia U Demonstrations," Fox News, April 19, 2024, https://www.foxnews.com/us/anti-israel-protesters-heard-shouting-we -hamas-long-live-hamas-columbia-university-demonstrations.

26. Ecclesiastes 1:9, *The Complete Jewish Bible with Rashi Commentary,* Chabad.org, https://www.chabad.org/library/bible_cdo/aid/16462/jewish/Chapter-1. htm.

27. See Daniel Arkin, "Antisemitic Incidents in the U.S. Surged after Oct. 7 Hamas Attack, Advocacy Group Say," NBC News, January 10, 2024, https:// www.nbcnews.com/news/us-news/antisemitic-incidents-us-jumped-360-oct -7-hamas-attack-advocacy-group-rcna133104; Nicole Chavez, "Antisemitic Incidents in the US Reached Record High Last Year, Up 140% from 2022, ADL Says," CNN, April 16, 2024, https://www.cnn.com/2024/04/16/us /adl-antisemtism-2023-audit-reaj/index.html; "New Study Shows Five-fold Increase in Online Antisemitism Since October ," *Haaretz,* March 26, 2024, https://www.haaretz.com/jewish/2024-03-26/ty-article/.premium /new-study-shows-five-fold-increase-in-online-antisemitism-since-october-7 /0000018e-7b1b-d680-a1cf-ff1f2c780000; "UK Jewish Group Records All-time High in Antisemitic Incidents after October 7," *Times of Israel,* February 5, 2024, https://www.timesofisrael.com/uk-jewish-group -records-all-time-high-in-antisemitic-incidents-after-october-7/.

28. See "We're Protecting You: Full Text of Netanyahu's Address to Congress."

29. See generally William F. Buckley Jr., God and Man at Yale: The Superstitions of 'Academic Freedom' (1951).

30. See generally Christopher R. Rufo, *America's Cultural Revolution: How the Radical Left Conquered Everything* (Broadside Books, 2023).

31. Josh Hammer, "The Peace Process That Never Was," *Tablet,* March 22, 2021, https://www.tabletmag.com/sections/israel-middle-east/articles /peace-process-that-never-was-josh-hammer.

32. "Remarks by President Biden on the United States' Response to Hamas's Terrorist Attacks Against Israel and Russia's Ongoing Brutal War Against Ukraine," October 20, 2023, https://www.whitehouse.gov/briefing-room/ speeches-remarks/2023/10/20/remarks-by-president-biden-on-the-unites -states-response-to-hamass-terrorist-attacks-against-israel-and-russias -ongoing-brutal-war-against-ukraine.

33. Jordan Schachtel, "The Unpopular Truth: Surveys Show That Most Palestinians Support Hamas and Fellow Jihadist Compatriot Groups," *The Dossier,* October 31, 2023, https://www.dossier.today/p/the-unpopular-truth -surveys-show.

34. Isaac Schor, "Tucker Carlson Launches Stunning Attack on Ben Shapiro: He 'Obviously' Doesn't 'Care About America,'" *MediaIte,* December 30, 2023, https://www.mediaite.com/news/tucker-carlson-launches-stunning-attack -on-ben-shapiro-he-obviously-doesnt-care-about-america/.

35. Brett Martin, "Jerry Seinfeld Says Movies Are Over. Here's Why He Made One Anyway," *GQ*, April 22, 2024, https://www.gq.com/story/jerry-seinfeld-gq-hype.

36. Franklin Foer, "The Golden Age of American Jews Is Ending," *The Atlantic*, April 2024, https://www.theatlantic.com/magazine/archive/2024/04/us-anti-semitism-jewish-american-safety/677469/.

37. "English Haggadah Text with Instructional Guide," Chabad.org, https://www.chabad.org/holidays/passover/pesach_cdo/aid/661624/jewish/English-Haggadah-Text.htm.

38. See, e.g., Genesis 12:2: "And I will make you into a great nation, and I will bless you, and I will aggrandize your name, and [you shall] be a blessing." https://www.chabad.org/library/bible_cdo/aid/8176/jewish/Chapter-12.htm.

39. See Tzvi Freeman, "What Is Emunah?" Chabad.org, n.d., https://www.chabad.org/library/article_cdo/aid/1398519/jewish/Emunah.htm.

40. See Franklin Foer, "The Golden Age of American Jews Is Ending."

41. See generally "Israel/Palestine Policy Debate: Peter Beinart vs. Josh Hammer," New Zionist Congress, YouTube Video, July 20, 2021, https://www.youtube.com/watch?v=mhiYAo5-ahU.

42. "The Size of the U.S. Jewish Population," Pew Research Center, May 11, 2021, https://www.pewresearch.org/religion/2021/05/11/the-size-of-the-u-s-jewish-population/.

43. John Spencer, "Israel Has Created a New Standard for Urban Warfare. Why Will No One Admit It?" *Newsweek*, March 25, 2024, https://www.newsweek.com/israel-has-created-new-standard-urban-warfare-why-will-no-one-admit-it-opinion-1883286.

44. See, e.g., Marina Medvin, April 24, 2024, https://twitter.com/MarinaMedvin/status/1783066947443130812; Ohad Merlin, "'Eradicate the US': American Student Group Publishes, Then Deletes Controversial Message," *Jerusalem Post*, September 8, 2024, https://www.jpost.com/diaspora/antisemitism/article-819216.

45. Stu, May 7, 2024, https://twitter.com/thestustustudio/status/178804 1873652646213.

46. Christopher F. Rufo, May 8, 2024, https://twitter.com/realchrisrufo/status/1788252106190889276.

CHAPTER 2

1. Exodus 19:3, *The Complete Jewish Bible with Rashi Commentary*, Chabad.org, https://www.chabad.org/library/bible_cdo/aid/9880/jewish/Chapter-19.htm#v3.

2. "Logical Proof of the Revelation at Mt. Sinai," *Letters from the Rebbe*, July 19, 1954, https://www.chabad.org/therebbe/letters/default_cdo/aid/2076252/jewish/Logical-Proof-of-the-Revelation-at-Mt-Sinai.htm.

3. See, e.g., Yoram Hazony, "The Bible and Leo Strauss," *Perspectives on Political Science* 45, no. 3 (2016), 190–207, http://dx.doi.org/10.1080/10457097.2016 .1175791.

4. Genesis 1:27, *The Complete Jewish Bible with Rashi Commentary*, Chabad.org, https://www.chabad.org/library/bible_cdo/aid/8165/jewish /Chapter-1.htm.

5. Exodus 20:2, *The Complete Jewish Bible with Rashi Commentary*, Chabad.org, https://www.chabad.org/library/bible_cdo/aid/9881/jewish/Chapter -20.htm.

6. Alfred Korzybski, *Manhood of Humanity: The Science and Art of Human Engineering*, 2nd ed (Lakeville, CT: The International Non-Aristotelian Library Publishing Company, 1968).

7. Cassius Jackson Keyser, "Lecture XX: Korzybski's Concept of Man," in *Mathematical Philosophy: A Study of Fate and Freedom Lectures for Educated Laymen*, 1st ed. (New York, NY: E. P. Dutton, 1922). Reprinted in Korzybski, *Manhood of Humanity*, 296.

8. Cassius Jackson Keyser, "Lecture XX: Korzybski's Concept of Man," 297.

9. Cassius Jackson Keyser, "Lecture XX: Korzybski's Concept of Man," 298–99.

10. Cassius Jackson Keyser, "Lecture XX: Korzybski's Concept of Man," 299.

11. Cassius Jackson Keyser, "Lecture XX: Korzybski's Concept of Man," 299.

12. See, e.g., Genesis 1:3 ("And God said, 'Let there be light," and there was light.'"), https://www.chabad.org/library/bible_cdo/aid/8165/jewish /Chapter-1.htm.

13. "The Morning Prayers, Upon Arising in the Morning," Sefaria. org, https:// www.sefaria.org/Weekday_Siddur_Sefard_Linear%2C_The _Morning_Prayers%2C_Baruch_She'amar.6?lang=bi.

14. Midrash Tanchuma, Naso 16a. See also Bamidbar Raba, 13 6a; Tanya Chapters 33, 36.

15. Schneur Zalman, *Likutei Amarim* (*Tanya*) by Rabbi Schneur Zalman of Liadi. Translated from the Hebrew, with an Introduction, 3rd rev. ed. (Brooklyn, NY: Kehot Publication Society, 1969), chapter 2.

16. See Menachem Mendel Schneerson, *I Will Choose The King: BeYom Ashtei-Asor Yom*, 5731. Translated by Eliyahu Touger and Sholom B. Wineberg (Brooklyn, NY: Sichos in English, 2011).

17. See, e.g., Liel Liebovitz, "The Return of Paganism," Commentary, May 2023, https://www.commentary.org/articles/liel-leibovitz/paganism-afflicts -america/.

18. Oren Cass, "Constructing Conservatism," First Things, October 2024, https://www.firstthings.com/article/2024/10/constructing-conservatism.

19. Oren Cass, "Constructing Conservatism."

20. Deuteronomy 5:30, Torah Reading for Va'etchanan, Chabad.org, https:// www.chabad.org/parshah/torahreading.asp?aid=2495794.

21. See generally Shimon Dovid Cowen, *The Theory and Practice of Universal Ethics—The Noahide Laws* (chapter 6).

22. Jeremy England, "Live by the Law or Die on the Cross," *Tablet*, May 28, 2024, https://www.tabletmag.com/sections/news/articles/live-law-die-cross-israel.

23. See Rabbi Menachem Mendel Schneerson, "Starting from a Moral Code that Unites All Mankind: Message from the Rebbe," available at https://asknoah.org/wp-content/uploads/7-Laws-Outreach-Booklet-AskNoah.pdf.

24. See generally Yoram Hazony, *The Virtue of Nationalism* (Hachette Book Group, 2018); Brad Littlejohn, "In Defense of Nationalism: Notes on Yoram Hazony and His Critics," Mere Orthodoxy, July 3, 2019, https://mereorthodoxy.com/defense-nationalism-notes-yoram-hazony-critics.

25. Steven Grosby, "Reading the Talmud in the Tower of London," Law and Liberty, July 31, 2013, https://lawliberty.org/reading-the-talmud-in-the-tower-of-london/.

26. See Cassius Jackson Keyser, "Lecture XX: Korzybski's Concept of Man."

27. Genesis 1:28, *The Complete Jewish Bible with Rashi Commentary*, Chabad.org, https://www.chabad.org/library/bible_cdo/aid/8165/jewish/Chapter-1.htm.

CHAPTER 3

1. Genesis Chapter 1, *The Complete Jewish Bible with Rashi Commentary*, Chabad.org, https://www.chabad.org/library/bible_cdo/aid/8165/jewish/Chapter-1.htm.

2. Leviticus Chapter 19, *The Complete Jewish Bible with Rashi Commentary*, Chabad.org, https://www.chabad.org/library/bible_cdo/aid/9920/jewish/Chapter-19.htm.

3. Leviticus Chapter 19.

4. See Shabbat 31a, https://www.sefaria.org/Shabbat.31a.

5. Shoshannah Brombacher, "On One Foot," Jewish Stories from the Midrash, Chabad.org, n.d., https://www.chabad.org/library/article_cdo/aid/689306/jewish/On-One-Foot.htm.

6. See, e.g., Zohar 117a, https://www.sefaria.org/Zohar%2C_Vayera.30.444-451.

7. Sotah 14a, https://www.sefaria.org/Sotah.14a.

8. See, e.g., *Gold from the Land of Israel: A New Light on the Weekly Torah Portion From the Writings of Rabbi Abraham Isaac HaKohen Kook*, 297–298.

9. See, e.g., Josh Hammer, "The Fifth Circuit Rejects the Lie of Transgender Pronouns," *National Review*, January 27, 2020, https://www.nationalreview.com/2020/01/transgender-pronouns-fifth-circuit-rejects-them-and-lie-they-stand-on.

10. Shabbat 88a, https://www.sefaria.org/Shabbat.88a.

11. Exodus 6:7, *The Complete Jewish Bible with Rashi Commentary*, Chabad.org, https://www.chabad.org/library/bible_cdo/aid/9867/jewish/Chapter-6.htm.

12. Exodus 8:18, *The Complete Jewish Bible with Rashi Commentary*, Chabad.org, https://www.chabad.org/library/bible_cdo/aid/9869/jewish/Chapter-8 .htm.

13. See generally Exodus Chapter 12, *The Complete Jewish Bible with Rashi Commentary*, Chabad.org, https://www.chabad.org/library/bible_cdo/aid /9873/jewish/Chapter-12.htm.

14. *Hirsch Chumash*, Exodus Chapter 12. See also: Rabbi Joseph B. Soloveitchik in *Gesher 1960*.

15. Josh Hammer, Overrule *Stare Decisis*," *National Review*, Fall, 2020, https:// nationalaffairs.com/publications/detail/overrule-stare-decisis.

16. Numbers 15:16, *The Complete Jewish Bible with Rashi Commentary*, Chabad.org, https://www.chabad.org/library/bible_cdo/aid/9943/jewish/Chapter -15.htm.

17. Michael Broyde, "The Hidden Influence of Jewish Law on the Common Law Tradition: One Lost Example," Emory Law Scholarly Commons, 2008, https://scholarlycommons.law.emory.edu/cgi/viewcontent.cgi?article=1039 &context=faculty-articles.

18. Deuteronomy Chapter 17, *The Complete Jewish Bible with Rashi Commentary*, Chabad.org, https://www.chabad.org/library/bible_cdo/aid/9981/jewish /Chapter-17.htm.

19. Pesach Wolicki, "Shoftim—Why Is the Rabbinic Law Legitimate?" *The Israel Bible*, September 7, 2024, https://theisraelbible.com/shoftim-why -is-the-rabbinic-law-legitimate/.

20. Leviticus Chapter 10, *The Complete Jewish Bible with Rashi Commentary*, Chabad .org, https://www.chabad.org/library/bible_cdo/aid/9911/jewish/Chapter -10.htm.

21. Aryeh Kaplan, "The Rules of Jewish Law," Aish.com, n.d., https://aish .com/48932007.

22. For more, see Joseph Karo, *Jewish Holy Scriptures: The Shulchan Aruch* (Jewish Virtual Library); Israel Meir Kagan, *Mishneh Brurah* (Jewish Virtual Library). An entire corpus of Jewish ethical works was particularly popular in the medieval period, with literature such as *Chovot HaLevavot* by Bahya ibn Paquda, *Ma'alot ha-Middot* by Jehiel ben Jekuthiel Anav, *Orchot Tzaddikim* by anonymous, and *Kad ha-Kemah* by Bahya ben Asher. This period was later referred to as the *Musar Movement*—literally, the "ethical movement."

23. Mark Goldfeder, "Defining and Defending Borders; Just and Legal Wars in Jewish Thought and Practice," *Touro Law Review* 30, no. 3 (2014), https:// digitalcommons.tourolaw.edu/lawreview/vol30/iss3/8.

24. Isaiah 2:4; Jeremiah 29:7, *The Complete Jewish Bible with Rashi Commentary*, Chabad.org, https://www.chabad.org/library/bible_cdo/aid/15933/jewish /Chapter-2.htm; https://www.chabad.org/library/bible_cdo/aid/16026 /jewish/Chapter-29.htm.

25. Yonatan Brafman, *Toward a Modern Jewish Virtue Ethics of Education* (Jewish Theological Seminary).

26. Joseph Garfinkle, *The Eight Chapters of Maimonides on Ethics (Shemonah Perakim): A Psychological and Ethical Treatise, Edited, Annotated, and Translated, With an Introduction (Classic Reprint)* (Forgotten Books, 2024).

27. Rambam on Pirkei Avot, Mishnah 3:15, https://www.sefaria.org/Rambam _on_Pirkei_Avot.3.15.1

28. Rambam on Pirkei Avot, Mishnah 3:15.

29. Mishnah Sanhedrin 4:5, https://www.sefaria.org/Mishnah_Sanhedrin.4.5; *see also* Sanhedrin 37a, https://www.sefaria.org/Sanhedrin.37a

30. See also Moshe Taragin, *Mai Chazit - Whose Blood Is Redder*. Talmudic Methodology - Choshen Mishpat - Lesson 31. Torat Har Etzion, February, 2015.

31. Eugene Korn, "Jewish Ethics," *St. Andrews Encyclopedia of Theology* (University of St. Andrews, 2024).

32. Norris Turner Piers, "Harm and Mill's Harm Principle," *Ethics* 124, no. 2 (January 2014), 299–326.

33. *See* Leviticus 19:28; Deuteronomy 21:20; Leviticus 19:14, *The Complete Jewish Bible with Rashi Commentary*, Chabad.org, https://www.chabad.org/library /bible_cdo/aid/9920/jewish/Chapter-19.htm; https://www.chabad.org /library/bible_cdo/aid/9985/jewish/Chapter-21.htm; https://www.chabad .org/library/bible_cdo/aid/9920/jewish/Chapter-19.htm. For the authentic Jewish and Halachic view of lust more generally, see: Rafi Eis, "What Judaism Teaches About Lust," First Things, May 5, 2023, https://www.firstthings .com/web-exclusives/2023/05/what-judaism-teaches-about-lust.

34. Shabbat 54b, https://www.sefaria.org/Shabbat.54b.20.

35. Leviticus 19:16, *The Complete Jewish Bible with Rashi Commentary*, Chabad.org, https://www.chabad.org/library/bible_cdo/aid/9920/jewish/Chapter-19 .htm.

36. See, *e.g.*, Nathan Schlueter, "No, But Classical Liberalism Can," Law & Liberty, March 5, 2018, https://lawliberty.org/forum/no-but-classical -liberalism-can/.

37. *Sanhedrin* 27b, https://www.sefaria.org/Sanhedrin.27b.19.

38. See Aharon Lichtenstein, *By His Light: Character and Values in the Service of God* (Maggid Books, 2016).

39. "Introducing Harav Lichtenstein ztl, Source Sheet," Torat Har Etzion, May, 2015, https://etzion.org.il/en/philosophy/great-thinkers/harav-aharon -lichtenstein/introducing-harav-lichtenstein-ztl-source-sheet.

40. Nechemia Coopersmith, *Rabbi Noach Weinberg's 48 Ways to Wisdom* (ArtScroll Publishing, 2017).

41. Mishneh Torah (Hilchot De'ot 4:4), https://www.sefaria.org/Mishneh _Torah%2C_Human_Dispositions.4.4. See also Orchot Rabbeinu 189.

42. Ecclesiastes 2:24, *The Complete Jewish Bible with Rashi Commentary*, Chabad.org, https://www.chabad.org/library/bible_cdo/aid/16463/jewish/Chapter -2.htm.

43. Tractate *Pesachim* 109a, https://www.sefaria.org/Pesachim.109a.

44. Psalms 2:11, *The Complete Jewish Bible with Rashi Commentary*, Chabad.org, https://www.chabad.org/library/bible_cdo/aid/16223/jewish/Chapter -2.htm.

45. Leviticus 19:1–2.

46. Binyamin Zimmerman, *Kedoshim Tihyu: The Holiness of Interpersonal Perfection* (Torat Har Etzion, 2016).

47. Binyamin Zimmerman, *Kedoshim Tihyu*.

48. Binyamin Zimmerman, *Kedoshim Tihyu*.

49. Shoshannah Brombacher, "On One Foot."

50. "From John Adams to Massachusetts Militia, 11 October 1798," Founders Online, https://founders.archives.gov/documents/Adams/99-02-02-3102.

51. See generally Ronen Shoval, *Holiness and Society: A Socio-Political Exploration of the Mosaic Tradition* (Routledge, 2024).

52. Genesis 6:20, *The Complete Jewish Bible with Rashi Commentary*, Chabad.org, https://www.chabad.org/library/bible_cdo/aid/8171/jewish/Chapter-6.htm.

53. Rambam on Pirkei Avot, Mishnah 3:15; Tractate Sanhedrin 37a.

54. Tractate Bava Metzia 62a-b, https://www.sefaria.org/Bava_Metzia.62a .1-62b.12.

55. Josh Hammer, "Common Good Originalism: Our Tradition and Our Path Forward," *Harv. J.L. & Pub. Pol'y* 44 (2021), 917, 942.

CHAPTER 4

1. Deuteronomy 16, *The Complete Jewish Bible with Rashi Commentary*, Chabad.org, https://www.chabad.org/library/bible_cdo/aid/9980/jewish/Chapter-16 .htm. https://www.nps.gov/liho/learn/historyculture/peoriaspeech.htm.

2. On Aristotle, see Glenn Ellmers, "'Conservatism' is no Longer Enough," The American Mind, March 24, 2021, https://americanmind.org/salvo/why -the-claremont-institute-is-not-conservative-and-you-shouldnt-be-either.

3. Josh Hammer, *Standing Athwart History: Anti-Obergefell Popular Constitutionalism and Judicial Supremacy's Long-Term Triumph*, 16 U. St. Thomas L.J. 178 (2020).

4. Rafi Eis, "National Unity and National Perpetuation," *National Affairs*, Number 61, Fall 2024, https://www.nationalaffairs.com/publications /detail/national-unity-and-national-perpetuation.

5. Second Inaugural Address of Abraham Lincoln, The Avalon Project, Yale Law School, https://avalon.law.yale.edu/19th_century/lincoln2.asp.

6. Soloveichik, Meir. *Lincoln's Almost Chosen People*. First Things, https://www .firstthings.com/article/2021/02/lincolns-almost-chosen-people.

7. See Dr. Yvette Alt Miller, "Abraham Lincoln and the Jews: 10 Fascinating Facts," Aish, https://aish.com/abraham-lincoln-and-the-jews-10-fascinating -facts/; "Ulysses S. Grant and General Orders No. 11," Ulysses S Grant National Historic Site, National Park Service, https://www.nps.gov/articles /000/ulysses-s-grant-and-general-orders-no-11.htm.

8. Rabbi David Wolpe, "Lincoln and the Jews," *Time*, March 20, 2015, https:// time.com/3753016/lincoln-and-the-jews/.

9. See Dr. Yvette Alt Miller, "Abraham Lincoln and the Jews: 10 Fascinating Facts," Aish, https://aish.com/abraham-lincoln-and-the-jews-10-fascinating-facts/; "Ulysses S. Grant and General Orders No. 11," Ulysses S Grant National Historic Site, National Park Service, https://www.nps.gov/articles/000/ulysses-s-grant-and-general-orders-no-11.htm.

10. John Marshall Gest, "The Influence of Biblical Texts Upon English Law," available at https://scholarship.law.upenn.edu/cgi/viewcontent.cgi?article=7211&context=penn_law_review.

11. John Marshall Gest, "The Influence of Biblical Texts Upon English Law," available at https://scholarship.law.upenn.edu/cgi/viewcontent.cgi?article=7211&context=penn_law_review.

12. Ofir Haivry and Yoram Hazony, "What Is Conservatism," *American Affairs*, Summer 2017, Vol. 1, No. 2, https://americanaffairsjournal.org/2017/05/what-is-conservatism/.

13. Ofir Haivry and Yoram Hazony, "What Is Conservatism," *American Affairs*, Summer 2017, Vol. 1, No. 2, https://americanaffairsjournal.org/2017/05/what-is-conservatism/.

14. Sara Lamm, "Justice, Justice, You Shall Pursue," The Israel Bible, November 4, 2024, https://theisraelbible.com/justice-justice-you-shall-pursue/.

15. See, e.g., James Madison's "Notes on the debates in the Federal Convention," available at https://avalon.law.yale.edu/subject_menus/debcont.asp.

16. *Sefer HaMitzvot*, Negative Commandments 290:1, available at https://www.sefaria.org/Sefer_HaMitzvot%2C_Negative_Commandments.290.1.

17. Exodus 23:7, available at https://www.chabad.org/library/bible_cdo/aid/9884/jewish/Chapter-23.htm.

18. Steven Crosby, "Reading the Talmud in the Tower of London," Law and Liberty, July 31, 2013, https://lawliberty.org/reading-the-talmud-in-the-tower-of-london/.

19. For the importance placed by Rabbinic Judaism on the intergenerational transmission of tradition, see, e.g., Pirkei Avot 1:1 ("Moses received the Torah from Sinai and gave it over to Joshua. Joshua gave it over to the Elders, the Elders to the Prophets, and the Prophets gave it over to the Men of the Great Assembly."), available at https://www.chabad.org/library/article_cdo/aid/2165/jewish/Chapter-One.htm.

20. See Ed Simon, *"Rabbi"* John Selden and the Restoration of the Jews to England," *Tablet*, December 15, 2017, https://www.tabletmag.com/sections/arts-letters/articles/john-selden-and-restoration-of-jews-to-england.

21. See Ofir Haivry and Yoram Hazony, "What Is Conservatism," *American Affairs*, Summer 2017, Vol. 1, No. 2, https://americanaffairsjournal.org/2017/05/what-is-conservatism?/.

22. See Ofir Haivry and Yoram Hazony, "What Is Conservatism?" *American Affairs*, Summer 2017, Vol. 1, No. 2, https://americanaffairsjournal.org/2017/05/what-is-conservatism/; Steven Grosby, "Reading the Talmud in the Tower of London," Law and Liberty. July 31, 2013, https://lawliberty.org/reading-the-talmud-in-the-tower-of-london/.

23. See Steven Grosby, "Reading the Talmud in the Tower of London," Law and Liberty, July 31, 2013, https://lawliberty.org/reading-the-talmud-in-the-tower -of-london/.

24. Haivry, Ofir. The British Christian Political Theorist Who Found the Answers in the Talmud. *Mosaic,* June 14, 2022, https://mosaicmagazine.com /picks/history-ideas/2022/06/the-british-christian-political-theorist-who -found-the-answers-in-the-talmud/.

25. *De Successionibus in Bona Defuncti* (1631). For a sampling of works displaying Selden's mastery of arcane Rabbinic law, see: *History of Tithes* (1617), *De Synhedriis* (1650), *De Successionibus* (1631), and others.

26. For more, see Ed Simon, "Rabbi' John Selden and the Restoration of the Jews to England," *Tablet,* December 15, 2017, https://www.tabletmag.com/sections /arts-letters/articles/john-selden-and-restoration-of-jews-to-england; Ofir Haivry and Yoram Hazony, "What Is Conservatism," *American Affairs,* Summer 2017, Vol. 1, No. 2, https://americanaffairsjournal.org/2017/05 /what-is-conservatism/; Steven Grosby, "Reading the Talmud in the Tower of London," Law and Liberty. July 31, 2013. https://lawliberty.org/reading -the-talmud-in-the-tower-of-london/.

27. See Yoram Hazony, *The Virtue of Nationalism* (Hachette Book Group, 2018).

28. See Ed Simon, "Rabbi' John Selden and the Restoration of the Jews to England," *Tablet,* December 15, 2017, https://www.tabletmag.com/sections /arts-letters/articles/john-selden-and-restoration-of-jews-to-england.

29. Ofir Haivry and Yoram Hazony, "What Is Conservatism," *American Affairs,* Summer 2017, Vol. 1, No. 2, https://americanaffairsjournal.org/2017/05 /what-is-conservatism/.

30. See Rich Tenorio, "Back in 1620, the Pilgrim Leader Behind Thanksgiving Was Hebrew-obsessed," *The Times of Israel,* November 20, 2020, https://www .timesofisrael.com/back-in-1620-the-pilgrim-leader-behind-the-1st -thanksgiving-was-hebrew-obsessed/.

31. Tsivya Fox, "How Hebrew Almost Became the Official Language of America," Israel365News, July 27, 2016, https://israel365news.com/309223/american -first-language-hebrew.

32. See, e.g., Eliezer Wenger, "Birkat Hagomel: The Laws of the Blessing of Thanksgiving," Chabad, https://www.chabad.org/library/article_cdo/aid /115308/jewish/Birkat-Hagomel.htm.

33. Daniel Slate, "Jewish Ideas in Plymouth Colony," *Mosaic,* November 25, 2020, https://mosaicmagazine.com/observation/history-ideas/2020/11/jewish -ideas-in-plymouth-colony/.

34. *From George Washington to the Hebrew Congregation in Newport, Rhode Island, 18 August 1790,* Founder Online, https://founders.archives.gov/documents /Washington/05-06-02-0135#:~:text=%E2%80%9CDeprived%20as%20 we%20heretofore%20have,%E2%80%9D%20(%20DLC:GW%20).

35. Josh Hammer, "Conservatives Should Aim Higher," Tomklingenstein.com, August 2, 2024, https://tomklingenstein.com/after-chevron-conservatives -should-aim-higher/.

36. Josh Hammer, "Conservatives Should Aim Higher," Tomklingenstein.com, August 2, 2024, https://tomklingenstein.com/after-chevron-conservatives -should-aim-higher/.

37. Josh Hammer, "Conservatives Should Aim Higher," Tomklingenstein.com, August 2, 2024, https://tomklingenstein.com/after-chevron-conservatives -should-aim-higher/.

38. Josh Hammer, "Conservatives Should Aim Higher," Tomklingenstein.com, August 2, 2024, https://tomklingenstein.com/after-chevron-conservatives -should-aim-higher/.

39. William Pencak, *Jews and Gentiles in Early America: 1654—1800.* (Ann Arbor) University of Michigan, 2005.

40. Article VI, Supreme Law, Clause 3: Oaths of Office, Constitution Annotated: Analysis and Interpretation of the US Constitution, https://constitution .congress.gov/browse/article-6/clause-3/.

41. Yosef Kaufmann, "Haym Salomon: The Man Who Financed the American Revolution," Chabad, https://www.chabad.org/library/article_cdo/aid /5175340/jewish/Haym-Salomon-The-Man-Who-Financed-the-American -Revolution.htm.

42. "The Great Seal," National Museum of American Diplomacy, March 19, 2018, https://diplomacy.state.gov/the-great-seal/.

43. Rich Tenorio, "When Moses Almost Parted the Red Sea on the Great Seal of the United States," *Times of Israel*, April 16, 2017, https://www.timesofisrael .com/when-moses-almost-parted-the-red-sea-on-the-great-seal-of-the -united-states/; see generally Philip Gorsky, *American Covenant: A History of Civil Religion from the Puritans to the Present,* (Princeton University Press, February 2017).

44. Lester Olson, *Emblems of American Community in the Revolutionary Era: A Study in Rhetorical Iconology* (Smithsonian Press, October 1991).

45. See, e.g., David Dalin, *Jews, Judaism, and the American Founding,* (Oxford University Press, April 2014).

46. For more on Judaism's contributions to the American political order, see Jonathan Silver, *Proclaim Liberty Throughout the Land: The Hebrew Bible in the United States: A Sourcebook,* (Toby Press, May 2019).

47. "The Founding Fathers and the Role of Hebrew in Shaping the United States," LangSouls, July 2023, https://langsouls.com/the-founding-fathers -and-the-role-of-hebrew-in-shaping-the-united-states/.

48. See Tsivya Fox, "How Hebrew Almost Became the Official Language of America," Israel365News, July 27, 2016, https://israel365news.com/309223 /american-first-language-hebrew.

49. Tsivya Fox, "How Hebrew Almost Became the Official Language of America," Israel365News, July 27, 2016, https://israel365news.com/309223 /american-first-language-hebrew.

50. "From John Adams to François Adriaan Van der Kemp, 16 February 1809," Founders Online, National Archives, https://founders.archives.gov /documents/Adams/99-02-02-5302; see generally Adams, Jefferson and the Jews: Supplementary Readings," Yeshiva University, https://www.yu.edu

/sites/default/files/inline-files/Adams-Jefferson-and-the-Jews
-Supplementary-Readings.pdf.

51. Ofir Haivry and Yoram Hazony, "American Nationalists," *The American Conservative*, July 2, 2020, https://www.theamericanconservative.com
/american-nationalists/.

52. "From John Adams to Massachusetts Militia, 11 October 1798," Founders Online, National Archives, https://founders.archives.gov/documents
/Adams/99-02-02-3102.

53. Joseph Prudhomme, "Zionism of the Founding Fathers," *Modern Age*, June 27, 2024, https://modernagejournal.com/zionism-of-the-founding-fathers
/241092/.

54. See Juliana Pilon, "Founding Philosemitism," *Law & Liberty*, October 3, 2023, https://lawliberty.org/book-review/founding-philosemitism/.

55. Ron Chernow, *Alexander Hamilton*, (Penguin Random House, March 29), 2005, p. 18, https://www.penguinrandomhouse.com/books/292945
/alexander-hamilton-by-ron-chernow.

56. Alexander Hamilton, "Comments on Jews, [N.P., N.D.]," Founders Online, National Archives, https://founders.archives.gov/documents/Hamilton
/01-26-02-0003-0009; Dr. Yvette Alt Miller, "Alexander Hamilton and the Jews," Aish, https://aish.com/alexander-hamilton-and-the-jews/.

57. See Tsivya Fox, "How Hebrew Almost Became the Official Language of America," Israel365News, July 27, 2016, https://israel365news.com/309223
/american-first-language-hebrew; see also Andrew Miller, "The Man Who Brought Hebrew to America," Armstrong Institute of Biblical Archaeology, January 14, 2023, https://armstronginstitute.org/828-the-man-who-brought
-hebrew-to-america.

58. See Meir Soloveichik, *Lincoln's Almost Chosen People*. First Things. https://
www.firstthings.com/article/2021/02/lincolns-almost-chosen-people.

59. Meir Soloveichik, *Lincoln's Almost Chosen People*. First Things. https://www
.firstthings.com/article/2021/02/lincolns-almost-chosen-people.

60. Meir Soloveichik, *Lincoln's Almost Chosen People*. First Things. https://www
.firstthings.com/article/2021/02/lincolns-almost-chosen-people.

61. Joseph Prudhomme, "Zionism of the Founding Fathers," *Modern Age*, June 27, 2024, https://modernagejournal.com/zionism-of-the-founding-fathers
/241092/.

62. See also: Porwancher, Andrew. *The Jewish World of Alexander Hamilton*. Princeton University Press. October, 2021.

63. See Joseph Prudhomme, "Zionism of the Founding Fathers," *Modern Age*, June 27, 2024. https://modernagejournal.com/zionism-of-the-founding
-fathers/241092/.

64. Joseph Prudhomme, "Zionism of the Founding Fathers," *Modern Age*, June 27, 2024. https://modernagejournal.com/zionism-of-the-founding-fathers
/241092/.

65. Joseph Prudhomme, "Zionism of the Founding Fathers," *Modern Age*, June 27, 2024. https://modernagejournal.com/zionism-of-the-founding-fathers
/241092/.

66. Joseph Prudhomme, "Zionism of the Founding Fathers," *Modern Age,* June 27, 2024. https://modernagejournal.com/zionism-of-the-founding-fathers /241092/.

67. "Balfour Declaration: U.S. Congress Endorses Declaration (September 21, 1922)," Public Resolution No. 73, 67th Congress, Second Session, Lodge–Fish Resolution, https://www.jewishvirtuallibrary.org/u-s-congress-endores -the-balfour-declaration.

CHAPTER 5

1. Deuteronomy 16.

2. See City of David, Ancient Jerusalem, https://cityofdavid.org.il/en/.

3. See Genesis 13:18: "And Abram pitched his tents, and he came, and he dwelt in the plain of Mamre, which is in Hebron, and there he built an altar to the Lord," https://www.chabad.org/library/bible_cdo/aid/8208/jewish /Chapter-13.htm.

4. See Nikki Main, "Archaeologists Find More Evidence of Bible Story About Moses Leading His People to the Promised Land 3,200 Years Ago," *Daily Mail,* July 12, 2024, https://www.dailymail.co.uk/sciencetech /article-13629323/Archaeologists-evidence-Bible-story-Moses.html; see also Joshua 15:34, 56, *The Complete Jewish Bible with Rashi Commentary,* Chabad.org, https://www.chabad.org/library/bible_cdo/aid/15799/jewish/Chapter-15 .htm.

5. Nikki Main, "Archaeologists Find More Evidence of Bible Story About Moses Leading His People to the Promised Land 3,200 Years Ago."

6. Nikki Main, "Archaeologists Find More Evidence of Bible Story About Moses Leading His People to the Promised Land 3,200 Years Ago."

7. Yair Netanyahu, "Why the Jewish People Are the Rightful Owners of the Land of Israel," *Newsweek,* October 20, 2022, https://www.newsweek.com /why-jewish-people-are-rightful-owners-land-israel-opinion-1752970.

8. Meir Loewenberg, "Did Maimonides Really Pray on the Temple Mount?" *Jewish Magazine,* October/November 2012, http://www.jewishmag. com/169mag/rambam_temple_mount/rambam_temple_mount.htm.

9. Genesis 15:18, The Complete Jewish Bible with Rashi Commentary, Chabad. org, https://www.chabad.org/library/bible_cdo/aid/8210/jewish /Chapter-15.htm.

10. Jonathan Bronitsky and Josh Hammer, "Beware of Media Sanitizing Antisemitism with Phony 'Jewish' Sources," *The Federalist,* December 1, 2023, https://thefederalist.com/2023/12/01/the-media-must-stop-sanitizing -antisemitism-with-jewish-groups/.

11. Psalms 137:5, *The Complete Jewish Bible with Rashi Commentary,* Chabad.org, https://www.chabad.org/library/bible_cdo/aid/16358/jewish/Chapter -137.htm.

12. See, e.g., Eugene Kontorovich, "Unesco Writes Jews Out of Ancient Jericho," *Wall Street Journal,* September 28, 2023, https://www.wsj.com/articles/unesco

-writes-jews-out-of-ancient-jericho-judaism-palestine-world-heritage
-site-c7590c69.

13. Deuteronomy 30:3–5, *The Complete Jewish Bible with Rashi Commentary*, Chabad.org, https://www.chabad.org/library/bible_cdo/aid/9994/jewish /Chapter-30.htm.

14. See Yair Netanyahu, "Why the Jewish People Are the Rightful Owners of the Land of Israel."

15. See, e.g., Nehemiah 9:8 ("And You found his heart faithful before You, and You made the covenant with him to give the land of the Canaanites, the Hittites, the Amorites, the Perizzites, the Jebusites, and the Girgashites, to give to his seed, and You kept Your words, for You are righteous,") https:// www.chabad.org/library/bible_cdo/aid/16516/jewish/Chapter-9.htm; see also Parshat Devarim (Deuteronomy 1:1–3:22), https://www.chabad.org /parshah/torahreading.asp?aid=2495789&jewish=Devarim-Torah-Reading .htm&p=complete.

16. Ryan Prior, "Ancient DNA Reveals That Biblical-Era Philistines May Have Originated in Europe," CNN, July 4, 2019, https://www.cnn.com/2019/07/04 /world/philistines-european-dna-trnd.

17. See Josh Hammer, "The Peace Process That Never Was."

18. See generally Josh Hammer, "How to Combat Anti-Israeli Hate on College Campuses," *National Interest*, October 13, 2020, https://nationalinterest.org /blog/middle-east-watch/how-combat-anti-israeli-hate-college-campuses -170622.

19. "The Balfour Daclaration", Modern History Sourcebook, https://www1.udel .edu/History-old/figal/Hist104/assets/pdf/readings/14balfour.pdf.

20. See Josh Hammer, "How to Combat Anti-Israeli Hate on College Campuses."

21. "The Palestine Mandate," Yale Law School, Lillian Goldman Law Library, July 24, 1922, https://avalon.law.yale.edu/20th_century/palmanda.asp.

22. See generally Abraham Bell and Eugene Kontorovish, "Palestine, *Uti Possidetis Juris*, and the Borders Of Israel," *Arizona Law Review* 58 (2016), https://arizonalawreview.org/pdf/58-3/58arizlrev633.pdf

23. See Abraham Bell and Eugene Kontorovish, "Palestine, *Uti Possidetis Juris*, and the Borders Of Israel," 644 ("By becoming independent, [the] new State acquires sovereignty with the territorial base and boundaries left to it by the [administrative boundaries of the] colonial power. . . . [The principle of *uti possidetis juris*] applies to the State as it is [at that moment of independence], i.e., to the 'photograph' of the territorial situation then existing. The principle of *uti possidetis* [*juris*] freezes the territorial title; it stops the clock. . . .")

24. See Ronen Shoval, *Holiness and Society*.

25. Ronen Shoval, *Holiness and Society*.

26. Ronen Shoval, *Holiness and Society*.

27. "Jordanian-Israeli General Armistice Agreement," Yale Law School, Lillian Goldman Law Library, April 3, 1949, https://avalon.law.yale.edu/20th _century/armo3.asp.

28. "Jordanian-Israeli General Armistice Agreement."

29. See, e.g., Michael Doran and Jonathan Silver, "How Israel Got Caught by Surprise in 1973 and 2023," *Mosaic*, October 26, 2023, https://mosaicmagazine.com/response/israel-zionism/2023/10/how-israel-got-caught-by-surprise-in-1973-and-2023/.

30. Liel Leibovitz, "The Most Legitimate State on Earth," November 28, 2021, *Tablet*, https://www.tabletmag.com/sections/israel-middle-east/articles/israel-most-legitimate-state.

31. Genesis 15:18–21, *The Complete Jewish Bible with Rashi Commentary*, Chabad.org, https://www.chabad.org/library/bible_cdo/aid/8210/jewish/Chapter-15.htm.

32. David P. Goldman, "Nationalism Is Dead. Long Live Nationalism," *Tablet*, August 14, 2018, https://www.tabletmag.com/sections/israel-middle-east/articles/nationalism-is-dead-long-live-nationalism.

33. See Yoram Hazony, *The Virtue of Nationalism*.

34. Michael Doran and Jonathan Silver, "How Israel Got Caught by Surprise in 1973 and 2023."

35. See Josh Hammer, "Israel's Judicial Reform 'Controversy' Is Much Ado About Nothing," *Newsweek*, January 20, 2023, https://www.newsweek.com/israels-judicial-reform-controversy-much-ado-about-nothing-opinion-1775181; Josh Hammer, "What Israel's Protests Are Really About," *Newsweek*, July 28, 2023, https://www.newsweek.com/what-israels-protests-are-really-about-opinion-1815892.

36. See, e.g., Yoram Hazony, "In Defense of Israeli Nationalism" (speech given at the University of Colorado-Boulder's Benson Center for the Study of Western Civilization on March 5, 2024), https://www.youtube.com/watch?v=O83iLS91JzI.

37. See Steven Grosby, "Reading the Talmud in the Tower of London."

38. Erick Erickson, "You Will Be Made to Care," RedState, March 29, 2013, https://redstate.com/erick/2013/03/29/you-will-be-made-to-care-n45747.

39. See generally Erick Erickson, *You Will Be Made to Care: The War on Faith, Family, and Your Freedom to Believe* (Regnery, 2016).

40. William F. Buckley Jr., "Our Mission Statement," *National Review*, November 19, 1955, https://www.nationalreview.com/1955/11/our-mission-statement-william-f-buckley-jr/.

41. David P. Goldman, "Christian Nationalism and Israel," *The American Mind*, May 2, 2024, https://americanmind.org/salvo/christian-nationalism-and-israel/.

42. "GDP Per Capita, Current Prices," International Monetary Fund, https://www.imf.org/external/datamapper/NGDPDPC@WEO/OEMDC/ADVEC/WEOWORLD/ISR.

43. See, e.g., Sharon Wrobel, "Tel Aviv Moves Up to 5th Place in Annual Ranking of Best Global Tech Ecosystems," *Times of Israel*, June 15, 2023, https://www.timesofisrael.com/tel-aviv-moves-up-to-5th-place-in-annual-ranking-of-best-global-tech-ecosystems/ ("Tel Aviv moved up two spots to fifth place in an annual survey ranking the world's most attractive ecosystems for startups and innovation by US research firm Startup Genome, rising from

seventh last time."); "High-Tech and High Life: Tel Aviv," *Porsche*, August 14, 2023, https://www.porsche.com/stories/innovation/high-tech--and -high-life-tel-aviv ("At the last count, there were some 7,000 start-ups in this fertile breeding ground they call The Big Orange. Tech giants from all over the world are setting up operations in 'Silicon Wadi,' the name given to the high-tech hub centered around Tel Aviv—a region ranked second only to the USA in global terms when it comes to developments in cyber security.").

44. Lyndsey Matthews and Michele Baran, "These Are the World's Happiest Countries in 2024," *Afar*, March 20, 2024, https://www.afar.com/magazine /the-worlds-happiest-country-is-all-about-reading-coffee-and-saunas.

45. Emily Bontrager, "Palestine's Christian Population Has Nearly Vanished," For the Martyrs, June 15, 2022, https://forthemartyrs.com/palestines-vanishing -christian-population/.

46. Emily Bontrager, "Palestine's Christian Population Has Nearly Vanished."

CHAPTER 6

1. Psalms Chapter 121, *The Complete Jewish Bible with Rashi Commentary*, Chabad .org, https://www.chabad.org/library/bible_cdo/aid/16342/jewish /Chapter-121.htm.

2. See "Hamas Covenant 1988."

3. See, e.g., Bassam Tawil, "Guess Which 'Moderate' Palestinian Terrorist Group Participated In the October 7 Massacre," Gatestone Institute, May 28, 2024, https://www.gatestoneinstitute.org/20668/fatah-october-7-atrocities.

4. See generally Josh Hammer, "Why We Fight," *RedState* (August 1, 2014), https://redstate.com/josh_hammer/2014/08/01/why-we-fight-3-n49954.

5. The IDF rejects this rumor. See Yonah Jeremy Bob, "IDF Rejects Allegations That Soldiers Working with Radar, Iron Dome Risk Cancer," *Jerusalem Post*, January 9, 2023, https://www.jpost.com/israel-news/article-728054.

6. See "Conference Sovereignty," Bible Lands Museum, n.d., https://tickchak .co.il/56669/en.

7. David Bernstein, "Sept. 11 Is Responsible for Overwhelming GOP Support for Israel—Not Sheldon Adelson," *Washington Post*, September 9, 2015, https://www.washingtonpost.com/news/volokh-conspiracy/wp/2015 /09/09/sept-11-is-responsible-for-overwhelming-gop-support-for -israel-not-sheldon-adelson/.

8. "Foreign Terrorist Organizations," US Department of State, n.d., https:// www.state.gov/foreign-terrorist-organizations/.

9. See Nick Schifrin and Ali Rogan, "In Foreign Policy Shift, Biden Lifts Terrorist Designation for Houthis in Yemen," *PBS Newshour*, February 16, 2021, https://www.pbs.org/newshour/show/in-foreign-policy-shift-biden -lifts-terrorist-designation-for-houthis-in-yemen.

10. See Gil Troy, "The U.S. Owes Israel $5 Million," *Wall Street Journal*, August 21, 2024, https://www.wsj.com/articles/the-u-s-owes-israel-5-million -fuad-shukr-bounty-assassination-947cocdo.

11. "Biden to Netanyahu After Killing of Fuad Shukr: 'Bibi, What the F-?'," Israel National News, October 8, 2024, https://www.israelnationalnews.com/news /397305.

12. See Haley Strack, "Israeli Strike Kills Hezbollah Commander Behind 1983 U.S. Embassy Bombing," National Review, September 20, 2024, https://www .nationalreview.com/news/israel-launches-targeted-strike-on-high -ranking-hezbollah-terrorist-in-beiruit.

13. Josh Hammer, "Hold Obama-Biden Foreign Policy Responsible for Iran's Unprecedented Attack on Israel," Newsweek, April 19, 2024, https://www .newsweek.com/hold-obama-biden-foreign-policy-responsible -irans-unprecedented-attack-israel-opinion-1891997.

14. See "Iran: U.S. and Israeli Threats & Options," The Iran Primer, United States Institute of Peace, January 26, 2023, https://iranprimer.usip.org /blog/2023/jan/26/iran-us-and-israeli-threats-options.

15. Josh Hammer, "After Hamas Pogrom, Qatar Must Finally Pay for Its Sponsor of Terrorism," Newsweek, November 17, 2023, https://www.newsweek.com /after-hamas-pogrom-qatar-must-finally-pay-its-sponsor-terrorism -opinion-1844586.

16. "State Sponsors of Terrorism," US Department of State, Bureau of Counterterrorism, n.d., https://www.state.gov/state-sponsors-of-terrorism/.

17. itrek home page, https://itrek.org/about-itrek/.

18. See, e.g., Maayan Jaffe-Hoffman, "Young Evangelical Support for Israel Plummets," Jerusalem Post, February 12, 2024, https://www.jpost.com /christianworld/article-786545.

19. See, e.g., Philip Klein, "Christian Support for Israel Rooted in Genesis Promises, Not End-Times Prophecy, Evangelicals Say," Washington Examiner, July 27, 2014, https://www.washingtonexaminer.com/opinion/885284 /christian-support-for-israel-rooted-in-genesis-promises-not-end-times -prophecy-evangelicals-say/.

20. "Jewish Americans in 2020: Marriage, Families, and Children," Pew Research Center, May 11, 2021, https://www.pewresearch.org/religion/2021/05/11 /marriage-families-and-children/.

21. See Keep God's Land home page, https://keepgodsland.com/leadership/; see also https://keepgodsland.com/about-us/.

22. Jacob Magid, "Dermer Suggests Israel Should Prioritize Support of Evangelicals over US Jews," Times of Israel, May 10, 2021, https://www .timesofisrael.com/dermer-suggests-israel-should-prioritize-support -of-evangelicals-over-us-jews/.

23. See Brooke Goldstein, "We Must Put an End to Palestinian Apartheid," Newsweek, April 10, 2022, https://www.newsweek.com/we-must -put-end-palestinian-apartheid-opinion-1698648.

24. Emily Bontrager, "Palestine's Christian Population Has Nearly Vanished."

25. Eugene Kontorovich, "Unesco Writes Jews Out of Ancient Jericho."

26. See Caroline Glick, "When Cultural Appropriation and Historical Revisionism Are Acts of War," Newsweek, March 19, 2021, https://www

.newsweek.com/when-cultural-appropriation-historical-revisionism
-are-acts-war-opinion-1576970.

27. Lior Dattel, "Israeli Schools Teach Three Times as Much Bible as Europe's
Schools," *Haaretz*, August 29, 2019, https://www.haaretz.com/
israel-news/2019-08-29/ty-article/.premium/israeli-schools-teach-three
-times-as-much-bible-as-europes-schools/0000017f-da77-dea8-a77f
-de778a3e0000.

28. Genesis 1:28, *The Complete Jewish Bible with Rashi Commentary*, Chabad.org,
https://www.chabad.org/library/bible_cdo/aid/8165/jewish/Chapter-1.htm.

29. See "Total Fertility Rate," ined, n.d., https://www.ined.fr/en/everything
_about_population/data/europe-developed-countries/fertility
-indicators/.

CHAPTER 7

1. Genesis Chapter 12, *The Complete Jewish Bible with Rashi Commentary*, Chabad.
org, https://www.chabad.org/library/bible_cdo/aid/8176/jewish/Chapter
-12.htm.

2. "President Bush's Second Inaugural Address," NPR, January 20, 2005,
https://www.npr.org/2005/01/20/4460172/president-bushs-second
-inaugural-address.

3. Thomas Gale Moore, "A Humbler Foreign Policy," Independent Institute,
February 18, 2003, https://www.independent.org/news/article.asp?id=444.

4. "Freedom Agenda," George W. Bush White House Archives, 2009, https://
georgewbush-whitehouse.archives.gov/infocus/freedomagenda/.

5. Bret Stephens, "Stephens: Paul Ryan's Neocon Manifesto," *The Wall Street
Journal*, August 14, 2012, https://www.wsj.com/articles/SB10000872396390
44431810457758732244643o152.

6. Bret Stephens, "Stephens: Paul Ryan's Neocon Manifesto."

7. Bret Stephens, "Stephens: Paul Ryan's Neocon Manifesto."

8. "Declaration of Independence," America's Founding Documents, National
Archives, https://www.archives.gov/founding-docs/declaration-transcript;
"Abraham Lincoln's Speech at Chicago, Illinois: July 10, 1858," https://
georgepwood.com/2012/07/04/abraham-lincolns-speech-at-chicago-illinois
-july-10-1858/.

9. "The Federalist Papers: No. 2," Yale Law School, Lillian Goldman Law
Library, https://avalon.law.yale.edu/18th_century/fed02.asp.

10. Bret Stephens, "Stephens: Paul Ryan's Neocon Manifesto."

11. John Quincy Adams, "Speech to the U.S. House of Representatives on
Foreign Policy," July 4, 1821, https://loveman.sdsu.edu/docs/1821secofstate
JQAdmas.pdf.

12. Dennis Ross, "Memories of an Anti-Semitic State Department," The
Washington Institute for Near East Policy, September 26, 2017, https://www
.washingtoninstitute.org/policy-analysis/memories-anti-semitic-state
-department.

13. Robert Mackey, "Kerry Reminds Congress Netanyahu Advised U.S. to Invade Iraq," *The New York Times*, February 25, 2015, https://www.nytimes .com/2015/02/26/world/middleeast/kerry-reminds-congress-netanyahu -advised-us-to-invade-iraq.html.

14. Yitzhak Benhorin, "Israel Warned Us Against Iraq Invasion, US Official Says," *Ynet News*, September 1, 2007, https://www.ynetnews.com/articles /0,7340,L-3444393,00.html.

15. Barbara Demick, "Not All Israelis Welcome Prospect of War with Iraq," *Los Angeles Times*, October 16, 2002, https://www.latimes.com/archives/la-xpm -2002-oct-16-fg-iziraq16-story.html.

16. See Daniel Pipes, "Israel Must Give Up Managing the Conflict and Choose Winning It," *Jerusalem Post*, August 18, 2024, https://www.jpost.com/opinion /article-815115.

17. See, e.g., Patrick Clawson, Hanin Ghaddar, Nader Uskowi, "Middle East FAQs Volume 1: What Is the Shia Crescent?" The Washington Institute for Near East Policy, January 17, 2018, https://www.washingtoninstitute.org /policy-analysis/middle-east-faqs-volume-1-what-shia-crescent.

18. "Peace in the Middle East," George W. Bush White House Archives, 2009, https://georgewbush-whitehouse.archives.gov/infocus/mideast /#:~:text=Building%20support%20for%20the%20two,Minister%20 Sharon's%20withdrawal%20from%20Gaza.

19. "President Bush Discusses Israeli-Palestinian Peace Process," George W. Bush White House Archives, January 10, 2008, https://georgewbush-whitehouse .archives.gov/news/releases/2008/01/20080110-3.html.

20. See Josh Hammer, "The Peace Process That Never Was."

21. See generally Walter Russell Mead, "The Jacksonian Tradition," *National Interest* (Winter 1999), https://pmachala.people.amherst.edu /Current%20Politics/Case%20Studies%20in%20American%20 Diplomacy%20-The%20Readings%20FOR%20the%20FIRST%20and%20 SECOND%20Class/Mead,%20The%20Jacksonian%20Tradition.htm.

22. See, e.g., Daniel Pipes, "My Six-Step Plan for a Two-State Solution," *Boston Globe*, April 12, 2024, https://www.bostonglobe.com/2024/04/04/opinion /two-state-solution-netanyahu-biden-palestinian-authority/.

23. To understand just how truly "bloodthirsty" the Palestinian-Arabs are, consider Dennis Prager, "Germans—Even During the Hitler Era—Were a Better People Than the Palestinians," Townhall, June 18, 2024, https:// townhall.com/columnists/dennisprager/2024/06/18/germans-even -during-the-hitler-era-were-a-better-people-than-the-palestinians-n2640610.

24. See, e.g., Josh Hammer, "The Peace Process That Never Was."

25. Walter Russell Mead, "The Jacksonian Tradition."

26. John Quincy Adams, "Speech to the U.S. House of Representatives on Foreign Policy."

27. See Josh Hammer, "Donald Trump May Be the Most Pro-Jewish President Ever," October 22, 2020, *New York Post*, https://nypost.com/2020/10/22 /donald-trump-may-be-the-most-pro-jewish-president-ever/; see also Josh Hammer, "The Jewish Case for President Donald Trump," Jewish Telegraphic

Agency, March 15, 2020, https://www.jta.org/2020/03/15/ideas/the-jewish
-case-for-president-donald-trump.

28. See, e.g., Josh Hammer, "Trump and Netanyahu Debunk the Failed
Consensus," American Greatness, August 20, 2020, https://amgreatness
.com/2020/08/20/trump-and-netanyahu-debunk-the-failed-consensus/.

29. See, e.g., Jennifer Bell, "UAE's First Fully Equipped Jewish Neighborhood to
Be Established, Says Rabbi," *Jerusalem Post*, April 15, 2022, https://www.jpost
.com/middle-east/article-704293.

30. "First-Ever Kosher Supermarket in Gulf Opens in Dubai," *Jerusalem Post*,
December 14, 2022, https://www.jpost.com/middle-east/article-724819.

31. See, e.g., Josh Hammer, "Donald Trump May Be the Most Pro-Jewish
President Ever"; Josh Hammer, "The Jewish Case for President Donald
Trump."

32. "What Was That Glowing Orb Trump Touched in Saudi Arabia?" *New York
Times*, May 22, 2017, https://www.nytimes.com/2017/05/22/world
/middleeast/trump-glowing-orb-saudi.html.

33. For my thoughts on what an "America First" foreign policy means (and does
not mean), see Josh Hammer, "What Exactly Is Meant by 'America First'?"
Newsweek, February 2, 2024, https://www.newsweek.com/what-exactly
-meant-america-first-1866209.

34. See, e.g., Josh Hammer, "Confronting the Chinese Communist Party Is
America's Generational Challenge," Real Clear Politics, May 22, 2020,
https://www.realclearpolitics.com/articles/2020/05/22/confronting_the
_chinese_communist_party_is_americas_generational_challenge_143270
.html.

35. Elbridge A. Colby, "Only One Priority Makes Sense for American Foreign
Policy," American Compass, July 10, 2024, https://americancompass.org
/only-one-priority-makes-sense-for-american-foreign-policy/.

36. Aryeh Lightstone, "Strengthening the Abraham Accords: American Foreign
Policy Priority," Real Clear Politics, August 13, 2024, https://www
.realclearpolitics.com/articles/2024/08/13/strengthening_the_abraham
_accords_american_foreign_policy_priority_151438.html.

37. See Jonathan Masters and Will Merrow, "U.S. Aid to Israel in Four Charts,"
Council on Foreign Relations, May 31, 2024, https://www.cfr.org/article/us
-aid-israel-four-charts; see also "What Every American Should Know About
U.S. Aid to Israel," AJC, October 1, 2024, https://www.ajc.org/news/what
-every-american-should-know-about-us-aid-to-israel (the American Jewish
Committee advocating for the current MOU).

38. See, e.g., Josh Hammer, "HAMMER: The Pro-Israel Case Against U.S.
Military Aid To Israel," *Daily Wire*, November 4, 2019, https://www.dailywire
.com/news/hammer-the-pro-israel-case-against-u-s-military-aid-to-israel.

39. "FACT SHEET: Memorandum of Understanding Reached with Israel,"
Barack Obama White House Archives, September 14, 2016, https://
obamawhitehouse.archives.gov/the-press-office/2016/09/14/fact-sheet
-memorandum-understanding-reached-israel.

40. See, e.g., Josh Hammer, "HAMMER: The Pro-Israel Case Against U.S. Military Aid To Israel."

41. On Israel's contentious 2023 judicial reform debate, see Josh Hammer, "Israel's Judicial Reform 'Controversy' Is Much Ado About Nothing"; I also debated Alan Dershowitz on this topic in Miami Beach, at the time https://www.eventbrite.com/e/alan-dershowitz-vs-josh-hammer-israels-judicial-reform-pro-and-con-tickets-538054685047.

42. See, e.g., Jacob Siegel and Liel Leibovitz, "End U.S. Aid to Israel," *Tablet,* July 16, 2023, https://www.tabletmag.com/sections/news/articles/end-american-aid-israel.

CHAPTER 8

1. Genesis Chapter 12, *The Complete Jewish Bible with Rashi Commentary*, Chabad.org, https://www.chabad.org/library/bible_cdo/aid/16216/jewish/Chapter-12.htm.

2. See "Defining Antisemitism," US Department of State, n.d., https://www.state.gov/defining-antisemitism/.

3. "Defining Antisemitism."

4. "Defining Antisemitism."

5. See Natan Sharansky, "Anti-Semitism in 3D," Aish, n.d., https://aish.com/48892657/.

6. Natan Sharansky, "Anti-Semitism in 3D."

7. See, e.g., "In Light of the Terrorist Attack on October 7th, What Are the Proper Limits of Speech on Campus?" Intercollegiate Studies Institute, YouTube video, April 11, 2024, https://www.youtube.com/watch?v=galD4OCGSIg (a two-on-two debate I participated in, in April 2024, on the moral limits of campus speech); see also Yoram Hazony, "Should Universities Protect Campus Anti-Semites?" Public Discourse, February 11, 2024, https://www.thepublicdiscourse.com/2024/02/92656/.

8. *See generally* Elisha Pearl, *Make Peace: A Strategic Guide for Achieving Lasting Peace In Israel | The Lubavitcher Rebbe's Timeless Vision for Israel's Security and the Ongoing Conflict in the Middle East* (Yonah Press/Sichos in English, 2024).

9. Uziel Scheiner, "New Book Delves into the Rebbe's Approach to Peace in Israel," Chabad.org, July 17, 2024, https://www.chabad.org/news/article_cdo/aid/6519937/jewish/New-Book-Delves-Into-the-Rebbes-Approach-to-Peace-in-Israel.htm.

10. Uziel Scheiner, "New Book Delves into the Rebbe's Approach to Peace in Israel."

11. Satmar Headquarters, December 5, 2023, https://x.com/HQSatmar/status/1732044496706363891; see also Satmar Headquarters, April 22, 2024, https://x.com/HQSatmar/status/1782463696481988927.

12. Satmar Headquarters, December 21, 2023, https://x.com/HQSatmar/status/1741665806499348935.

13. See Baruch Green, "WATCH: Candace Owens Shows 'Profound Ignorance' About Neturei Karta and Antisemitism," Vinnews, November 7, 2023,

https://vinnews.com/2023/11/07/watch-candace-owens-shows-profound
-ignorance-about-neturei-karta-and-antisemitism/; see also Josh Hammer,
November 6, 2023, https://x.com/josh_hammer/status/172167836433
7988072.

14. Elliot Kaufman, "To Break the 'Moral Spine' of the Jews," *Wall Street Journal*,
August 22, 2024, https://www.wsj.com/opinion/to-break-the-moral-spine-of
-the-jews-anti-zionist-loyalty-oaths-progressive-culture-82d094f2.

15. 378 US 184 (Stewart, J., concurring).

16. See Jaryn Crouson, "Violent Protesters Disrupt Speech Condemning Hamas;
University Police Sit Back & Do Nothing."

17. See Robby Soave, "Activists Disrupt Law Professor's Talk at the University of
Chicago," Reason, April 9, 2019, https://reason.com/2019/04/09/university
-of-chicago-law-kontrovich-bds/.

18. See Josh Hammer, "The Peace Process That Never Was."

19. Josh Hammer, "The Peace Process That Never Was."

20. See generally "Hamas Covenant 1988."

21. See, e.g., Daniel Pipes, "The Uniqueness of the Israeli-Palestinian Conflict,"
Jerusalem Post, July 16, 2024, https://www.jpost.com/opinion/article-810433.

22. See Josh Hammer, "The Peace Process That Never Was."

23. See, e.g., Jay Sekulow, "UNRWA Has Changed the Definition of Refugee,"
Foreign Policy, August 17, 2018, https://foreignpolicy.com/2018/08/17
/unrwa-has-changed-the-definition-of-refugee.

24. See Josh Hammer, "The Peace Process That Never Was."

25. Josh Hammer, "The Peace Process That Never Was."

26. Josh Hammer, "The Peace Process That Never Was."

27. Josh Hammer, "The Peace Process That Never Was."

28. See generally Josh Hammer, "How to Combat Anti-Israeli Hate on College
Campuses."

29. See generally Caroline Glick, *The Israeli Solution: A One-State Plan for Peace in
the Middle East* (Forum Books, 2014) Caroline Glick; David Friedman, *One
Jewish State: The Last, Best Hope to Resolve the Israeli-Palestinian Conflict*
(Humanix Books, 2020).

30. See Josh Hammer, "The Peace Process That Never Was."

31. Rachel Avraham, "Dr. Mordechai Kedar: 'The Eight State Solution Is the
Best,'" Foreign Policy Association, March 20, 2014, https://
foreignpolicyblogs.com/2014/03/20/dr-mordechai-kedar-the-eight-state
-solution-is-the-best/.

32. Rachel Avraham, "Dr. Mordechai Kedar: 'The Eight State Solution Is the
Best.'"

33. See, e.g., Josh Hammer, "The Only Way Out Is Through," *Newsweek*, April 14,
2023, https://www.newsweek.com/only-way-out-through-opinion-1794353.

CHAPTER 9

1. II Kings Chapter 17, *The Complete Jewish Bible with Rashi Commentary*, Chabad .org, https://www.chabad.org/library/bible_cdo/aid/15923/jewish/Chapter -17.htm.

2. Sohrab Ahmari, "The New Racist Right Are Uniquely Dangerous," *New Statesman*, April 10, 2024, https://www.newstatesman.com/comment /2024/04/the-new-racist-right-are-uniquely-dangerous.

3. See, e.g., Ofir Haivry and Yarom Hazony, "What Is Conservatism?" *American Affairs*, Summer 2017, https://americanaffairsjournal.org/2017/05/what -is-conservatism/.

4. Russell Kirk, *The Conservative Mind: From Burke to Eliot* (Regnery, 2001); see also "Russell Kirk: Quotes," https://www.goodreads.com/author/quotes /50252.Russell_Kirk.

5. Russell Kirk, *The Conservative Mind*.

6. "Washington's Farewell Address," https://www.senate.gov/artandhistory /history/resources/pdf/Washingtons_Farewell_Address.pdf.

7. See Genesis 1:27, *The Complete Jewish Bible with Rashi Commentary*, Chabad.org, https://www.chabad.org/library/bible_cdo/aid/8165/jewish/Chapter -1.htm.

8. Proverbs Chapter 22, *The Complete Jewish Bible with Rashi Commentary*, Chabad .org, https://www.chabad.org/library/bible_cdo/aid/16393/jewish/Chapter -22.htm.

9. Sohrab Ahmari, "America's Dime-Store Nietzscheans," *New Statesman*, May 16, 2024, https://www.newstatesman.com/ideas/2024/05/americas-dime -store-nietzscheans.

10. Gregory Davis, "Egg-sposed: We Reveal the Identity of Far Right Bodybuilder 'The Raw Egg Nationalist,'" Hope Note Hate, June 24, 2020, https:// hopenothate.org.uk/2024/06/20/egg-sposed-we-reveal-the-identity-of-far -right-bodybuilder-the-raw-egg-nationalist/.

11. Sohrab Ahmari, "The New Racist Right Are Uniquely Dangerous."

12. Tamara Berens, "From Coy to Goy," Mosaic, June 5, 2023, https:// mosaicmagazine.com/essay/politics-current-affairs/2023/06/from-coy -to-goy/.

13. I hesitate to use the word "paleoconservative" in a negative sense for the very simple reason that I agree with many, and perhaps most, paleoconservative arguments (though not this one, naturally). I use it here for the simple reason that I cannot think of anything more precise and accurate to use instead.

14. See generally Matthew Walther, "Rise of the Barstool Conservatives," The Week, February 1, 2021, https://theweek.com/articles/964006/rise-barstool -conservatives.

15. See generally Nate Hochman, "What Comes After the Religious Right?" *The New York Times*, June 1, 2022, https://www.nytimes.com/2022/06/01 /opinion/republicans-religion-conservatism.html.

16. Yoram Hazony, "Conservative Democracy," First Things, January, 2019, https://www.firstthings.com/article/2019/01/conservative-democracy.

17. Hank Berrien, "Columbia University Anti-Israel Groups Call for 'Total Eradication Of Western Civilization,'" Daily Wire, August 9, 2024, https:// www.dailywire.com/news/columbia-university-anti-israel-groups-call -for-total-eradication-of-western-civilization.

18. See Genesis 12:3, The Complete Jewish Bible with Rashi Commentary, Chabad.org, https://www.chabad.org/library/bible_cdo/aid/8176/jewish/Chapter -12.htm.

19. "From George Washington to the Hebrew Congregation in Newport, Rhode Island, 18 August 1790," https://founders.archives.gov/documents /Washington/05-06-02-0135.

20. Ecclesiastes 1:9, The Complete Jewish Bible with Rashi Commentary, Chabad.org, https://www.chabad.org/library/bible_cdo/aid/16462/jewish/Chapter -1.htm.

21. Yoram Hazony, "The Challenge of Marxism," Quillette, August 16, 2020, https://quillette.com/2020/08/16/the-challenge-of-marxism/.

22. James Kirchick, "Rock, Paper, Scissors of PC Victimology," Tablet, February 26, 2015, https://www.tabletmag.com/sections/news/articles /victimhood-olympics.

23. James Kirchick, "Rock, Paper, Scissors of PC Victimology."

24. See generally Josh Hammer, "Common Carriage Now," The American Mind, October 4, 2022, https://americanmind.org/salvo/common-carriage-now/.

25. Josh Hammer, "The Coalition of the Un-Woke," Newsweek, April 2, 2021, https://www.newsweek.com/coalition-un-woke-opinion-1580601.

26. Matthew Schmitz, "The Woke and the Un-Woke," Tablet, September 24, 2020, https://www.tabletmag.com/sections/news/articles/woke-religion-america.

27. Bari Weiss, "End DEI," Tablet, November 7, 2023, https://www.tabletmag .com/sections/news/articles/end-dei-bari-weiss-jews.

28. Max Eden, "Ban Critical Race Theory Now," Newsweek, May 5, 2021, https:// www.newsweek.com/ban-critical-race-theory-now-opinion-1588362.

29. Bari Weiss, "End DEI."

30. See Noah Lewin-Epstein and Yinon Cohen, "Ethnic Origin and Identity in the Jewish Population of Israel," Journal of Ethnic and Migration Studies 45, no. 11 (2018), 2118–2137, https://doi.org/10.1080/1369183X.2018.1492370.

31. League of United Latin American Citizens v. Perry, 548 US 399 (2006) (Roberts, C.J., dissenting).

32. 600 US 181 (2023) (Thomas, J., concurring).

33. See Deuteronomy 5:9, The Complete Jewish Bible with Rashi Commentary, Chabad.org, https://www.chabad.org/library/bible_cdo/aid/9969/jewish /Chapter-5.htm.

34. Josh Hammer, "Reparations Would Be Unjust and Tear Our Nation Apart," New York Post, March 3, 2021, https://nypost.com/2021/03/03/reparations -would-be-unjust-and-tear-our-nation-apart/.

35. Genesis 1:27, *The Complete Jewish Bible with Rashi Commentary*, Chabad.org, https://www.chabad.org/library/bible_cdo/aid/8165/jewish/Chapter-1.htm.

CHAPTER 10

1. Isaiah Chapter 42, *The Complete Jewish Bible with Rashi Commentary*, Chabad.org, https://www.chabad.org/library/bible_cdo/aid/15973/jewish/Chapter-42.htm.

2. See generally Josh Hammer, "Standing Athwart History: Anti-Obergefell Popular Constitutionalism and Judicial Supremacy's Long-Term Triumph," *University of St. Thomas Law Journal* 16, No. 2 (2020), https://ssrn.com/abstract=3588899.

3. Leviticus 23:27, *The Complete Jewish Bible with Rashi Commentary*, Chabad.org, https://www.chabad.org/library/bible_cdo/aid/9924/jewish/Chapter-23.htm.

4. Pirkei Avot 1:1, https://www.chabad.org/library/article_cdo/aid/2165/jewish/Chapter-One.htm.

5. I looked up Rabbi Modek in 2024, and I came across a very well-written and well-argued (if not quite entirely agreeable) blog post he had written about the war in Gaza for *Times of Israel*: https://blogs.timesofisrael.com/the-gaza-death-chamber-a-centrists-take/. The piece motivated me to email Rabbi Modek, which made for our first correspondence in over two decades.

6. Harold J. Berman, "The Origins of Historical Jurisprudence: Coke, Selden, Hale," *Yale Law Journal* 103 (1994).

7. Pirkei Avot 1:1, https://www.chabad.org/library/article_cdo/aid/2165/jewish/Chapter-One.htm.

8. Mark Twain, "Concerning the Jews," *Harper's Magazine*, September, 1899 (Internet History Sourcebooks), https://sourcebooks.fordham.edu/mod/1898twain-jews.asp.

9. Deuteronomy 4:31, https://www.chabad.org/parshah/torahreading.asp?aid=2495794.

10. See "English Haggadah Text with Instructional Guide," Chabad.org, https://www.chabad.org/holidays/passover/pesach_cdo/aid/661624/jewish/English-Haggadah-Text.htm.

11. See generally Ronen Shoval, *Holiness and Society*.

12. Jacob Ausubel, Gregory A. Smith, and Alan Cooperman, "Denominational Switching Among U.S. Jews: Reform Judaism Has Gained, Conservative Judaism Has Lost," Pew Research Center, June 22, 2021, https://www.pewresearch.org/short-reads/2021/06/22/denominational-switching-among-u-s-jews-reform-judaism-has-gained-conservative-judaism-has-lost/.

13. See "Comment on the Impact of the 1883 Trefa Banquet," https://www.newspapers.com/article/the-american-israelite-comment-on-the-im/31422833/.

14. Max Freedman, "Searching for the Jewish Future in South Florida," *Jewish Currents*, Summer 2024, https://jewishcurrents.org/searching-for-the-jewish-future-in-south-florida.

15. See generally Ronen Shoval, *Holiness and Society.*

16. "Jewish Americans in 2020: Marriage, Families, and Children."

17. Barak Ravid, "Israeli Education Minister Calls Intermarriage Rate of U.S. Jews 'Second Holocaust,'" Axios, July 9, 2019, https://www.axios.com/2019/07/09/rafi-peretz-second-holocaust-intermarriage-jews-us#.

18. See "One in Five Young Americans Believes the Holocaust Is a Myth, Poll Finds," *Times of Israel*, December 11, 2023, https://www.timesofisrael.com/one-in-five-young-americans-believes-the-holocaust-is-a-myth-poll-finds/.

19. Elliott Hamilton, "The Real Story of Chanukah and What It Should Mean for American Jewry Today," *Daily Wire*, December 22, 2016, https://www.dailywire.com/news/real-story-chanukah-and-what-it-should-mean-jewish-elliott-hamilton.

20. See, e.g., https://aish.com/light-unto-the-nations/ ("Jewish law consistently exhorts us to act in a way which will effect a sanctification of the Divine Name, and thereby brings us respect as a holy and upright people.")

21. Josh Hammer, "HAMMER: The Lesson of Chanukah Is Deeply Relevant in 2019. Here's Why," *Daily Wire*, December 23, 2019, https://www.dailywire.com/news/hammer-the-lesson-of-chanukah-is-deeply-relevant-in-2019-heres-why.

22. See Isaiah Chapter 42, *The Complete Jewish Bible with Rashi Commentary*, Chabad.org, https://www.chabad.org/library/bible_cdo/aid/15973/jewish/Chapter-42.htm.

23. 328 F.3d 567, https://scholar.google.com/scholar_case?case=1659953 8532304446493.

24. See Ashley R. Williams, "With Threats on the Rise, Many Jews in America Are Buying Guns and Seeking Firearms Training," CNN, November 6, 2023, https://www.cnn.com/2023/11/06/us/american-jews-guns-antisemitism/index.html; Linda Dayan, "'It Wasn't Even a Thought Until Now': After October 7, These U.S. Jews Are Buying Guns," *Haaretz*, January 4, 2024, https://www.haaretz.com/us-news/2024-01-04/ty-article-magazine/.premium/it-wasnt-even-a-thought-until-now-after-october-7-these-u-s-jews-are-buying-guns/0000018c-cf5e-d4e1-ad8f-fffffc3a0000.

25. See AJC 2018 Survey of American Jewish Opinion, June 10, 2018, https://www.ajc.org/news/survey2018.

26. Marc Rod, "FBI Reports Record-High Antisemitic Hate Crimes in 2023, up 63% from 2022," *Jewish Insider*, September 23, 2024, https://jewishinsider.com/2024/09/fbi-reports-record-high-antisemitic-hate-crimes-in-2023-up-63-from-2022/.

27. See Carl Campanile, "Nearly Half of Jewish Voters Believe NY Is Unsafe for Them, Shocking Poll Finds," *New York Post*, July 10, 2024, https://nypost.com/2024/07/10/us-news/nearly-half-of-jewish-voters-believe-ny-is-unsafe-for-them-shocking-poll-finds/.

28. Carl Campanile, "Nearly Half of Jewish Voters Believe NY Is Unsafe for Them, Shocking Poll Finds."

29. Josh Hammer, "HAMMER: Jews Simply Must Arm Themselves. Now," *Daily Wire*, April 29, 2019, https://www.dailywire.com/news/hammer-jews -simply-must-arm-themselves-now-josh-hammer.

30. Josh Hammer, "HAMMER: Jews Simply Must Arm Themselves. Now."

31. *See* Etan Nechin, "Israeli Civilians Are Taking Up Arms," *Foreign Policy*, March 22, 2024, https://foreignpolicy.com/2024/03/22/israel-gun-laws-ben -gvir-hamas-war-gaza/.

32. Sanhedrin 72a, https://www.sefaria.org/Sanhedrin.72a.4.

33. Josh Hammer, "HAMMER: An Armed and Trained Jew Is the Best Kind of Jew," *Daily Wire*, December 30, 2019, https://www.dailywire.com/news /hammer-an-armed-and-trained-jew-is-the-best-kind-of-jew.

34. Psalms 144:1, *The Complete Jewish Bible with Rashi Commentary*, Chabad.org, https://www.chabad.org/library/bible_cdo/aid/16365/jewish/Chapter -144.htm.

35. Josh Hammer, "The Virtue of Gun Ownership and the Decline of Manliness," *Newsweek*, March 26, 2021, https://www.newsweek.com/virtue-gun -ownership-decline-manliness-opinion-1578908.

36. Josh Hammer, "The Virtue of Gun Ownership and the Decline of Manliness."

37. See Josh Hammer, "HAMMER: Jews Simply Must Arm Themselves. Now"; see also Josh Hammer, "HAMMER: An Armed and Trained Jew Is the Best Kind of Jew."

38. See Josh Hammer, "HAMMER: Jews Simply Must Arm Themselves. Now"; see also Josh Hammer, "HAMMER: An Armed and Trained Jew Is the Best Kind of Jew."

39. Psalms 111:10, *The Complete Jewish Bible with Rashi Commentary*, Chabad.org, https://www.chabad.org/library/bible_cdo/aid/16332/jewish/Chapter -111.htm.

40. Pesach Wolicki, "Destroying Amalek: Timing Is Everything," *The Israel Bible*, September 14, 2024, https://theisraelbible.com/ki-tezte-destroying-amalek -timing-is-everything/.

41. Ecclesiastes 12:13, https://www.sefaria.org/Ecclesiastes.12.13.

42. Abraham Lincoln, "Lyceum Address," https://www.abrahamlincolnonline .org/lincoln/speeches/lyceum.htm.

43. See, e.g., Josh Hammer, "HAMMER: The Lesson of Chanukah Is Deeply Relevant in 2019. Here's Why."

CHAPTER 11

1. Proverbs Chapter 3, *The Complete Jewish Bible with Rashi Commentary*, Chabad .org, https://www.chabad.org/library/bible_cdo/aid/16374/jewish/Chapter -3.htm.

2. Viktor Orbán, "Orbán: The Point of NATO Is Peace, Not Endless War," *Newsweek*, July 5, 2024, https://www.newsweek.com/orban-point-nato -peace-not-endless-war-opinion-1915287.

3. See Abraham Lincoln, "Lyceum Address."

4. See, e.g., M. Zuhdi Jasser, "How to Understand the Red-Green Axis," *Newsweek*, January 25, 2021, https://www.newsweek.com/how-understand -red-green-axis-opinion-1603891.

5. See Abraham Lincoln, "Lyceum Address"; Viktor Orbán, "Orbán: The Point of NATO Is Peace, Not Endless War."

6. Eric Hoffer, "Israeli Premonition" (1968), reprinted at Aish.com, n.d., https://aish.com/48892687/.

7. For the lyrics to "Imagine," *see* https://www.azlyrics.com/lyrics/johnlennon /imagine.html.

8. See Robert P. George, "Catholic Teaching on Jews and Judaism," Public Discourse, December 26, 2022, https://www.thepublicdiscourse.com /2022/12/86231.

9. Robert P. George, "Catholic Teaching on Jews and Judaism."

10. Robert P. George, "Catholic Teaching on Jews and Judaism."

11. Andrew Doran and Mary Eberstadt, "Candace Owens Doesn't Speak for Catholics," First Things, September 5, 2024, https://www.firstthings.com /web-exclusives/2024/09/candace-owens-doesnt-speak-for-catholics; Bishop Robert Barron, "Catholics Cannot Be Anti-Semites," Word on Fire, December 21, 2023, https://www.wordonfire.org/articles/barron/catholics -cannot-be-anti-semites/.

12. Andrew Doran and Mary Eberstadt, "Candace Owens Doesn't Speak for Catholics"; Bishop Robert Barron, "Catholics Cannot Be Anti-Semites."

13. See Genesis Chapter 1, *The Complete Jewish Bible with Rashi Commentary*, Chabad.org, https://www.chabad.org/library/bible_cdo/aid/8165/jewish /Chapter-1.htm.

14. Leviticus 19:15, *The Complete Jewish Bible with Rashi Commentary*, Chabad.org, https://www.chabad.org/library/bible_cdo/aid/9920/jewish/Chapter-19.htm.

15. See, e.g., Bava Batra 30a.

16. See, e.g., Numbers 35:16–24, *The Complete Jewish Bible with Rashi Commentary*, Chabad.org, https://www.chabad.org/library/bible_cdo/aid/9963/jewish/ Chapter-35.htm.

17. See Steven Grosby, "Reading the Talmud in the Tower of London,"

18. See Robert P. George, "Catholic Teaching on Jews and Judaism."

19. https://theisraelbible.com/the-danger-of-attacking-israel (interpreting Zechariah 2:12, "For thus said the lord of Hosts—He who sent me after glory—concerning the nations that have taken you as spoil: 'Whoever touches you touches the pupil of his own eye.'")

20. See, e.g., Elliott Abrams, "Hunting Jews," *Tablet*, March 10, 2024, https:// www.tabletmag.com/sections/news/articles/hunting-jews-europe-ban -kosher-slaughter.

21. Robert P. George, "Catholic Teaching on Jews and Judaism."

22. See Genesis 15:18, *The Complete Jewish Bible with Rashi Commentary*, Chabad. org, https://www.chabad.org/library/bible_cdo/aid/8210/jewish/Chapter -15.htm.; *see also* Keep God's Land home page, https://keepgodsland.com /leadership/.

23. See Robert P. George, "Catholic Teaching on Jews and Judaism."

24. See Jonathan Bronitsky and Josh Hammer, "Beware of Media Sanitizing Antisemitism with Phony 'Jewish' Sources"; see also the first half of this book's chapter 9.

25. See Robert P. George, "Catholic Teaching on Jews and Judaism."

26. "First Amendment," Cornell Law School, Legal Information Institute, https://www.law.cornell.edu/constitution/first_amendment.

27. See "Jefferson's Letter to the Danbury Baptists," January 1, 1802, https://www.loc.gov/loc/lcib/9806/danpre.html.

28. "George C. WALLACE, Governor of the State of Alabama, et al., Appellants v. Ishmael JAFFREE et al. Douglas T. SMITH, et al., Appellants v. Ishmael JAFFREE et al.," Cornell Law School, Legal Information Institute, https://www.law.cornell.edu/supremecourt/text/472/38.

29. Alexander Ward and Heidi Pryzbyla, "Trump Allies Prepare to Infuse 'Christian Nationalism' in Second Administration," *Politico*, February 20, 2024, https://www.politico.com/news/2024/02/20/donald-trump-allies-christian-nationalism-00142086.

30. "Obama's 2006 Speech on Faith and Politics," *The New York Times*, June 28, 2006, https://www.nytimes.com/2006/06/28/us/politics/2006obamaspeech.html.

31. "Religious Freedom: Protect Civil Rights," ADL, n.d., https://www.adl.org/what-we-do/protect-civil-rights/religious-freedom.

32. "ADL Deeply Disappointed in Supreme Court Ruling Allowing Maryland Cross to Stand on Public Ground," press release, ADL, June 20, 2019, https://www.adl.org/resources/press-release/adl-deeply-disappointed-supreme-court-ruling-allowing-maryland-cross-stand.

33. "AJC Disappointed by Supreme Court Decision Upholding Maryland Cross," AJC, June 20, 2019, https://www.ajc.org/news/ajc-disappointed-by-supreme-court-decision-upholding-maryland-cross; "AJC Critical of Supreme Court Ruling on Prayer in Public Schools," AJC, June 27, 2022, https://www.ajc.org/news/ajc-critical-of-supreme-court-ruling-on-prayer-in-public-schools.

34. Stephanie Gallman and Diane Gallagher, "Louisiana Classrooms Now Required by Law to Display the Ten Commandments," CNN, June 19, 2024, https://www.cnn.com/2024/06/19/politics/louisiana-classrooms-ten-commandments/index.html.

35. "The 13 Principles of Faith," https://www.sefaria.org/sheets/417740.

36. Jackie Hajdenberg, "Jewish Parents Join Lawsuit Challenging Louisiana Law Requiring Ten Commandments in Schools," Jewish Telegraphic Agency, June 25, 2024, https://www.jta.org/2024/06/25/united-states/jewish-parents-join-lawsuit-challenging-louisiana-law-requiring-ten-commandments-in-schools.

37. Isaiah Chapter 42, *The Complete Jewish Bible with Rashi Commentary*, Chabad.org, https://www.chabad.org/library/bible_cdo/aid/15973/jewish/Chapter-42.htm.

38. Tuly Weisz, "Jews Should Advocate for Public Displays of the Ten Commandments in All 50 States," Israel 365, July 3, 2024, https://israel365news.com/392624/jews-should-advocate-for-public-displays-of-the-ten-commandments-in-all-50-states.

39. See, e.g., https://www.sefaria.org/sheets/87620.4 (As the Radak, a 12th–13th century rabbi and biblical commentator, wrote about the underlying concept in Isaiah 42:6: "The light is the Torah that goes out of Zion. Israel will sustain the nations of the world through two ways: One is that there will be peace amongst all the nations because of the Jewish people. . . . The second reason is that because of the Jewish people, the other nations will keep the seven Noahide laws and they will go in a good path.")

40. Exodus 19:6, *The Complete Jewish Bible with Rashi Commentary*, Chabad.org, https://www.chabad.org/library/bible_cdo/aid/9880/jewish/Chapter-19.htm.

41. For the basic case against the façade of a "values-neutral" public order, see Josh Hammer, "The Only Path Forward Is National Conservatism," *The American Conservative*, November 5, 2021, https://www.theamericanconservative.com/the-only-path-forward-is-national-conservatism/.

42. Michael Feldberg, "John Adams and the Jews," My Jewish Learning, n.d., https://www.myjewishlearning.com/article/john-adams-and-the-jews/.

43. Michael Feldberg, "John Adams and the Jews."

44. "From George Washington to the Hebrew Congregation in Newport, Rhode Island, 18 August 1790."

45. See Robert P. George, "Catholic Teaching on Jews and Judaism."

46. See generally Christopher F. Rufo, *America's Cultural Revolution*.

47. See Josh Hammer, "Common Good Originalism: Our Tradition and Our Path Forward."

48. See Josh Hammer, "Against 'Principled Loserdom,'" *Newsweek*, April 21, 2022, https://www.newsweek.com/against-principled-loserdom-opinion-1699917; *see also* Josh Hammer, "The Only Way Out Is Through."

49. See, e.g., Josh Hammer, "There Is No Escape Hatch," *The American Mind*, June 15, 2023, https://americanmind.org/features/the-constitution-citizenship-and-the-new-right/there-is-no-escape-hatch/.

50. See, e.g., Meir Y. Soloveichik, "Lincoln's Almost Chosen People," First Things, February 2021, https://www.firstthings.com/article/2021/02/lincolns-almost-chosen-people.

ACKNOWLEDGMENTS

It is often said that writing a book is a labor of love. And so it was for me too.

It is thus only fitting that the love of my life and my *eishet chayil* ("woman of valor"), my wife, Shir, be thanked first. Shir always accommodates my, at times, unusual working hours, but this book project was different: We found out she was pregnant with our first child right around the time I began working on the manuscript. She exhibited tremendous patience and selflessness throughout, enduring her first pregnancy with a husband who was often working late nights and weekends. I hope it was worth it—and that our daughter, Esther, will look back on this book decades from now with pride, having already decided to be a modern Maccabee.

I am deeply grateful to my parents, Bill and Leslee, for raising me in such a loving home, for encouraging me to pursue my dreams, for supporting me even as my ambitions have changed, and for encouraging me to become a bar mitzvah even as I stubbornly resisted it. In their unyielding love, care, and concern, they have always exhibited exemplary parenting—traits I now wish to emulate, as a father. I am also grateful to my remarkable in-laws, Moshe and Miriam, for their incredible warmth and generosity, and for showing me the beauty of the Sephardic Jewish traditions. My father-in-law is my model for how a humble, God-fearing Jew should think and act.

I am thankful to both Shabbos Kestenbaum and Jordan Goldstein for their assistance with some of the book's earlier, more philosophically and historically dense chapters. They both have bright futures ahead of them in whatever fields they pursue.

I am additionally grateful to Jonathan Bronitsky of ATHOS for his literary representation—and for being a good friend. The truth is that I had initially planned to write my first book on an entirely different subject. But in the aftermath of the October 7, 2023, terrorist attack, Jonathan suggested I alter my plans. He was right, and it quickly "clicked": This, indeed, was the book I was meant to write. But it would not have been possible were it not for Jonathan. I am thankful as well to Scott Waxman and Keith Wallman of Diversion Books / Radius Book Group. Keith always tolerated my deadline delays with aplomb, and his substantive edits were usually spot-on.

I am thankful to my friend and Edmund Burke Foundation colleague, Yoram Hazony, for helping me understand not merely what it means to be a better conservative, but also what it means a better Jew. Many of Yoram's ideas clearly weave their way throughout this entire book; it is sometimes impossible to miss. I am also grateful to Ben Shapiro, a friend of many years, for continuing to model how a religious Jew can engage with the broader world and for helping to demonstrate that any Jew can keep the Sabbath—no matter how "busy" he may appear.

Various other friends of mine have, over the years, encouraged me to pursue a career doing what I love the most: namely, engaging in the battle of ideas. Two of those friends who have had the biggest impact on my life are Adam Mortara and Judge (and hopefully future Justice) James C. Ho. Without each of them, it is entirely possible that I would still be working a boring law firm job today. They helped alter the trajectory of my life toward something greater and more fulfilling, and for that I will always be grateful.

Since I first started making the turn toward greater Jewish observance, I have had the tremendous honor of befriending, and often studying with, a number of rabbis. They are too many to name, but in particular I will always cherish my friendship with Rabbi Zvi Drizin of The Intown Chabad of Dallas, Texas. Rabbi

Drizin co-officiated our wedding in 2023, and in him I have a lifelong friend and an abundant source of Jewish wisdom. I am grateful to Rabbi Reuben Modek for praying for me and preparing me for my bar mitzvah after I nearly bailed on it back in 2002. And I am grateful for Taglit-Birthright Israel, an organization that helped spark my soul's yearning for the Jewish people and the Jewish state by taking me to Israel in 2010.

I am grateful for all my wonderful Christian friends who support the Jewish people and the Jewish state of Israel. Your staunch support for another people and another religion is deeply inspiring—and touching. I have been passionate about Jewish–Christian relations for my entire life, and this book was written with Christian readers in mind just as much as (if not more than) Jewish readers. I hope that many, many Christians read this book, take something powerful away, and then act on that conviction.

Last but certainly not least, I am grateful to the brave men and women of the Israel Defense Forces for their valiant, never-ending defense of the Jewish people and the Land of Israel. Each and every one of the soldiers of the IDF is a hero—perhaps especially so after October 7, 2023. May they always bear in mind the words of Joshua 1:9: "Be strong and have courage, do not fear and do not be dismayed, for the Lord your God is with you wherever you go."

ABOUT THE AUTHOR

JOSH HAMMER is senior editor-at-large of *Newsweek*, a syndicated columnist through Creators Syndicate, and a fellow with both the Edmund Burke Foundation and the Palm Beach Freedom Institute. He also hosts *The Josh Hammer Show*, a *Newsweek* podcast and syndicated radio show, as well as *America on Trial with Josh Hammer*, a *First TV* podcast. A frequent pundit and essayist on political, legal, and cultural issues, Josh is a constitutional attorney by training.

Josh has been published by many leading outlets, including the *Los Angeles Times*, the *New York Post*, *Daily Mail*, *National Review*, *The Spectator*, *Townhall*, *Fortune*, Fox Business, *Deseret Magazine*, the *Times of Israel*, *The Forward*, *Jewish Telegraphic Agency*, and the *Jewish Journal*. His legal scholarship has been published by the *Harvard Journal of Law & Public Policy* and the *University of St. Thomas Law Journal*. Josh is a college campus speaker through Young America's Foundation and the Intercollegiate Studies Institute, and a law school campus speaker through the Federalist Society.

Prior to *Newsweek* and the *Daily Wire*, where he was an editor, Josh practiced law at Kirkland & Ellis LLP and clerked for Judge James C. Ho on the US Court of Appeals for the Fifth Circuit. Josh has also served as a John Marshall Fellow with the Claremont Institute and as a Fellow with the James Wilson Institute. Josh graduated from Duke University, where he majored in economics, and from the University of Chicago Law School. He lives in Florida with his wife, Shir, and their daughter, Esther.